FUNDAMENTAL DETERMINANTS OF EXCHANGE RATES

JEROME L. STEIN, POLLY REYNOLDS ALLEN,
AND ASSOCIATES

CLARENDON PRESS · OXFORD

Oxford University Press, Great Clarendon Street, Oxford OX2 6DP
Oxford New York
Athens Auckland Bangkok Bogota Bombay Buenos Aires
Calcutta Cape Town Dar es Salaam Delhi Florence Hong Kong Istanbul
Karachi Kuala Lumpur Madras Madrid Melbourne Mexico City
Nairobi Paris Singapore Taipei Tokyo Toronto Warsaw
and associated companies in
Berlin Ibadan

Oxford is a registered trade mark of Oxford University Press

Published in the United States
by Oxford University Press Inc., New York

First published 1995
Revised paperback edition published 1997

British Library Cataloging in Publication Data
Data available

Library of Congress Cataloging in Publication Data
The fundamental determinants of exchange rates / Jerome L. Stein,
Polly Reynolds Allen, and associates.
Includes bibliographical references and index.
1. Foreign exchange rates. 2. Foreign exchange administration.
I. Stein, Jerome L. II. Allen, Polly Reynolds.
HG3851.F86 1995   95–17010
332.4′56—dc20
ISBN 0 19 828799 2 (hbk)
ISBN 0 19 829306 2 (pbk)

1 3 5 7 9 10 8 6 4 2

Typeset by Pure Tech India Ltd, Pondicherry
Printed in Great Britain
on acid-free paper by
Bookcraft (Bath) Ltd, Midsomer Norton, Avon

FUNDAMENTAL DETERMINANTS OF EXCHANGE RATES

PREFACE

Economists have been dismayed at the failure of extant models to explain exchange-rate movements. These models encounter two basic problems. First, many models concentrate on modelling short-run movements in exchange rates. In the short run, exchange rates are determined largely by speculative capital flows, depending upon expectations. It is very difficult to claim that these expectations are based upon a wide set of fundamentals. Since the 'fundamentals' evolve gradually, short-run movements in exchange rates are largely noise. Second, the real fundamentals are generally ignored by assuming purchasing-power parity, that the mean and variance of the real exchange rate are invariant over time, and that the real exchange rate converges relatively rapidly to the unchanging mean. That is, it is assumed that the real exchange rate is stationary. Very little attempt has been made to explain what economic forces determine the mean. Since the period of floating, it is apparent that the real exchange rates of the major countries are not stationary in the sense defined.

The short-run models of monetary dynamics with rational expectations have given way to the newer representative agent intertemporal optimization models. The newer models have generally not been subject to empirical verification. In the few cases where they have been, they are inconsistent with the evidence. The reasons are that these models make highly restrictive assumptions and their crucial variables are not objectively measurable.

We therefore began thinking of an alternative approach. We ignore the short run and focus upon the medium to longer run. We concentrate upon the real rather than upon the nominal exchange rate. Our fundamentals are productivity of capital and thrift both at home and abroad. We reasoned that since floating, social thrift (which includes both private and public saving) and the productivity of capital were the most important fundamentals determining the longer-run movements in the real exchange rate and capital flows. We needed a manageable, testable model which simultaneously explained the equilibrium real exchange rates and non-speculative capital flows. We called our equilibrium real exchange rate the Natural Real Exchange Rate (NATREX), since it is the equilibrium rate when there is both internal and external balance, in the sense that Nurkse used the term equilibrium.

We have independent saving and investment functions, instead of a representative agent who makes the joint saving and investment decision. People attempt to optimize when they know that they do not know what will be the evolution of the fundamentals. Our optimization process relies upon feedback controls and dynamic programming which guarantees that the ratio of net foreign assets to GDP will converge to an evolving unpredictable steady-state value. Then, the present value of the constant ratio of net foreign assets to GDP converges to zero as time goes to infinity. We do not believe that a country faces an intertemporal budget constraint whereby the initial and terminal foreign debt are the same, or that the terminal debt must be zero. We allow countries to change from debtor to creditor and vice versa. In our model, the steady-state ratio of net foreign assets to GDP depends upon the evolution of the fundamentals. The net foreign assets to GDP ratio may converge to a positive, negative, or zero value, depending upon the path of the fundamentals. Our model guarantees that the foreign debt stabilizes so that the trade balance is sufficient to make the interest payments on the debt.

The empirical results are encouraging, when the model was applied to different types of economies. Stein applied it to the United States and the G-10, two large economies where the terms of trade are endogenous. Others joined our project in applying the NATREX to different pairs of countries. G. C. Lim joined Stein in applying the model to Australia, a small economy where the terms of trade are exogenous. Michael Connolly and John Devereux examined a subset of the small economy version of the model to explain real exchange rates in Latin American countries. Liliane Crouhy-Veyrac and Michèle Saint Marc considered the bilateral real exchange rate between the French franc and Deutschmark.

The results are encouraging. Proxies for productivity and thrift do explain trends in the real exchange rate and in some cases also the ratio of the current account to GNP in the countries examined. The NATREX is more general than purchasing-power parity. The real exchange rates are not stationary because the underlying fundamentals, productivity and thrift, do not have means that are independent of time. If the fundamentals are stationary, so would be the equilibrium real exchange rates.

Since no one has 'world enough and time', Chapter 1 presents a complete exposition of our contribution. The underlying framework, implications, evaluation of results, and relation to other approaches are developed. The emphasis in Chapter 1 is on the economic scenarios and meaning of both the mathematical models and econometrics contained in the subsequent chapters.

Polly Reynolds Allen and Jerome L. Stein

CONTENTS

CONTRIBUTORS

JEROME L. STEIN is Visiting Professor of Applied Mathematics and Professor of Economics, Eastman Professor of Political Economy, emeritus, Brown University, Providence, Rhode Island, USA.

POLLY REYNOLDS ALLEN is Professor of Economics, University of Connecticut, Storrs, Connecticut, USA.

GUAY C. LIM is Director of the programme in monetary and financial economics, Department of Economics, University of Melbourne, Melbourne.

LILIANE CROUHY-VEYRAC is Professor of Economics and Finance, Hautes Etudes Commerciales (HEC), Jouy-en-Josas, France.

MICHÈLE SAINT MARC is Directeur de Recherche au Centre Nationale de la Recherche Scientifique (CNRS), Paris, France.

MICHAEL CONNOLLY and JOHN DEVEREUX are Professor of Economics and Associate professor of Economics, University of Miami, Coral Gables, Florida, USA.

1

The Economic and Policy Implications of the NATREX Approach

POLLY REYNOLDS ALLEN

The large fluctuations in the real exchange rates of most currencies over the past twenty years have not been adequately explained. Much of the research on determination of exchange rates has focused on short-run movements of exchange rates. Fluctuations in real exchange rates are often treated as temporary deviations from the 'long-run' equilibrium real exchange rate, for which purchasing power parity (PPP) remains the prevailing paradigm. Since PPP yields a constant real exchange rate, it follows that movements in real exchange rates must be deviations from the equilibrium level. While purchasing power parity must serve as an ultimate benchmark for the relative values of currencies, it provides a poor measure of equilibrium exchange rates in the presence of numerous fundamental real disturbances to both the current and long-term capital accounts.

The NATREX approach offers an alternative paradigm for equilibrium real exchange rates. NATREX is the acronym for NATural Real EXchange, referring to a medium-run, inter-cyclical equilibrium real exchange rate, determined by real, fundamental factors. Importantly, the NATREX is a *moving* equilibrium real exchange rate, responding to continual changes in exogenous and endogenous real fundamentals. In a world of high capital mobility, the fundamentals of thrift, productivity, capital intensity, and net debt to foreigners become particularly important, influencing desired long-term capital flows and altering the equilibrium real exchange rate. The NATREX approach identifies and models the fundamental determinants of equilibrium real exchange rates, consistent with their recent empirical movements in various countries.

The goal of the NATREX approach is primarily empirical—to explain movements of medium-to long-run real exchange rates in terms of the fundamental real variables of thrift and productivity, assuming that real exchange rates do adjust toward their equilibrium level, although with a lag. A family of consistent general equilibrium models—of rational, optimizing behaviour, determining medium-run equilibrium real exchange rates—forms the core of the NATREX approach. These models provide logical economic justifications for the empirical results.

Economists studying exchange-rate determination have had little success in developing empirically verifiable explanations of movements in nominal exchange rates. None of the existing empirical studies of which we are aware satisfactorily explains the nominal and real appreciation and subsequent depreciation of the US dollar during the 1980s. The state of the art in this literature on exchange-rate determination is discussed and evaluated in the Appendix.

The results from the NATREX approach are more promising. The NATREX model can account for both the rise and the fall of the dollar. Jerome Stein tests a version of the NATREX model for the US relative to the G-10 in Chapter 2. In the model, a moving equilibrium real exchange rate for the US dollar responds to changes in US thrift and productivity and G-10 productivity. The estimated model closely predicts movements in both the real exchange rate and the current account. The evidence also supports important assumptions of the model—the absence of any constant mean value for the real exchange rate and the convergence of real long-term interest rates. McKibbin and Sachs (1991) predict that expansionary fiscal policy will produce a trajectory of real appreciation and subsequent real depreciation. Their dynamic simulation model is consistent with and complements the predictions and evidence from the NATREX model of the United States.

Whereas the United States is a large economy that can influence its terms of trade and the world real interest rate, Australia is a relatively small country facing an exogenous terms of trade and a fixed world interest rate. A different version of the NATREX model, depicting a small country producing tradable and non-tradable goods, better describes the Australian economy. Guay Lim and Jerome Stein find in Chapter 3 that real fundamentals explain changes in the Australian real exchange rate also. In this case, real fundamental disturbances include exogenous changes in the terms of trade and the world interest rate, as well as changes in Australian thrift and productivity.

Germany and France are modelled as medium-size economies, unable to influence world interest rates, but large enough to influence world prices of tradable goods and the country's terms of trade. The bilateral real exchange rate between France and Germany strongly depends on the respective exchange rates with the US dollar, as well as on relative price levels between the two countries. Liliane Crouhy-Veyrac and Michèle Saint Marc estimate the determinants of the French/German real exchange rate in Chapter 4. To explain movements in the bilateral real exchange rate between the French franc and the Deutschmark, they use a NATREX model, depicting interactions of the French and German economies, respectively, with the US economy. The fundamentals are French and German thrift and productivity. With a pegged nominal exchange rate under the European Monetary System, changes in the French/German bilateral real exchange rate must come through relative price changes. The actual real exchange rate between France and Germany does respond to fundamental disturbances, but adjusts more slowly than in the cases where the nominal exchange rate is flexible. These three cases show that the NATREX approach is not a single model, but a family of models, each tailored to the particular characteristics of the country or countries under consideration. The family of NATREX models shares a number of common attributes. NATREX models, by focusing on the equilibrium real exchange rate in the medium to long run, focus attention on changes in investment, saving, and long-term net capital flows; on the resulting changes in stocks of real physical capital, wealth, and net debt to foreigners; and on the implications of these changes for the moving equilibrium real exchange rate.

In one other case study, Michael Connolly and John Devereux (Chapter 5) look at the fundamental determinants of real exchange rates in Latin America. The terms of trade, technological progress, and country size are shown to have significant influence on real exchange rates in Latin American countries. Although Connolly and Devereux do not present a full NATREX model—not considering endogenous changes in capital, wealth, and net debt to foreigners—their model of fundamental determinants of the real exchange rate closely resembles and complements the NATREX approach.

We believe that, among industrialized countries characterized by fairly high capital mobility, exogenous changes in thrift and productivity account for many of the changes in the NATREX in recent years. Both a fall in thrift, lowering desired saving, and an increase in the marginal product of capital, raising desired investment, lead to new borrowing from foreigners. The purpose of the borrowing determines how the economy develops through time, whether wealth and consumption will rise or fall in the long run. The theory supporting the NATREX approach suggests the following outcomes.

When borrowing finances new consumption, in a well-behaved stable economy the rising debt to foreigners steadily reduces wealth, gradually reducing consumption and increasing saving. The rising saving continually reduces the need to borrow from foreigners, until the borrowing ceases. In the long run, the country faces higher net debt and larger interest payments to foreigners. And what of the country's capital stock? Nothing works to increase it, and it may decline, if the increased borrowing raises the world interest rate, or if the higher debt raises the risk premium. With consumption equal to net national product (NNP) in the long run, consumption per unit of effective labour will clearly be lower.

By contrast, when borrowing finances new productive investment, the country's capital stock rises even more rapidly than its debt to foreigners. Wealth and consumption gradually rise, how much depending on the eventual increase in average productivity. Sufficiently productive new investment implies repayment of the newly incurred debt to foreigners and eventual lending to foreigners. Borrowing to finance productive investment will eventually contribute to a country's net creditor position, bringing in net interest payments *from* foreigners. Consumption, equal to NNP in the long run, is clearly higher.

Long-run outcomes depend on whether a country's borrowing is for consumption or investment. This is a major message of the NATREX approach. In the long run, borrowing from foreigners will reduce wealth and consumption when the funds are used to finance new consumption, and will increase wealth and consumption when the funds are used to finance productive investment.

The use of borrowed funds influences the trajectory of the NATREX also. Exogenous decreases in thrift or increases in productivity first appreciate the NATREX, to facilitate the long-term capital inflow, and then gradually depreciate it, as changes in capital and debt reduce the investment–saving differential. Borrowing for consumption steadily depreciates the NATREX, ending in a long-run net depreciation. Borrowing for investment may produce a more complex trajectory, possibly reversing a gradual deprecia- tion and ending in long-run net appreciation if the country becomes a net creditor.

This emphasis on the *trajectory* of the equilibrium exchange rate distinguishes the NATREX approach from other empirical studies that stress the role of saving and investment for the real exchange rate. Bosworth (1993), for example, argues that fundamental changes in S and I are important influences on real exchange rates, but does not distinguish between equilibrium and disequilibrium real exchange rates nor consider the trajectory.

The empirical studies of the US, Australia, and France/Germany in the coming chapters each identify proxies for changes in the country's thrift and productivity, along with selected other fundamentals. By means of cointegration analysis, these studies test the explanatory power of the proxies for changes in the countries' real exchange rates. In each case, the real exchange rate and the fundamental variables are non-stationary and cointegrated. The cointegrating equations track trends in the actual real exchange rate surprisingly well, with R-squares ranging from 0.85 to 0.96. The proxies for domestic thrift and productivity are significant and consistent with the theoretical NATREX models. For all three cases, reductions in thrift lead to long-run depreciation, while increases in productivity produce mixed effects on the long-run NATREX.

These empirical results are consistent with three main assertions of the NATREX approach:

(i) The trends in real exchange rates can be explained by the fundamentals of productivity and thrift and, for small countries, by the exogenous terms of trade and world real interest rate.

(ii) The actual rate adjusts to a moving equilibrium real exchange rate, the NATREX.

(iii) The long-run effects on the NATREX of borrowing from foreigners depend on whether borrowing is for new consumption or new investment.

The following sections of this chapter lay out the characteristics of the NATREX approach, its applications to the different coun- tries studied, and the implications for economic policies—in general, non-technical terms. Subsequent chapters present in detail the models and empirical results for each case study.

1. WHAT IS THE NATREX?

The NATREX (or NATural Real EXchange rate) is the *equilibrium real exchange rate that clears the balance of payments in the absence of cyclical factors, speculative capital flows, and movements in international reserves.* Nurkse (1945) identified these same standards for an equilibrium exchange rate, although he did not call his rate the NATREX. He believed that this definition of an equilibrium exchange rate was appropriate for giving economic content to the IMF's loose definition of 'fundamental equilibrium' under the Bretton Woods system.

We focus on the *real* exchange rate for two reasons. First, the real, rather than the nominal, rate determines basic economic decisions about consumption, growth, and resource allocation. Second, a moving inter-cyclical equilibrium, neutral with respect to money, can be expressed wholly in real terms, making the equilibrium *real* exchange rate independent of the nominal exchange-rate regime.

In the short run, changes in the real exchange rate closely follow movements in the nominal exchange rate, because prices of goods adjust only slowly. With flexible nominal rates, systematic explanations for short-run movements in exchange rates are elusive, due to the dominant influence of speculative capital flows and the problems of modelling and estimating these flows. By comparison, the real fundamentals, changing relatively little in the short run, have only a minor influence on short-run exchange rates.

The NATREX approach, always describing equilibrium situations, avoids the problems of modelling speculative capital flows and cyclical factors. A NATREX model starts at some hypothetical inter-cyclical medium run, in which prices have adjusted and output has returned to its inter-cyclical potential level. The real exchange rate has adjusted to its current equilibrium level. Demand for money equals the prevailing supply of money, with no foreign-exchange intervention by the central banks. This medium-run equilibrium, constituting the 'long-run equilibrium' of most monetary models, is the starting point of a NATREX model.

The medium-run market-clearing equilibrium of a NATREX model can be described by the familiar national-income-accounts equation,

$$I - S + CA = 0 \qquad (1.1)$$

where I is desired national investment, S is desired national saving, and CA is the desired current account, all measured when the economy is at capacity output and expectations about inflation are met. The real exchange rate, R, appreciates in response to an excess demand for goods, insuring that equilibrium is maintained.

In this medium-run equilibrium, equation (1.1) can be interpreted as the equilibrium condition for the balance of payments, as well as for the goods market. Desired investment minus desired saving, $I - S$, always describes the sum of the country's excess flow supplies of financial assets—of non-tradable securities (X_N), tradable long-term securities (X_L), tradable short-term speculative securities (X_S), and domestic money (X_M). Given the medium-run conditions—that (a) the domestic securities markets clear ($X_N = 0$), (b) short-term speculative capital flows cancel out ($X_S = 0$), and (c) money equilibrium prevails with no official foreign-exchange intervention ($X_M = 0$), any difference between investment and saving represents the excess flow supply of tradable long-term securities ($I - S = X_L$). Under these conditions, $I - S$ describes desired net long-term capital inflows, and equation (1) is the sum of the current and capital accounts, or balance-of-payments equilibrium. The equilibrium real exchange rate, R, simultaneously clears the goods market and assures balance-of-payments equilibrium.

In the clearing of the market, the current account responds to changes in R. Desired saving and desired investment are assumed to be either independent of the real exchange rate or relatively unresponsive to it, compared to the responses of the current account. In spite of much concern about ongoing US trade deficits in the face of dollar depreciation, empirical evidence suggests that current accounts do respond to the real exchange rate. Bosworth (1993, ch. 4), testing the effects of real exchange rates on the non-oil trade balances of fourteen industrialized countries, concludes that changes in real exchange rates are effective means of altering trade flows.

An assumption that the real exchange rate does not influence $I - S$ simplifies the NATREX models and has implications for the trajectory of the real exchange rate, but is not crucial to the NATREX approach. For many countries, the assumption seems reasonable. A long literature, starting with Laursen and Metzler (1950), discusses whether and how saving is influenced by the real exchange rate, with no strong theoretical evidence in either direction

(Svensson and Razin, 1983). On the other side, desired investment is independent of the real exchange rate, as long as domestically priced capital goods are used to produce domestically priced final goods, while capital goods purchased at world prices are used to produce goods sold at world prices. In the coming chapters, the real exchange rate influences investment in the model used for Australia, where non-traded and imported capital goods are used to produce exportables sold at the world price, but in the models for the United States, France, and Germany, investment is independent of the real exchange rate.

Desired investment and saving, relatively independent of the real exchange rate, depend on the existing stocks of capital, wealth, and net debt to foreigners. When these stocks are changing, the NATREX, an equilibrium exchange rate, becomes a moving equilibrium. NATREX models focus on the results of investment, saving, and net capital flows over time. Investment (I) and saving (S), both net of depreciation, and net capital inflows $(I - S)$ produce changes in the real stocks of physical capital (k), wealth $(w = k - F)$, and net debt to foreigners (F), respectively. These changes in stocks in turn alter desired I, S, and CA, calling for new equilibrium real exchange rates. The NATREX reaches a constant level only when and if the economy reaches its long-run equilibrium, where both the fundamentals, Z, and the stocks of real assets (per unit of effective labor) remain constant. In an economy with no growth of labor, I, S, and CA would all be zero in this long-run steady state.

Exogenous fundamental disturbances (Z)—such as changes in thrift and productivity, at home and abroad, and for small countries, changes in the terms of trade and the world real interest rate—influence the NATREX in two ways. They first affect desired investment, saving, or the current account, inducing a change in the NATREX in the medium run. Second, by changing the rates of accumulation of k, w, and F, the exogenous fundamentals alter the trajectory of the NATREX as it moves toward its new long-run equilibrium. At any point other than long-run equilibrium, the NATREX is a function of both exogenous (Z) and endogenous $(A = k, F)$ fundamentals $(w = k - F)$.

A full NATREX model determines the medium-run equilibrium real exchange rate, R (the NATREX); its subsequent trajectory; and its eventual long-run equilibrium value, R^*. Frequent real fundamental disturbances, such as occur in the world, are continually sending the NATREX toward new long-run equilibria, so it never actually reaches a steady-state level. The empirical evidence supports this assumption of continual movement in the equilibrium R: real exchange rates are non-stationary (that is, they do not tend toward a given mean or trend), because the exogenous fundamentals are non-stationary. If the real fundamentals were stationary, so too would be the NATREX.

This medium-run equilibrium of the NATREX models is an artificial construct toward which the economy tends, but which never actually prevails. Similarly, we can never observe the NATREX itself, but only the actual real exchange rate, which tends to adjust toward its moving equilibrium, the NATREX.

The real exchange rate can be depicted at different stages of adjustment:

$R_t = R_t(Z, A, C)$ actual (disequilibrium) rate,
$R = R(Z, A)$ equilibrium rate (NATREX),
$R^* = R^*(Z)$ steady-state rate,

where Z represents real exogenous fundamental factors, A represents stocks of net real assets, and C represents short-run cyclical and speculative factors. We empirically estimate the equilibrium real exchange rate on the trajectory between R and R^*, as a function of the exogenous fundamental factors, Z, but we observe only the actual rate, R_t. So the empirical estimates are simultaneously testing two hypotheses: (1) that the NATREX, R, as it moves toward the steady-state rate, R^*, can be explained by the real fundamentals, Z, in a manner consistent with the predictions of a NATREX model; and (2) that the quarterly actual real exchange rate, R_t, converges to the moving NATREX, R.

The NATREX is a positive, not a normative, concept of the equilibrium real exchange rate. It is the rate implied by the real fundamentals and by the existing economic policies. We make no claims that these policies are socially optimal or welfare maximizing, or that the NATREX is the optimal real exchange rate, only that it is the equilibrium rate implied by the prevailing fundamentals. Like Nurkse (1945), we take existing trade policy as a given, but do not allow for adjustments in the degree of protectionism as a means of achieving an equilibrium real exchange rate. Similarly, we take the prevailing fiscal policies as given. For example, an exogenous fall in public or private saving in the United States, considered undesirable and inconsistent with long-run social goals of growth and productivity, will affect the NATREX. A NATREX model predicts how such a change will affect the equilibrium real exchange rate, without considering the desirability of the disturbance or the outcome. NATREX models imply no judgement as to whether the real fundamentals themselves are consistent with welfare.

In this respect, the NATREX differs from John Williamson's (1983) concept of a fundamental equilibrium exchange rate (FEER). Williamson is looking for a measure of the real exchange rate that will serve as a guide for policy. His FEER is the real exchange rate that will bring the current account, measured at potential output, into line with some measure of 'desirable capital flows'. Williamson's desirable capital flows equal the difference between levels of investment and saving that are not distorted by public policy. This normative element is the major difference between the definitions of the NATREX and Williamson's FEER. Although prescribed optimal policies are not part of the definition of the NATREX, such policies could, of course, be put into a NATREX model to determine the implied equilibrium real exchange rate.

Most work on the determination of real exchange rates has focused on the short to medium run, with cyclical adjustments of output, slow or no adjustment of prices, speculative capital flows, or balance-of-payments disequilibrium. Open-economy Keynesian models described *cyclical* changes in real exchange rates, fully reflecting changes in nominal rates, with prices of goods fixed. Such intra-cyclical real exchange rates can be seen as short-run deviations from the NATREX. Similarly, monetary-type models that allow for changes in real exchange rates depict short-run changes due to lagged adjustment in prices (e.g.: Dornbusch, 1976). Rational expectations models show short-run deviations from equilibrium as a result of either lagged price adjustment or unexpected disturbances. In monetary models, the 'long-run' equilibrium exchange rates (comparable to the medium-run NATREX) are assumed to be unchanging. Although the authors of monetary models often acknowledge the possibility of real disturbances influencing the equilibrium real exchange rate, monetary models seldom incorporate any real disturbances, their equilibrium real exchange rate being determined by purchasing-power parity.

Economists studying developing countries have done most of the recent work on the determinants of *equilibrium real* exchange rates. Edwards (1989) is a good example of such work. Although these development models of real exchange rates, often with no investment, saving, or capital flows, do not distinguish between medium- and long-run equilibria, they are close in spirit to the NATREX approach. A NATREX model starts with the fundamental determinants of the equilibrium real exchange rate, depicted in a model like that of Edwards, and carries the analysis forward through time to examine the long-run implications of investment, saving, and net capital flows.

Like the work of Edwards, Connolly's and Devereux's study of equilibrium real exchange rates in Latin America (Chapter 6 below) does not allow for investment, saving, or capital flows, and so produces no changes in stocks of assets. Their equilibrium, requiring a balanced current account, differs slightly from a medium-run NATREX equilibrium, where net capital flows can offset a current-account imbalance. Because they do not allow for endogenous changes in capital, wealth, and net foreign debt, theirs is not a full NATREX model. At the same time, their model is more disaggregated and describes behavioural and policy decisions that are not included in the simple NATREX models we have used. The two approaches are complementary.

2. MEASUREMENT OF THE NATREX

The real exchange rate is always a relative price between some goods produced in the home country and other goods produced in the foreign country. Economists differ in their choice of relative price. The oldest and most general measure of the real exchange rate is the nominal exchange rate deflated by the ratio of overall purchasing powers in the two countries.

$$R = P + N - P', \qquad (1.2)$$

where N is the nominal exchange rate (the foreign-currency price of domestic currency), P and P' are overall price indexes (such as GDP deflators) in the home country and in the foreign country, and all prices and exchange rates are written in logarithms. A rise in R (or N) is an appreciation of the currency in real (or nominal) terms.

Traditionally, analysis of exchange-rate adjustment focused on the relative price between export and import goods, or the terms of trade. In simple macro-models of countries producing a single good both for domestic use and for export, the overall price index is simply the price of this single exportable good. The real exchange rate becomes the terms of trade.

$$R_t = P_1 + N - P'_2 = T, \tag{1.3}$$

where good 1 is the home country's good, good 2 is the foreign country's good, T is the terms of trade, and the prime denotes a price in the foreign currency.

The terms of trade are exogenous for small countries facing exogenous world prices of traded goods. Endogenous relative price adjustment can only occur between the prices of non-tradable and tradable goods. Simple models of small countries standardly depict two goods produced by the home country, a non-tradable good N and a tradable good T. The real exchange rate is often defined as the relative price of non-tradable to tradable goods,

$$R_n = P_n - P_t. \tag{1.4}$$

Such a definition is natural in a model where $P_n - P_t$ is the only relative price. In such a model, changes in R_n are proportional to changes in R, given prices in the rest of the world.

As real exchange rates, both the terms of trade, R_t, and the relative price of non-tradables/tradables, R_n, are special cases of the general R. Each is applicable only to disturbances affecting that single relative price.

We can see how R_t and R_n are special cases, by writing out R in terms of the GDP deflators and applying the law of one price to tradable goods. For generality, we allow for production of three types of goods—exportables, importables, and non-tradables. First, define the GDP deflators for the two countries as

$$P = \alpha P_n + \beta P_2 + (1 - \alpha - \beta) P_1, \tag{1.5a}$$

$$P' = \alpha' P'_n + \beta' P'_1 + (1 - \alpha' - \beta') P'_2, \tag{1.5b}$$

where good 1 is the home country's exportable good, good 2 is the foreign country's exportable good, α and α' are the weights of the non-tradable good and β and β', the weights of the respective importable goods in the countries' GDP deflators. Second, assume the law of one price for tradable goods,

$$P_i + N = P'_i, \quad i = 1, 2. \tag{1.6}$$

Using (1.5a), (1.5b), and (1.6), we can rewrite the real exchange rate, equation (1.2), as the weighted sum of the relative prices of non-tradables to exportables in each country and of the home country's terms of trade,

$$R = \alpha(P_n - P_1) - \alpha'(P'_n - P'_2) + (1 - \beta - \beta')T. \qquad (1.2a)$$

A rise in the relative price of non-tradables to exportables in the home country will appreciate the real exchange rate, as in equation (1.4). An increase in the country's terms of trade, given the other relative prices, will appreciate its real exchange rate, as long as the weights of the importables in the GDP deflators sum to less than unity. This is consistent with equation (1.3), where the weights of non-tradables and importables are implicitly zero.

Harberger (1986) argues strongly for defining the real exchange rate in terms of some general theoretical price index, such as the GDP deflator, precisely because R_n is unable to accommodate changes in the terms of trade. A further, empirical argument for using R is the difficulty of finding adequate definitions and price indexes for non-tradable goods. The distinction between tradable and non-tradable depends on prices and transportation costs: a non-tradable becomes a tradable when the difference between its domestic and foreign prices exceed the transportation costs. Even services, once considered the quintessential non-tradables, are a growing proportion of US exports—in education, finance, and insurance.

For all of these reasons, the NATREX approach always uses the general definition R for the real exchange rate, from equations (1.2) and (1.2a).

3. GENERAL CHARACTERISTICS OF NATREX MODELS

Several other general characteristics are common to all NATREX models:

(i) The saving and investment functions of NATREX models are the products of intertemporal optimizations using all available, relevant information. The optimization, using dynamic programming, produces the same eventual outcome as if participants could perfectly predict the future. However, this type of optimization, based on current, knowable information, is far more stable than popular optimization procedures that depend on perfect foresight (where any small error can knock the economy off the path to equilibrium), and more closely approximates decisions made in the real world.

(ii) NATREX models focus on *national* saving and *national* investment for an entire economy of a country, making no distinction between private and public sources. This aggregation of public and private does not imply that private and government behaviour are determined in the same way. Rather, by aggregating public and private expenditures, we can focus on the differences between the uses of borrowed funds for consumption and for productive investment—and their effects on the economy over time.

The NATREX approach side-steps the theoretical issues of the relationships between public and private saving and investment. A NATREX model examines the effects of net changes in public plus private saving, saying nothing about whether private saving adjusts to offset changes in government saving (Ricardian equivalence). Similarly, NATREX models examine changes in total social investment, making no assumptions about the relative productivity of public and private investment. The difference between national investment and national saving defines net long-term capital inflows, regardless whether the net borrowing reflects investment or saving, or whether it is public or private.

The NATREX approach is positive, examining the effects on the economy of fundamental disturbances to national saving and national investment. Whether these fundamentals are optimal is another question. The theoretical NATREX models assume that private firms and individuals rationally maximize profits or utility, using all available information efficiently, but lacking information on future fundamental disturbances. Many models of intertemporal optimization incorporate an assumption of perfect foresight, or at least an ability to predict mean values and variances of crucial variables. For fundamental disturbances to investment and saving, such assumptions are not warranted empirically—the proxies for these fundamentals are not stationary (they do not tend toward any constant mean) and cannot be predicted. For this reason, we use an optimization procedure that continually adjusts for any new information but does not base actions on predictions of unknowable future events. Government purchases are treated either as consumption or investment, as appropriate for the relevant country. We do not assume government fiscal policies to be socially optimal, so desired national saving, public plus private, may not be socially optimal. Desired national investment, reflecting optimization by private decision-makers, also may not be socially optimal due to externalities, suboptimal government investment, or other inappropriate government policies.

(iii) The NATREX approach posits exogenous changes in investment (due to changes in productivity) and saving (due to changes in thrift) as important determinants of the equilibrium real exchange rate, implying an assumption of relatively high long-term capital mobility.

Long-term capital mobility, in the sense of real capital formation in one country financed by the saving of another country, can occur directly or indirectly. Direct long-term capital mobility means that the long-term liabilities financing domestic capital formation are close substitutes internationally and are freely tradable between countries. Alternatively, indirect long-term capital mobility requires (a) short-term capital mobility (close substitutability and trade internationally among short-term liabilities), combined with (b) a high degree in each country of domestic arbitrage and substitution between the non-traded long-term liabilities financing capital formation and the short-term financial liabilities traded internationally. Both types of long-term capital mobility pull long-term interest rates toward parity, though indirect international integration of long-term markets likely produces greater slippage.

How much an exogenous change in I or S affects the equilibrium real exchange rate depends on the degree of long-term capital mobility. Consider the basic market equation that determines R:

$$I - S + CA = 0. \qquad (1.1)$$

At one extreme, a small country with perfect long-term capital mobility can borrow or lend any amount at the world interest rate. Any change in I or S produces a corresponding change in net capital inflows, $I - S$. The real exchange rate adjusts to produce the necessary change in the current account. An exogenous change in I or S affects both the real exchange rate and the current account. At the other extreme, with zero long-term capital mobility, the domestic real interest rate adjusts to ensure that $I = S$. Any exogenous change in I or S produces the necessary adjustment in the real interest rate, r, affecting neither the real exchange rate nor the current account.

The NATREX approach does not require perfect capital mobility, but also accommodates intermediate cases, where changes in productivity and thrift influence both the NATREX and the real interest rate. Such intermediate cases occur whenever capital mobility is less than perfect, as in Australia, or the home country is large enough to affect the world real interest rate, as the United States.

Feldstein and Horioka (1980) concluded that long-term capital mobility is quite low, when their regression of investment on to saving produced a coefficient close to unity—a finding that has been much debated. The NATREX approach provides an alternative test of the capital mobility hypothesis, by estimating the explanatory power of productivity and thrift for the NATREX and for the current account. In the absence of capital mobility, changes in productivity and thrift would produce changes in the interest rate to maintain the equality of investment and saving, also maintaining a balanced current account. Any initial influences of thrift and productivity on the current account would be reversed through induced changes in the real exchange rate. The trajectory of the real exchange rate would differ substantially from that predicted for the case of high capital mobility.

All three cases studied here (the United States, Australia, and France/Germany) show strong influences of exogenous changes in I and S on the NATREX, as predicted by the NATREX models when capital mobility is assumed to be high, lending support to the assumption of high long-term capital mobility. Two other results support an assumption of high long-term capital mobility between the US and the G-10: real long-term interest rates, both between the US and the G-10 and between the US and Germany, converge with a lag of about two years; and exogenous changes in productivity and thrift are strong determinants of the US current account.

(iv) Under high capital mobility, the long-term real interest-rate differential between countries converges to the expected rate of change of the real exchange rate. Yet empirical evidence suggests that rational market participants can do no better than to expect the future exchange rate to equal the current exchange rate. First, proxies for the exogenous real fundamentals are not stationary (that is, they do not tend toward any mean level). With a fundamental disturbance today providing no information of use in predicting future disturbances, future fundamental disturbances must be considered almost totally unpredictable. Second, the real exchange rate itself is not stationary. It continually moves, with no tendency toward a mean level or trend. A real appreciation or depreciation today provides no new information about future changes in real exchange rates.

In the face of such empirical evidence, market participants have no basis for predicting the future NATREX. They know that new disturbances will almost certainly alter the long-run NATREX, but they do not know the direction. As the time horizon lengthens, predictions about the real exchange rate become ever more unreliable, due to the accumulation of unpredictable fundamental disturbances. We specifically avoid making distinctions, popular in the literature, between anticipated and unanticipated, or between permanent and transitory, disturbances. They are subjective concepts, operational only with *ad hoc* arbitrary assumptions. For decisions on long-term capital flows, one needs to know the expected average annual change in the NATREX over the full long-term horizon. Anticipating numerous, wholly unpredictable disturbances within this time horizon, market participants are left with no choice but to act *as if* the NATREX will not change from its current level.

Theoretically, the NATREX is a moving equilibrium on a trajectory toward a long-run steady state. Every new fundamental disturbance changes both the long-run equilibrium and the trajectory of the NATREX. Even assuming market participants fully understand the structure of the economy and know with certainty the trajectory implied by the current known fundamentals, they cannot predict the annual rate of change of the NATREX over the relevant time horizon, *because they cannot predict the future fundamental disturbances*. Empirically, the expected value of the change in the real exchange rate is zero. Stein's empirical findings on the convergence of long-term real interest rates provide further evidence to this effect—long-term expectations about future real exchange rates are not well formulated.

This continually changing, but wholly unpredictable NATREX is at the heart of the NATREX approach. Because fundamental disturbances are empirically non-stationary and unpredictable, long-term expectations play almost no role in the NATREX models. This absence of long-run expectations for the real exchange rate is fundamentally different from purchasing-power parity.

Under purchasing-power parity, the real exchange rate always returns to the constant PPP level. In NATREX models, the NATREX is expected to change, but in an unpredictable direction. With speculative capital flows cancelled out in the medium run, NATREX models also ignore short-run expectations.

Although the NATREX and the monetary models appear superficially similar in their assumptions of no specific expected change in the real exchange rate, the underlying rationale is entirely different. In the monetary models, market participants correctly predict that the equilibrium real exchange rate will not change. In the NATREX models, *R does* change, and is expected to do so. The unanswerable question is: in which direction?

(v) In other ways, NATREX and monetary models are truly similar. Both describe a world in which money is neutral. Nominal money supplies, nominal prices, and the nominal exchange-rate regime have no effect on real values in the medium-run equilibrium, where the NATREX models start (and monetary models end). Our interest being in real values, and nominal values being assumed to have no real effects, NATREX models are written in real terms, with real exchange rates and relative prices.

How the actual real exchange rate adjusts to its NATREX equilibrium depends on the nominal exchange-rate regime. Under a pegged nominal exchange rate, flows of reserves clear the foreign-exchange market, and relative nominal prices of goods must change to alter the real exchange rate. By contrast, a flexible nominal exchange rate can combine with relative nominal price adjustments to produce the same equilibrium real exchange rate more easily.

Since NATREX models, starting at medium-run equilibrium, do not treat short-run deviations of the actual real exchange rate, R_t, from the NATREX, R, we must draw on the results of other, short-to medium-run models to see how and why the deviations of R_t from R differ across exchange-rate regimes.

The short run is characterized by lagged adjustments of the prices of goods, with the goods markets either cleared by adjustments in output (Mundell–Fleming) or remaining in disequilibrium (Dornbusch, 1976). With a pegged nominal exchange rate, lagged adjustment of prices unambiguously slows the adjustment of the real exchange rate. When the nominal rate is allowed to float, the short-run behaviour of the real exchange rate is less obvious, depending on the origin of disturbances (in the goods or money markets) and whether or not output adjusts to clear the goods markets.

Perhaps more important, short-run speculative capital flows dominate the foreign-exchange market under flexible exchange rates, producing short-run volatility in both nominal and real exchange rates. Despite this short-run volatility under flexible nominal exchange rates, empirical results in subsequent chapters show that the real exchange rate adjusts more rapidly to the NATREX, with no evidence of systematic overshooting, and that the fundamentals have more explanatory power for the real exchange rate, when the nominal exchange rate is flexible.

4. DIFFERENT VERSIONS OF THE NATREX MODELS

All of our NATREX models are based on the market equation,

$$I - S + CA = 0, \tag{1.1}$$

describing both goods-market and balance-of-payments equilibria (discussed in Section 1). Given clearing of the asset and money markets, the NATREX simultaneously assures aggregate goods-market equilibrium and basic balance-of-payments equilibrium at capacity output. The real exchange rate adjusts, bringing the current account into line with $I - S$.

The precise version of a NATREX model depends on several characteristics: the size of the economy relative to its trading partners in markets for tradable goods and assets; foreign elasticities of demand and supply for goods and assets; and substitutabilities among goods and among assets, between countries and within the home country. We categorize versions of NATREX models, by the treatments of asset markets and of goods markets.

4.1 Asset Markets

We consider three sets of assumptions about asset markets and capital mobility:

(i) A country small in world asset markets, with high capital mobility, can borrow as much as it wishes, $I - S$, at the world real interest rate r'. Market adjustment falls on R to bring the current account into line with $I - S$. France and Germany are modelled this way in Chapter 4.

(ii) In a country like the US, large enough to influence the world interest rate and characterized by high capital mobility, the world real interest rate and the real exchange rate are determined simultaneously by the interaction of two countries' basic market equations: $I - S + CA = 0$, for the home country, and $I' - S' - CA = 0$, for the foreign country. An increase in $I - S$, desired borrowing by the home country, raises the world real interest rate as well as appreciating the NATREX in the medium run. Because the higher real interest rate reduces $I - S$, the required appreciation will be smaller than if the country had faced a fixed world real interest rate.

(iii) A third possibility is that capital mobility is less than perfect. A small country, like Australia, facing a fixed r', cannot borrow as much as it wants, but faces a finite foreign demand, K, for its new liabilities. The domestic securities market clears, but the world markets impose a risk premium over the world interest rate. The domestic real interest rate adjusts to assure portfolio balance, in flow terms, $I - S + K = 0$, yielding a domestic interest equal to the world rate plus the risk premium. The real exchange rate clears the basic market equation, $I - S + CA = 0$, describing both goods-market and basic balance-of-payments equilibria. Here, a rise in desired borrowing, $I - S$, raises the domestic real interest rate, reducing $I - S$ and lessening the required adjustment of the NATREX, as compared to a small country borrowing at the fixed world interest rate.

4.2 Goods Markets

We turn next to the specifications of the goods markets. The general case of the two versions we adopt is a model with three goods: an exportable good, 1; an importable good, 2; and a non-tradable good, n. Two endogenous relative prices clear the goods markets: the terms of trade, $T = P_1 - P_2$, clears the basic market equation, $I - S + CA = 0$; and the relative price of non-tradables to exportables, $P_n - P_1$, clears the excess demand for non-tradable goods, X_n. The equilibrium prices are determined simultaneously, as both of the relative prices influence the excess demand in each goods market. In this general model, the real exchange rate,

$$R = \alpha(P_n - P_1) - \alpha'(P'_n - P'_2) + (1 - \beta - \beta')T, \qquad (1.2a)$$

is influenced by the endogenous prices, $(P_n - P_1)$ and T, $(P'_n - P'_2)$ being assumed exogenous. We follow popular practice by adopting two special cases of this general model, each of which has only one endogenous price.

The first (version 1) assumes perfect substitutability between exportables and non-tradables ($P_n = P_1$, $P'_n = P'_2$) and complete specialization in production of the exportable good (β, $\beta' = 0$). Each country's GDP deflator collapses to the price of its exportable good ($P = P_1$, $P' = P'_2$) and the real exchange rate becomes simply the terms of trade, T. This is the standard macroeconomic assumption for large, open economies, such as the Mundell–Fleming and other Keynesian-type open-economy models.

The second (version 2) assumes that the country is small in the tradable goods markets and faces perfectly elastic world demand for and supply of tradable goods, making the terms of trade exogenous. The relative price of non-tradables, $P_n - P_1$, is the only endogenous relative price. Endogenous changes in the real exchange rate are proportional to the changes in the relative price of non-tradables, an increase appreciating the real exchange rate $[dR = \alpha(dP_n - dP_1)]$. Exogenous changes in T also influence the real exchange rate, directly and through any effects on $P_n - P_1$.

Both versions of the model can be written in terms of the basic market equation, $I - S + CA = 0$, cleared by the real exchange rate. In the general model, where goods n, 1, and 2 are produced, excess demands for all domestic and tradable goods can be written as the basic national-income-accounts equation or as the sum of domestic and world excess demands for goods.

$$I - S + CA \equiv (X_n + X_1 + X_2) + (X'_1 + X'_2), \tag{1.7}$$

where X_i and X'_i are domestic and foreign excess demands for good i.

In version 1, with the endogenous terms of trade, the world's demand for exports of good 1, X'_1, is finite, but the world offers a perfectly elastic supply of the import good 2 ($X'_2 = -X_2 < 0$). Non-tradables are perfect substitutes for exportables, all domestic goods being counted as good 1, so $X_n = 0$. Equation (1.7) collapses to

$$I - S + CA \equiv X_1 + X'_1 \equiv (X_1 + X_2) + (X'_1 - X_2), \tag{1.7a}$$

where $(X_1 + X_2) = I - S$, or expenditure minus production, and $(X'_1 - X_2) = CA$. The current account is negatively related to the terms of trade, and the terms of trade is the real exchange rate.

In version 2, with an endogenous relative price of non-tradables, the world's excess demands for tradable goods 1 and 2 are perfectly elastic at world prices ($X_1' = -X_1 > 0$; $X_2' = -X_2 < 0$). Equation (1.7) collapses to

$$I - S + CA \equiv (X_n + X_1 + X_2) + (-X_1 - X_2) \equiv X_n. \tag{1.7b}$$

With the country's excess demands for tradable goods always met by the rest of the world, the excess demand for all goods becomes the excess demand for non-tradables. Endogenous changes in R, reflecting adjustments of $P_n - P_1$, clear the basic market equation. With the world's excess demands for tradable goods perfectly elastic at world prices, the desired trade balance is defined by the sum of the home country's excess supplies of tradable goods $(-X_1 - X_2)$.

In our case studies, the economies of the United States (Chapter 2) and France/Germany (Chapter 4) are assumed to be closer to version 1 and are so modelled. Australia (Chapter 3) and the Latin American countries (Chapter 5) are assumed to be closer approximations to small economies and are modelled along the lines of version 2.

Desired investment and saving are essentially the same in both versions and so, too, are the trajectories and long-run levels of the stocks of capital, wealth, and net debt to foreigners. Casting the market equation always in the same basic form, $I - S + CA = 0$, emphasizes this similarity of the various NATREX models and focuses attention on the effects of investment and saving over time.

5. RESPONSES OF THE *NATREX* TO CHANGES IN THRIFT AND PRODUCTIVITY

The trajectory of the NATREX following an exogenous increase of borrowing from foreigners depends on the uses of the borrowed funds. The role of non-tradable goods and the responsiveness of the terms of trade also influence the adjustment of the NATREX, making some theoretical outcomes ambiguous. Adding empirical results to the theoretical predictions, we draw from the NATREX approach two basic conclusions about exogenous disturbances to desired investment and saving:

(i) Borrowing to finance consumption leads in the long run to higher indebtedness and interest payments to foreigners, to lower wealth, and to lower consumption. The NATREX initially appreciates, then gradually depreciates, with a net long-run depreciation.

(ii) Borrowing to finance productive investment unequivocally increases long-run wealth and consumption–possibly making the country a net creditor, with even greater long-run wealth and consumption. The NATREX initially appreciates, then gradually depreciates. If the country becomes a net creditor, the NATREX may eventually reverse itself, for a net long-run appreciation.

The importance of productivity and thrift in explaining the movements in the equilibrium real exchange rate warrant a more detailed discussion here of the response to these two disturbances.

5.1 Response of the NATREX to a Fall in Thrift

A decline of saving raises $I - S$, increasing borrowing from foreigners and producing net long-term capital inflows. The desired balance of payments—current account plus net long-term capital inflows—moves toward surplus. In the medium run, the NATREX appreciates, a standard conclusion from the Mundell–Fleming and many other models with high capital mobility.

With the rising debt to foreigners, wealth and consumption gradually decline, saving begins to rise, and the situation is reversed: desired capital inflows decline and interest payments to foreigners rise, dominating any improvement in the desired trade balance. The NATREX gradually depreciates. In the long run, the NATREX depreciates below its initial level, producing the trade surplus needed to offset higher interest payments to foreigners. *Increased borrowing to finance consumption appreciates the NA-TREX in the medium run, but leads to net real depreciation in the long run.*

Changes in desired capital inflows are the dominant force in explaining these changes in the NATREX, both the initial appreciation and subsequent depreciation. In both versions of the NA-TREX model, the NATREX adjusts to produce whatever current-account balances are needed to match changing long-term capital flows. In version 1, changes in the terms of trade move the NATREX and bring about the adjustments in the current account. In version 2, changes in the relative price of non-tradables/tradables accomplish the same thing.

The empirical evidence strongly supports this prediction of long-run real depreciation in response to an exogenous fall in saving. Theoretically, if new consumption were strongly biased toward endogenously priced domestic goods, medium-run appreciation would be larger and might not be completely reversed in the long run, but the empirical results in the following chapters show long-run depreciation in all cases.

5.2 Response of the NATREX to a Rise in Productivity

A rise in productivity allows more possibilities for the trajectory of the NATREX, due to the sector specificity of investment demand and productivity increases.

In the medium run, the response of the NATREX depends on which sectors produce the capital goods purchased for new investment. In version 1, a rise in I appreciates the NATREX (terms of trade), to the extent that new capital goods are produced domestically. In version 2, the NATREX appreciates ($P_n - P_1$ rises), to the extent that new capital goods are *non-tradable*, such as construction of buildings and infrastructure. If all the new capital goods were imported, the new imports would exactly equal the capital inflow, with no change in the NATREX.

Through time, the induced investment becomes smaller, but output is increased, as the new capital is brought on line. The longer-run changes in the NATREX depend in which industry the increase of productivity, the new investment, and the higher output occur.

In a country producing a single domestic good (version 1), the rise in productivity affects output of *all* domestic goods, as the new capital is gradually installed. If interest payments to foreigners were unchanged, the increased world supply of domestic goods would clearly depreciate the terms of trade (the NATREX) in the long run. Long-run real appreciation (leading to a trade deficit) would require that the country eventually become a net creditor, with interest payments *from* foreigners large enough to offset the increased imports of a wealthier country.

When the country produces both non-tradables and tradables, the sectoral location of the productivity increase becomes a factor. (i) Increased productivity in the non-tradable industry gradually raises output of non-tradables relative to the exportables, creating an excess supply of non-tradables. Rising incomes and a probable shift of resources from exportables to non-tradables create excess demand for exportables. The relative price of non-tradables, and the real exchange rate, depreciate. *Increased productivity in non-*

tradables leads to real depreciation in the long run, given the foreign debt.

As in version 1, a long-run appreciation is possible, if the country becomes a strong net creditor. In that case, consumption demand for non-tradables will have risen even more than output of non-tradables, due to the greatly increased wealth.

(ii) Increased productivity in tradables, sold at the world price, has the opposite effect on the NATREX over time. Three factors raise the relative price of non-tradables: (a) greater output of tradables raises income and demands for both goods, creating an excess demand for non-tradables; (b) higher real wages in the tradables sector, in response to greater marginal labour productivity, force up real wages and also prices in the non-tradable sector; and (c) if the productivity increase in tradables is non-factor augmenting, resources are drawn away from the non-tradables sector, further increasing excess demand for non-tradables (see Connolly and Devereux, Chapter 5). If the country eventually becomes a net creditor, the NATREX appreciates even more. *When the terms of trade are exogenous, increased productivity in the tradable industry leads to long-run real appreciation.*

In summary, the NATREX models provide two reasons to expect long-run appreciation from an increase of productivity: (a) the increase in output is so large, that higher saving turns the country first into a net lender, and then a net creditor with interest payments from foreigners; or (b) the increase of productivity occurs in a tradable sector where excess supply has little effect on the terms of trade, and the resulting rise in the relative price of non-tradables appreciates the NATREX. The subsequent empirical tests do not identify which of these two factors is more responsible for the long-run appreciation. But in the following empirical estimates for the US/G-10, France/Germany, and Latin America, a general increase in productivity (unspecified by sector) produces significant long-run appreciation. In Australia, by contrast, a rise in productivity leads to long-run real depreciation, suggesting that productivity increases have occurred primarily in the non-tradable sectors.

The argument that increasing productivity in the tradable sector appreciates a country's real exchange rate has traditionally been based on rising wages in both sectors (Balassa, 1964; Samuelson, 1964; and Bhagwati, 1984). Connolly and Devereaux (Chapter 5) generally support this conclusion, but show that the effects on the real exchange rate can be ambiguous, depending on how the rise in productivity affects the allocation of resources between the sectors. Their empirical work for Latin America shows that growth of GDP, their proxy for productivity growth, leads to appreciation of the NATREX, whereas Edwards (1989: 136–9) got the opposite empirical results for several developing countries. Neither the Balassa argument, Edwards, nor Connolly and Devereux consider investment, net capital flows, or the change in the foreign debt (those factors the NATREX approach emphasizes).

6. FUNDAMENTAL DISTURBANCES TO THE CURRENT ACCOUNT

We have focused the NATREX approach on fundamental disturbances to investment, saving, and net long-run capital flows, $I - S$, because we think these disturbances play an important role in explaining real exchange rate movements in recent years. In particular, exogenous changes in I and S have produced large fluctuations in the NATREX levels of large countries, in large part reflecting endogenous changes in their terms of trade. Such endogenous fluctuations in the terms of trade of large countries are experienced by their small-country trading partners as exogenous fluctuations in the small countries' terms of trade. For this and other reasons, small countries have faced substantial fluctuations in their exogenous terms of trade—disturbances to their current accounts. Changes in the terms of trade of both Australia (Chapter 3) and the Latin American countries (Chapter 5) lead to corresponding fluctuations in their equilibrium real exchange rates.

In a NATREX model, a disturbance directly affecting only the desired current account calls for an adjustment of the real exchange rate to return the current account to its original level ($CA = S - I$). If neither saving nor investment are affected, the disturbance induces no changes in stocks of assets, and the medium-run response of the NATREX becomes the long-run response. Disturbances to the current account lead to the same responses in a pure trade model, such as Connolly's and Devereux's in Chapter 5, as in a comparable version of a NATREX model. The current-account disturbance considered here is an exogenous change in the terms of trade (in version 2).

Recall that the real exchange rate is written as

$$R = \alpha(P_n - P_1) - \alpha'(P'_n - P'_2) + (1 - \beta - \beta')T \qquad (1.2a)$$

A rise in T itself appreciates the real exchange rate, as long as the weights of the importable goods are small ($\beta + \beta' < 1$), and given the relative prices of non-tradables. The effect of a rise in T on the endogenous relative price of non-tradables ($P_n - P_1$) is ambiguous, depending on the various demand and supply elasticities, but in any event is negligible, compared to the direct effects of T on the real exchange rate.

An exogenous rise in the world terms of trade appreciates the real exchange rate of a small country. Both empirical studies of small countries, Australia and the Latin American countries, strongly support this conclusion. Of more interest is how R differs from the exogenous terms of trade, as the relative price of non-traded good responds to other real fundamentals.

7. EMPIRICAL TESTING OF THE NATREX MODELS

We have developed the NATREX models to test empirically whether movements in quarterly real exchange rates can be explained by changes in exogenous real fundamentals. Our fundamental disturbances are exogenous changes in thrift and productivity and, for small countries, the terms of trade and world real interest rate.

The NATREX models, cast in real terms and based on an assumption of monetary neutrality, do not treat as fundamental any monetary disturbances (changes in nominal money supplies, prices of goods, interest rates, or exchange rates). With monetary neutrality in the medium to long run, monetary disturbances can cause the actual real exchange rate to deviate from its current equilibrium level, but cannot affect the equilibrium real exchange rate. We do not try to estimate the short-run fluctuations, but rather look for fundamental determinants of the trends in the equilibrium real exchange rate (the NATREX).

As described above, a single exogenous disturbance to investment or saving produces an entire new trajectory for the equilibrium real exchange rate, reflecting gradual induced changes in stocks of real assets. The empirical chapters try to determine the influence of the fundamentals on the endogenous moving equilibrium real exchange rate—the NATREX.

In all three of the estimations of NATREX models (US/G-10, France/Germany, and Australia), the real exchange rate is non-stationary, but cointegrated with the proxies for the real fundamental disturbances. This cointegration suggests the random movements of the real exchange rate can be attributed to the randomness of the disturbances, some predictable relationships existing between them. If the fundamentals were stationary, so too would be the real exchange rate, in the long-run steady state when the capital and debt ratios reached their equilibrium levels. But as long ·as the fundamentals that influence the real exchange rate are not stationary, neither will the real exchange rate be stationary.

Cointegration analysis is designed to estimate both the long-run influence of independent variables on the dependent variable and also, when adjustment takes some time, the deviations of the dependent variable from its long-run equilibrium. Ideally, if a NATREX model accurately described the structure and behaviour of the economy, the long-run cointegration equation would estimate the effects of the fundamentals on the long-run, steady-state NATREX. At the same time, the error-correction estimate would capture the direct medium-run response of the NATREX, as stocks of real assets begin to change.

The empirical results are encouraging, the cointegration equations producing R-squares of 0.70 to 0.96 and significant coefficients on the proxies for productivity and thrift. In all three cases, the thrift variables have positive coefficients, indicating that borrowing to finance consumption (a *decline* of thrift) leads to eventual real depreciation. The productivity variables produce different results in different countries. Borrowing to finance productive investment (an *increase* of productivity) leads to eventual real appreciation for the United States and France/Germany, but to depreciation for Australia. These differences may reflect true differences in the steady-state responses, consistent with the theory, or may result from the estimates capturing different points on the trajectory of the NATREX, rather than its steady-state value. The initial medium-run influence of the fundamentals on the real exchange rate did not produce significant coefficients when measured directly and, for the United States and Australia, is picked up indirectly through the long-term real interest-rate differential.

The strong relationships between the fundamentals and the real exchange rates in the cointegration equations clearly suggest some regular influence, consistent with the predictions of the NATREX models. In particular, the coefficients on the proxies for thrift suggest that the cointegration equations are capturing longer-run responses. The predicted longer-run depreciation, in response to a fall in thrift, is the opposite sign from the predicted short-to medium-run appreciation, in the face of capital inflows.

We believe that the estimated cointegration equations are capturing the NATREX at some point on the trajectory toward the steady state, where the capital stock and net foreign debt are endogenous, but before the long-run steady state is reached. Several factors suggest that the cointegration equations are not measuring the full long-run, steady-state responses of the NATREX.

(i) The dependent variable is not directly observable. In the NATREX models, the dependent variable is the medium-run *equilibrium* real exchange rates. We can observe only the actual real exchange rates, R_t, usually short-run deviations from the current equilibrium rate. Because we cannot actually observe the equilibrium rate, the estimated equations must simultaneously test two hypotheses: (a) the actual real exchange rate adjusts fairly quickly to its equilibrium, and (b) the equilibrium rate (the NATREX) can be explained by the fundamentals as predicted by the NATREX models.

(ii) The independent variables of exogenous thrift and productivity also are not directly observable.

Changes in various rates of saving serve as proxies for exogenous changes in thrift. Without some external information, we have no way of separating the exogenous changes in thrift from endogenous responses of saving, as levels of real assets change. All three NATREX studies use a ratio of national saving (GNP-C-G) to GNP (GDP for Australia and France) as a proxy for thrift. Changing stocks of real assets alter these ratios, as they affect the numerator and denominator differently, making the saving ratios less than perfect proxies for exogenous changes in thrift. The French–German chapter addresses this problem by creating also a derived saving ratio, in which the influence of the capital–employment ratio has been removed. But all the proxies for exogenous thrift reflect endogenous changes in net foreign debt.

The proxies for productivity are also imperfect measures of exogenous productivity, in part reflecting endogenous increases in the capital stock. Again, the choice of proxies differs across the three studies: for the US and G-10, the twelve-quarter moving averages of rates of growth of their respective GNPs; for Australia, the average product of labour; and in France/Germany, the capital–employment ratio. The influence of endogenous changes in the stock of capital is most apparent in the capital–employment ratio, as well as problems of cyclical movements in employment.

(iii) A cointegration equation can estimate true long-run relationships between variables, only if the sample period is long enough to cover full adjustment for many observations. When the sample period is too short, the estimated equation reflects earlier, more short- and medium-run responses, rather than the true long-run relationship. The resulting coefficient will be the wrong size and possibly the wrong sign for the long-run influence.

The sample periods for the three NATREX studies range from 12 years for France/Germany, to 15 years for the US/G-10 and Australia. In NATREX models, adjustment to the long run implies that stocks of real capital and net debt to foreigners have reached their steady-state levels (or steady-state ratios to the labour force). We have no estimate of the length of time needed for the capital/labour ratio and the ratio of net foreign debt/labour to reach their steady-state values. But we seriously doubt whether 12 to 15 years is long enough for full adjustment to occur for several disturbances.

(iv) Finally, the medium run is an artificial construct, drawing a false dichotomy between the short- to medium-run period of cyclical, price, and speculative adjustments and the medium- to long-run period of adjustments in stocks of real assets. Ideally, the error-correction estimates should capture the medium-run responses of the NATREX to changes in the fundamentals, holding stocks of assets constant. In reality, stocks of assets start changing soon after an exogenous disturbance to investment or saving, before the inter-cyclical conditions of the medium run are met. The medium run cannot be observed, because it does not actually exist.

How then should we interpret the empirical results, in light of these qualifications? We are not sure what stage of adjustment the estimated cointegration equation is capturing. We suspect the cointegration equation may be estimating a relationship between the fundamentals and the equilibrium real exchange rate somewhere on its trajectory toward the steady state, partly because our proxies for the exogenous fundamentals include some of the effects of changing stocks, effectively incorporating endogenous changes in real assets into the independent variables.

We also believe that the cointegration equations may be estimating different points on the trajectories for different disturbances. The positive coefficients on proxies for thrift are consistent with the long-run predictions of the NATREX model, but opposite in sign to the standard short-to-medium run responses predicted by most models with high capital mobility, suggesting a point near the end of the trajectory. However, for the United States, the appreciation of the real exchange rate and the worsening of the current account in response to an increase in domestic productivity together suggest that the estimates may be picking up a point on the earlier part of the trajectory, when capital is still flowing in and the initial appreciation of the real exchange rate has not yet been fully reversed.

A further complication in trying to capture the medium-run responses is the slow convergence of real long-term interest rates. The NATREX models use long-term real interest rates, rather than the short-term nominal interest rates so much examined in the literature. In the study of the US/G-10, Stein found that US long-term real interest rates converge to G-10 and to German rates only with a considerable lag. Increased borrowing by the US, for either consumption or investment, initially increases the US real long-term interest more than the G-10 rate. The differential gradually converges to zero, but only half the differential is eliminated in one and one-half years. For a large country like the United States, increased borrowing $(I - S)$ will eventually raise the world long-term real interest rate. But initially, the adjustment falls more on the domestic, and less on the foreign, rate, reducing the required medium-run appreciation of the NATREX. This initial substitution of real interest-rate adjustment for real exchange-rate adjustment further suggests why some of the coefficients for the changes in the fundamentals are insignificant.

As an alternative means of capturing the early response of the NATREX, for both the US and Australian cases the long-run real interest-rate differential is included as an independent variable. The coefficient is significant and positive, as expected, but interpretation of this coefficient is not obvious. Could the appreciation of the real exchange rate in response to the increased differential between interest rates reflect a short-run deviation of R_t from the NATREX, due to monetary factors, rather than an equilibrium response of the NATREX to a change in the fundamentals? We do not think so, for monetary policy should not affect the long-term real interest rates. The slow convergence of long-term real interest rates across countries, following fundamental real disturbances, suggests that the differential between long-term real interest rates does provide a reasonable proxy for medium-run effects of fundamental disturbances.

In spite of these problems in interpreting the empirical results, we are struck by the strong cointegration of the real exchange rates with the proxies for the fundamentals, by the significance of the coefficients in the cointegration equations, consistent with the predictions of the NATREX models, and by the high explanatory power of the estimations for the movements in real exchange rates. These results are consistent for different countries and using different proxies for the exogenous fundamental variables. In addition, the study of the United States included tests on the relation of the fundamentals to the current account, also finding cointegration and strong explanatory power, consistent with the theory.

8. IMPLICATIONS FOR NOMINAL EXCHANGE-RATE POLICIES

The large year-to-year changes in real exchange rates over the past twenty years have often been seen as evidence that real exchange rates deviate seriously from their equilibrium levels. Others claim that all observed real exchange rates are the results of intertemporal optimization with random deviations. The major finding from these NATREX studies is that real fundamentals can largely explain trends in real exchange rates. Changes in thrift and productivity, and for small countries changes in the terms of trade and world interest rate, account for most of the movements in the real exchange rates.

We conclude that changes in the fundamentals are the only effective means of reducing movements in the real exchange rate. Monetary policies, aimed at nominal money supplies, interest rates or exchange-rates, will not substantially influence the year-to-year trajectory of the real exchange rate.

The choice of nominal exchange-rate regime does influence the speed at which the real exchange rate adjusts to its equilibrium

NATREX. The estimated cointegration equations in the subsequent chapters produce a better fit when the nominal exchange rate is not pegged. The three case studies include a country with a flexible nominal exchange rate (US/G-10), countries with an adjustable pegged nominal exchange rate (France/Germany), and a country operating under both during the sample period (Australia). The Australian real exchange rate tracked the predicted equilibrium exchange rate more closely when the nominal exchange rate was flexible. The overall fit of the estimated equation for the United States, with a flexible rate ($R^2 = 0.95$), is better than that for France/Germany, with a pegged nominal rate ($R^2 = 0.70$).

So in spite of the complications from speculative capital flows, the empirical evidence somewhat supports the traditional argument for a flexible nominal exchange rate, and for the traditional reasons. Under a pegged nominal exchange rate, real exchange-rate adjustment depends on the often slow changes in relative prices of goods and services. A rapidly changing flexible nominal exchange rate can speed up the adjustment. In spite of short-run volatility of real exchange rates, we find no evidence of systematic deviations of nominal and real exchange rates under a flexible nominal rate, the one exception being the large appreciation of the dollar in 1985, suggesting a speculative bubble.

However, we should emphasize that the NATREX approach does not model differences between fixed and flexible exchange rates. Theoretically, the assumption of monetary neutrality asserts that the medium run, the starting point of the NATREX model, is identical for either nominal exchange-rate regime. Empirically, we look only at the real exchange rate and do not distinguish between changes in the nominal exchange rate and changes in relative prices.

The strong influences of thrift and productivity on the real exchange rate lend support to two basic assumptions of the NATREX approach—a relatively high degree of long-term capital mobility and desired saving and investment relatively independent of the real exchange rate, compared with the response of the current account. For the US, Stein finds that both the real exchange rate and the current account/GNP ratio respond to the same measures of thrift and productivity in the way predicted by the NATREX model. This provides further evidence that the current account adjusts to match exogenous changes in long-term capital flows, responding to induced changes in the real exchange rate. We conclude that the most effective way to change the current account is to alter national investment minus national saving, rather than trying to influence the current account directly by altering demands and supplies for tradable goods through monetary and trade policies.

In summary, the empirical evidence from our NATREX studies tells us that actual real exchange rates have tracked their moving equilibrium levels fairly closely. Changes in the real fundamentals of thrift and productivity account for much of the real appreciations and depreciations. The real exchange rate moves to its equilibrium trajectory under either pegged or flexible nominal exchange rates, but more quickly under flexible nominal rates.

To say that the real exchange rate responds to real fundamentals is not to say that the outcome is optimal. The NATREX approach is positive rather than normative, and does not imply a judgement about the desirability of the outcome or the ability of policy-makers to influence that outcome. We believe that rapid adjustment to the equilibrium real exchange rate is preferable on balance to continued deviations from the real equilibrium rate. But the equilibrium real exchange rate may not be optimal, reflecting less than optimal policies. Because the ratio of social saving to GNP empirically is not stationary, we reject Ricardian equivalence. We believe the fundamentals of thrift and productivity can be influenced by government policies, changes in government saving being the most direct way for a government to influence $I - S$. On these issues, many may disagree. But, independent from questions of the optimality and effectiveness of government policies, the empirical evidence from the NATREX studies stands: real exchange rates and the current account/GNP ratios do respond to the fundamentals.

The evidence from these NATREX studies also provides a warning that changes in $I - S$ have both medium-run and long-run effects, possibly in opposite directions, and with complex trajectories. Long-run policies to achieve socially desirable rates of investment and saving make sense. Policies aimed at a single 'equilibrium' level of the real exchange rate do not make sense, for the equilibrium real exchange rate is continually changing.

Finally, I want to conclude this chapter on non-speculative real exchange rates with a speculative note. What does the NATREX approach tell us about the recent turmoil of exchange rates in Europe? In particular, can the market pressures for appreciation of the Deutschmark relative to the other European currencies be explained by the fundamentals or do these pressures simply reflect short-run monetary and speculative factors? The estimated empirical equation for France/Germany does not perform well for the most recent period, in large part because of the sudden change in the definition of the German economy. Lacking empirical evidence, we ask what the theoretical NATREX model would predict.

We must first define the basic fundamental economic disturbances resulting from German reunification. Despite the enormity of the economic problems in the former East Germany, I suggest that the real economic effects of reunification have been (a) an exogenous increase in the marginal productivity of investment in Germany, and (b) an exogenous decline in German national thrift, as the German government has borrowed to finance increased government consumption expenditures. Both disturbances should lead to real appreciation of Germany's NATREX in the medium run. The long-run effects on the NATREX are ambiguous, depending on the relative strength and duration of the two disturbances—that is, on the strength and speed of economic development in eastern Germany. Rapid growth of output and average productivity in eastern Germany could lead either to long-run real depreciation or, if a strong productivity effect on output dominated the decline in saving, to long-run appreciation of the German NATREX. But if the eastern German economy is very slow to recover, requiring large continued social assistance from the government, the fall in saving will dominate, clearly leading to long-run depreciation of the German NATREX.

What does this tell us of the recent exchange-rate pressures for appreciation of the mark? Given that Germany's equilibrium real exchange rate had appreciated, under fixed nominal exchange rates within the European Monetary System, a rise in the relative prices of German goods and services was the only way to achieve a real appreciation. With the high rate of German unemployment, the German economy is not at a medium-run equilibrium and the real exchange rate cannot be the equilibrium rate, but pressures toward the equilibrium rate remain. German inflation has risen somewhat, working in the direction of achieving the equilibrium real exchange rate, but German monetary policy has been working to reduce that inflation. Absent price inflation in Germany, the only way to achieve an equilibrium real exchange rate with a fixed nominal rate is price deflation in the other European countries. Participants in the financial markets, apparently doubting the willingness of the other European countries to accept the needed price deflation, successfully speculated on the nominal appreciation of the Deutschmark.

Have real disturbances or monetary policies been responsible for the turmoil in European financial markets? The answer—probably both. The underlying disturbances from German reunification are real, fundamental, and large, producing substantial changes in the equilibrium real exchange rates. *How* the real exchange rate will change—through prices of goods and services or the nominal exchange rate—depends on nominal monetary and exchange-rate policies. When domestic monetary and exchange-rate policies, combined with lagged price adjustment, do not promote adjustment to the equilibrium real exchange rate, speculation in the financial markets is the likely outcome.

This chapter has discussed the NATREX approach in intuitive terms—its purpose and characteristics—and summarized the supporting empirical evidence. Subsequent chapters present the empirical studies in detail, specifying the particular theoretical models and the method and results of the empirical tests. While the results are far from definitive, we believe they are too promising to be ignored. Fundamental economic variables provide systematic explanations for trends in real exchange rates, consistent with the predictions of the NATREX models.

REFERENCES

Balassa, Bela. 1964. 'The purchasing power parity doctrine: a reappraisal'. *Journal of Political Economy*, 72, 584–96.

Bhagwati, Jagdish N. 1984. 'Why are services cheaper in the poor countries?'. *Economic Journal*, 94 (June), 279–86.

Bosworth, Barry P. 1993. *Saving and Investment in a Global Economy*. Washington, DC, Brookings Institution.

Dornbusch, Rudiger. 1976. 'Expectations and exchange rate dynamics'. *Journal of Political Economy*, 84 (Dec.) 1161–76.

Edwards, Sebastian. 1989. *Real Exchange Rates, Devaluation, and Adjustment*. Cambridge, Mass., MIT Press.

Feldstein, Martin and Charles Horioka. 1980. 'Domestic saving and international capital flows'. *Economic Journal*, 90, 314–29.

Fleming, J. M. 1962. 'Domestic financial policy under fixed and under floating exchange rates'. *IMF Staff Papers*, 9, 369–79.

Harberger, Arnold. 1986. 'Economic adjustment and the real exchange rate'. In Sebastian Edwards and Liaquat Ahamed, eds., *Economic Adjustment and Exchange Rates in Developing Countries*. Chicago, University of Chicago Press, 371–414.

Laursen, Svend and Lloyd A. Metzler. 1950. 'Flexible exchange rates and the theory of employment'. *The Review of Economics and Statistics*, 32 (4), 281–99.

McKibbin, Warwick J. and Jeffrey D. Sachs. 1991. *Global Linkages: Macroeconomic Interdependence and Cooperation in the World Economy*. Washington, DC, Brookings Institution.

Mundell, R. A. 1963. 'Capital mobility and stabilization policy under fixed and flexible exchange rates'. *Canadian Journal of Economics and Political Science*, 29, 475–85.

Nurkse, Ragnar. 1945. *Conditions of International Monetary Equilibrium*. Essays in International Finance, no. 4 (spring), International Finance Section, Princeton University. [Reprinted in Ellis, Howard S. and Lloyd A. Metzler, eds., *Readings in the Theory of International Trade*, American Economic Association, Homewood, Illinois (Richard D. Irwin, 1950)].

Samuelson, Paul. 1964. 'Theoretical notes on trade problems'. *The Review of Economics and Statistics*, 46, 145–54.

Svensson, Lars E. O. and Assaf Razin. 1983. 'The terms of trade and the current account: the Harberger–Laursen–Metzler effect'. *Journal of Political Economy*, 91 (11), 94–125.

Williamson, John. 1983. *The Exchange Rate System*. Institute for International Economics, Washington, DC (Sept.). Distr. by MIT Press, Cambridge, Mass.

2

The Natural Real Exchange Rate of the United States Dollar, and Determinants of Capital Flows

JEROME L. STEIN

The aim of this chapter is show to what extent the NATREX model can be used to answer the following (Q) questions, concerning the real international value of the US dollar and current account.

Q1. To what extent has the real exchange rate of the US dollar been as stable as is justified by the 'fundamentals', and to what extent are its variations noise? What are the fundamentals? What factors can explain the persistent and large deviations from purchasing power parity? Can we calculate whether the US dollar is over or undervalued?[1] If we can answer these questions, we can evaluate the performance of the free exchange-rate regime for the US dollar.

Q2. How do international financial markets affect the responses of the US economy to internal and external disturbances? What are the determinants of capital mobility?

Q3. What has produced the US current-account deficits? What policies could be adopted to reverse them? One theory claims that they have been the result of increases in the expected return on investment in the US relative to other countries; and another theory attributes the inflows to the strong US fiscal policy stimulus and the declining private saving ratio. What are the long-run effects of government budget deficits upon the trade balance?

---

[1] We do not start with the assumption that at each moment of time the value of the dollar represents the value implied by a perfect-foresight intertemporal optimization model.

1. HOW THE *NATREX* MODEL RESPONDS TO THESE QUESTIONS

1.1 The NATREX Concept

Part 1 explains, in a relatively intuitive and non-technical manner, how the NATREX approach answers the above questions. Then, the more technical structure of the model and econometrics are presented. The NATREX, again, is the '*nat*ural *r*eal *ex*change rate', the equilibrium real exchange rate that would prevail if speculative and cyclical factors could be removed and the unemployment rate is at its natural rate. This is exactly what Nurkse had in mind in defining what he means by the 'equilibrium exchange rate'.

The nominal exchange rate N (a rise signifies an appreciation of the US dollar) is the number of units of foreign currency purchased by a unit of domestic currency. The real exchange rate R (a rise is an appreciation of the US dollar) is the amount of goods that \$1 can purchase abroad relative to what it can purchase at home. The relation between the real and nominal rates is $R = N/(p'/p) = Np/p'$ where N is the nominal exchange rate, p is the domestic and p' is the foreign GDP deflator. Our fundamentals are the disturbances to productivity and social thrift at home and abroad denoted by vector $Z(t)$, and are exogenous to the model. For the US, the terms of trade and world rate of interest are endogenous. The fundamentals $Z(t)$ affect the real exchange rate $R(t)$, the real interest rate, the rate of capital formation dk/dt and the rate of change of the foreign debt dF/dt equal to the current-account deficit.

The actual real exchange rate $R(t)$, which does not always equal the equilibrium (NATREX), may be decomposed as the sum of three elements in identity equation (2.1).

$$R(t) = [R(t) - R(k(t), F(t); Z(t))] + [R(k(t), F(t); Z(t)) - R^*(Z(t))]$$

$$+ R^*[Z(t)] = Np/p' \tag{2.1}$$

The conditions determining the NATREX are that the basic balance of payments, or goods markets, is in equilibrium at capacity output and there is portfolio balance between the holding of assets denominated in the home and in the foreign currency. The NATREX is $R(k(t), F(t); Z(t))$, where the stocks of capital $k(t)$ and foreign debt $F(t)$ per unit of effective labour are given.

The term $[R(t) - R(k(t), F(t); Z(t))]$ represents the deviation of the actual real exchange rate from the NATREX. In the *longer run*, the disturbances $Z(t)$ affect the evolution of capital and foreign debt, via the investment function and the current account. As the stocks of capital and foreign debt evolve, the equilibrium values of the real exchange rate and interest rate change. In the steady state when capital and debt converge to the values determined by the fundamentals $Z(t)$, the NATREX converges to $R^*(Z(t))$. The second term $[R(k(t), F(t); Z(t)) - R^*(Z(t))]$ is the deviation of the NATREX at any time from its steady-state value $R^*(Z(t))$. The interaction of the medium and longer run is the contribution of the NATREX model. The NATREX itself is a moving equilibrium rate, because exogenous $Z(t)$ and endogenous capital $k(t)$ and debt $F(t)$ evolve over time.

The actual real exchange rate $R(t)$ often differs from the NATREX (the first term) as a result of speculative and cyclical factors, which are definitely not included in our Z fundamentals. For example, in 1993, the expectations of a recovery in the US and an easing of monetary policy in Germany in view of their recession, affected the short-run nominal exchange rate and, given the slow change in relative prices, also the real exchange rate. Short-run exchange-rate variations are noise and not reflections of rational expectations, for the following reason.

The hypothesis of uncovered interest-rate parity with rational expectations states that there will be speculative short-term capital flows to produce an equality between the expected returns on a short-term asset denominated in dollars and a comparable asset denominated in foreign currency. If the foreign short-term nominal interest rate exceeds the corresponding dollar rate, the dollar will fall very quickly relative to its rationally expected value at the maturity of the short-term asset. If short-term speculative capital flows are produced by rational expectations, then the mathematical expectation of the percentage change in the nominal value of the dollar (over a one-or three-month horizon), is equal to the appropriate current short-term foreign less US interest-rate differential. Thereby, expected returns are equal in the two currencies. This is the uncovered interest-rate parity theory with rational expectations.

The covered interest-rate parity theory (which does not involve rational expectations) states that the forward premium (discount) on the $US is equal to the foreign less US interest-rate differential.

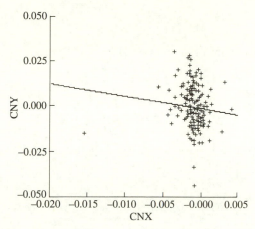

FIG. 2.1   *CNY = per cent change in spot price, CNX = forward premium one month earlier, monthly, 1981.05–1989.09, Canada*

Therefore, we may state the uncovered interest-rate parity theory with rational expectations as follows. On average, the points in a graph relating the percentage change in the nominal exchange rate (over a one-month horizon) to the forward premium or discount (equal to the interest-rate differential) on assets with a comparable maturity lie along a 45 degree line. Empirically, this is not the case. Figures 2.1 and 2.2 for Canada and Germany illustrate this point.[2] The regression coefficient is not significantly different from zero. It is well known that the current short-term nominal interest-rate differential (equal to the forward premium or discount) conveys no information about subsequent exchange rate changes.[3] Studies by the Bank of Canada[4] have shown that one cannot account for this failure by invoking an objective risk premium. Therefore, the short-term variations in the nominal exchange rate cannot be explained

---

[2] We used daily data at non-overlapping intervals.

[3] Almost everyone who has examined the data agrees that there is no informational content in the forward rate concerning subsequent exchange-rate changes. The adjusted R-square is close to zero. See the Appendix chapter, Table A2. Some do not feel that the lack of relation indicates that short-run changes are noise but claim that the fact that the means are the same is sufficient reason to accept rationality. We cannot accept this. Suppose that a watch is permanently stopped at 6:00. It gives an unbiased estimate of the time; but how much is one willing to pay for such a watch?

[4] Boothe, Clinton, Côté, and Longworth (1985).

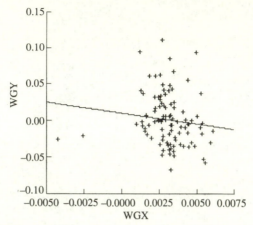

FIG. 2.2 *WGY = per cent change in spot price, WGX = forward premium one month earlier, monthly, 1981.05–1989.09, Germany*

by short-term interest-rate differentials. Short-term speculative capital flows are noise, not reflections of rational expectations.

Although the exchange rate does not reflect the fundamentals Z in the short run, it does so in the longer run. We show that, as the time horizon lengthens, market pressures push the real exchange rate toward the NATREX, as they push the nominal exchange rate and relative prices to clear the goods markets and produce equilibrium in the basic balance of payments. Component $[R(t) - R(k(t), F(t); Z(t))]$, which is the deviation of the actual real exchange rate from the NATREX, converges to zero. The fundamentals $Z(t)$ which change over time determine the moving equilibrium natural real exchange rate. Since $Z(t)$ evolves over time, NATREX changes over time. *A variable is said to be stationary if its mean and variance are both independent of time.*

The reason why the purchasing-power parity hypothesis[5] is often incorrect is that it fails to take into account the evolution of the fundamentals Z which have not been stationary during the free exchange-rate period. The PPP hypothesis is that R is stationary. A

---

[5] The PPP hypothesis is the relative PPP hypothesis whereby the index number of the nominal value of the dollar at any time relative to a base period is equal to the index number of the foreign GDP deflator relative to the index number of the US GDP deflator, relative to the same base period.

variable $R(t)$ is stationary at constant value C if its mathematical expectation denoted $E(R(t))$ converges to C as time increases. That is, the mean of $R = C$ is independent of time and $\lim E[R(t)] \Rightarrow C$, as t grows. In that case, variations in the nominal exchange rate are explained simply by changes in relative prices (PPP). Our Natural Real Exchange Rate (NATREX) generated by the fundamentals replaces the PPP theory. The PPP hypothesis arbitrarily assumes that $R[k(t), F(t); Z(t)]$ is constant. It ignores both the changing fundamentals and the resulting evolution of capital and debt.

It is agreed that the real exchange rate has not been stationary during the past twenty years since the nominal exchange rates were allowed to float.[6] Some authors take very long views and ask if the real exchange rate is stationary over a century or more. Corbae and Ouliaris (1991) test the stationarity hypothesis on the Australian real exchange rate for the period 1890–1984 and reject the stationarity hypothesis. Lothian and Taylor (1992) find that for a period of almost two centuries, the pound and French franc real exchange rates are stationary. However, the speed of convergence to stationarity is slow. They claim that the reason the real exchange rate is not considered to be stationary over shorter periods, such as post-World War II or the last two decades, is that the unit root tests are low powered.

What is the economic point of these stationarity tests? Suppose that over an horizon of a century or two, for example (Lothian–Taylor) during the period 1770–1944, the real exchange rate $R(t)$ is stationary at value $C(0)$. Does that mean that $C(0)$ is the equilibrium rate that should have been set at the Bretton Woods conference in 1946? Does this mean that the European Monetary System (EMS) should use $C(0)$ to set real exchange rates from 1984–2004? Does this mean that the deviation $[R(t) - C(0)]$ measures market disequilibrium? Given that the convergence to stationarity is slow, what are the economic implications for the EMS of the sustained deviations? When there is a deviation, does this mean that policy measures should or should not be undertaken to correct the situation? I think that this is a 1993 way of understanding Nurkse's objection to the use of PPP in determining what are equilibrium exchange rates.

The issue is not whether or not the real exchange rate is stationary over an arbitrary period, but whether it reflects the

---

[6] See Table 2.4 for stationarity tests.

fundamentals Z. If by chance Z is stationary over an arbitrary period, our real exchange rate will tend to be stationary, subject to qualifications below concerning the evolution of capital and debt. Then PPP will be valid for that period. If, as is the case, the fundamentals Z are $I(1)$ not stationary, then neither will be the real exchange rate. Our model focuses upon the second and third terms in equation (2.1) and is an economic generalization of PPP. The NATREX is a moving equilibrium, based upon explicit fundamentals and endogenous changes in capital and debt. Our object is to explain why the real exchange rate varies and how it responds to changes in the specific fundamentals. The PPP hypothesis ignores these questions.

The NATREX model does not specify whether changes in the real exchange rate $R = Np/p'$ will be reflected in changes in the nominal exchange rate or in changes in relative prices. In point of fact for the US since 1973, the variation is in the nominal exchange rate and not in relative prices.[7] We know that prices are less flexible than nominal exchange rates. This implies that the real exchange rate will converge faster to the NATREX under a regime of free rates than under fixed rates, where the entire burden of adjustment is on relative prices, with adverse effects upon unemployment and inflation.

1.2 *The NATREX Model; Theoretical and Empirical Results*

We describe and summarize in an intuitive way our answers to questions Q1–Q3 posed at the beginning of this chapter.

First: to what extent has the real exchange rate been as stable as is justified by the fundamentals, and what are the fundamentals? For the US relative to the G-10, the fundamentals Z are (a) the productivity of capital at home and abroad, measured by the moving average of the growth of domestic and foreign real GDP; (b) the US index of social time preference measured by the ratio $(C + G)/GNP$ of consumption C plus government purchases G to GNP; and (c) the ephemeral difference between the US and G-10 *real long-term* rates of interest. We use a twelve-quarter moving average of the growth of real GDP to abstract from the cyclical elements which are excluded from our concept of the NATREX, as a moving equilibrium real exchange rate.

---

[7] See Figure 2.7 where the real and nominal rates practically coincide. This is not necessarily true for other countries.

Neither the real exchange rate R nor the fundamentals $Z(t) = \{\text{the}$ index of time preference, the US and the foreign growth rates}, have not been stationary, during the past twenty years.[8] Hence the PPP assumption of stationarity of the real exchange rate and of the fundamentals is not valid during the period of floating. Moreover, we shall explain why endogenous variables such as the current account/GNP have not been stationary.

Second: we describe two scenarios. In the first, there is a rise in the index of social time preference, the social consumption ratio $(C + G)/$ GNP. We make no distinction between the private sector and the public sector, and assume for the US that government expenditures are consumption rather than investment.[9] For example, the Reagan tax cut which increased private consumption but which was not offset by a decline in government consumption is an exogenous rise in time preference. This means that social (private plus public) saving[10] declines. Then we describe the scenario where the growth rate of the US or the foreign economy has increased as a result of a rise in investment. This may occur either because the Keynes–Tobin q-ratio has increased or because growth has increased due to greater immigration.[11]

Tables 2.1 and 2.2 describe the theoretical and empirical results, respectively. In Table 2.1 column 1 are the effects of a rise in the index of time preference which lowers social saving. Column 2 describes the effects of a rise in the growth rate resulting from a rise in investment. In both cases investment less saving $(I - S)$ rises initially. Although the medium-run effects are the same in both cases, the longer-run (growth) effects are fundamentally different.

---

[8] See Table 2.6 for stationarity tests. My data come primarily from the Federal Reserve. The real exchange rate of the dollar is *vis-à-vis* the G-10. The foreign growth rate refers to the G-18.

[9] This assumption need not be true for other countries nor even for the US during some time period. For example, German government expenditures in Eastern Germany contain a large investment component.

[10] Social saving is private saving $S' = \text{GNP} - C - T$ (disposable income less consumption) plus government saving $S'' = (T - G)$. Consumption $= C$, taxes $= T$, government purchases $= G$. Hence social saving $S = S' + S'' = \text{GNP} - (C + G)$, and index of time preference $(C + G)/\text{GNP}$.

[11] Investment per unit of effective labour $I = dk/dt + nk$, where k is capital per unit of effective labour, n is the growth rate of effective labour. A rise in immigration raises n and raises investment. A rise in the q-ratio raises dk/dt and raises investment. Growth is associated either with a rise in the q-ratio or a rise in n. Immigration is less important for the US during the period considered than for countries such as Israel or even Germany.

TABLE 2.1   *Summary of the effects of two disturbances in the NATREX model: a rise in time preference, a rise in investment and growth*

	Rise in time preference	Rise in investment and growth
A. Medium run when the capital and debt intensities are given	Both disturbances have the same effect. There is a rise in the domestic less foreign real rate of interest and a capital inflow. The real exchange rate appreciates and there is a current account deficit and rising debt.	
B. Trajectory where capital and debt evolve	There are a growing debt, current account deficits, and a depreciating exchange rate.	The capital intensity and real GDP rise. Initially investment exceeds saving, there are current account deficits, and the debt rises. As saving rises due to the higher GDP, and investment declines due to the rising capital intensity, the current account increases. Capital inflows change to capital outflows. As the foreign debt is lowered, the real exchange rate appreciates.
C. Steady state where the capital and debt intensities are constant and the trade balance is equal to the interest payments.	Debt rises and capital declines. The real exchange rate depreciates.	The capital intensity rises and the debt intensity declines. The lower debt tends to appreciate and the higher capital intensity tends to depreciate the real exchange rate. Theoretically the net effect is ambiguous.

In both cases in the medium run, investment rises relative to saving. Since domestic social saving is inadequate to finance investment, this tends to raise the domestic less foreign real rate of interest, which leads to a portfolio adjustment and a capital inflow. The capital inflow appreciates the real exchange rate and leads to a current-account deficit. The portfolio adjustment and capital inflow will tend to equalize the real rates of interest. As long as investment less saving is not zero, the capital flow will continue even after real interest rates have been equalized.[12] The foreign debt rises as a

---

[12] See Niehans (1994) on why the convergence of real interest rates does not imply very much about capital mobility, which concerns the difference between saving and investment.

result of the current account deficits. The evolution of the economy is different in the two cases. The next phase is where capital and debt evolve in response to the change in the fundamentals.

The rise in the index of time preference leads to a rise in the foreign debt without a rise in the capital intensity and capacity output. The rise in the foreign debt reduces wealth, and the decline in wealth reduces consumption. Thereby, social saving rises to equal investment; and the foreign debt stabilizes at a higher level. For example, if the decline in social saving were the result of a decline in government saving, the decline in wealth would raise private saving to offset the decline. This is not Ricardian equivalence but an equilibrating mechanism whereby the foreign debt converges to a sustainable level. The government budget deficit is sustainable, but the foreign debt stabilizes at a higher level.

Finally, the economy reaches a steady state where the capital and debt intensities are constant at levels determined by the fundamentals. The higher steady-state foreign debt, with no change in the profile of investment, implies higher interest payments on the debt. The real exchange rate will depreciate to produce a higher trade balance to finance the higher interest payments on the debt. The medium-run effect of a rise in the index of time preference was to appreciate the real exchange rate. The longer-run effect is to depreciate the real exchange rate below its initial level.

In the second case where the growth rate increased as a result of a rise in investment, the *evolution* of the economy is quite different. The capital inflow equal to the current account deficit finances investment not consumption. As a result of the greater rate of investment, the capital intensity rises and increases capacity output. The rise in capital gradually reduces the marginal product of capital and in turn the rate of investment. The rise in real GDP increases saving. The decline in investment and rise in saving then reduce the capital inflow matched by falling current account deficits. Eventually, the rise in capacity output leads to a situation where saving exceeds investment, and there are capital outflows.

In the steady state, the foreign debt will decline, and stabilize at a lower level; and the capital intensity will converge to a higher level than initially.

There are conflicting effects on the real exchange rate, as capital and debt converge to their steady-state values. (a) The lower debt or possible conversion to a creditor will reduce interest payments to foreigners and tend to appreciate the real exchange rate. (b) The rise in capital lowers investment and increases saving, reducing desired capital inflows, and also increases desired imports, tending to depreciate the exchange rate. From another viewpoint, the rise in capital increases the output of exportables, depreciating the real exchange rate through a reduction in the terms of trade.[13]

Empirically, the econometric results in the tables below are summarized in Table 2.2 for the US/G-10. We believe that the econometric cointegration results are picking up the trajectory effects (part B of Table 2.1). The first column of Table 2.2 refers to the fundamental variables denoted Z: a rise in the index of time preference $(C+G)/GNP$, a rise in the moving average of the US growth rate, a rise in the moving average of the foreign growth rate. The second column refers to the change in the equilibrium real exchange rate R. The third column refers to the change in the equilibrium current account/GNP. These are the equilibrium effects along the growth trajectories as capital and debt vary endogenously.[14] The last row represents the medium-run effects of changes in the fundamentals dZ, given capital and debt. The medium-run effect of a rise in investment less social saving is to raise the real interest-rate differential. This leads to portfolio adjustments and capital inflows which eliminate the differential, although the capital inflow continues as long as $I-S$ is not zero. The medium-run effect dZ is therefore measured by the US less G-10 *real long-term* interest-rate differential, lagged one quarter to avoid a simultaneous estimation problem, denoted USFINT (-1). We show that real interest rates converge with a half-life of six quarters, so that the dZ effect is ephemeral.

The *medium-run* effects (dZ) indicate that a rise in $I-S$ which leads to a rise in the real long-term interest-rate differential appreciates the real value of the dollar. The medium-run effect upon the current account is not significant. The reason may be that the current account responds with a long lag to exchange-rate variations.

---

[13] This chapter has not introduced non-tradables as a separate, imperfect substitute for exportables. If it had, in the context of a large country, a rise in capital in the exportable industry would not only lower the terms of trade, but would also raise the relative price of non-tradables/exportables, making the net effect upon the real exchange rate ambiguous.

[14] The technical discussion of the econometric cointegration analysis and its relation to the theory will make these concepts more precise.

TABLE 2.2   *Summary of the empirical results*

Fundamental Z	Real exchange rate ($\$$appreciate = +)	*Current account/GNP*
$(C+G)$GNP	–	–
US GROWTH	+ ns	–
Foreign growth	–	+
dZ		
USFINT(-1)	+	ns

The longer-run effects (Z) *along the trajectories*, the middle part of Table 2.1 above, are as follows. (i) A rise in the index of time preference $(C+G)/GNP$ leads to a depreciated dollar and decreases in the current account. (ii) Foreign growth leads to a depreciation in the dollar and increases the current account. US growth leads to decreases in the current account and an appreciated dollar, but the appreciation effect is not significant.

The explanatory power of the NATREX model is summarized in Figure 2.6 for the real exchange rate and Figure 2.8 for the ratio of the current account/GNP. Three curves are plotted in Figure 2.6: the actual real value R of the $\$$US, the NATREX implied by the model and the estimating equation,[15] and the nominal value of the $\$$US denoted NEXR. We conclude the following. First: the graph of NATREX tracks the basic movement of the real exchange rate very well. This means that we are able to explain the movements in the real exchange rates by the fundamentals in the model. Second: there are significant short-period deviations of the actual R from the NA-TREX, due to speculative and cyclical factors. However, the actual R converges to the NATREX the rate implied by the fundamentals. There is long-period rationality in the foreign exchange market, but not short-period rationality. *We explain trends not short-term movements.* Third: the real and nominal values of the dollar move closely together $(R = Np/p')$. This indicates that relative prices are not able to explain much of the movement of the nominal exchange rate.[16] This answers question Q1 above.

---

[15] The derivation of the curve NATREX is based upon the econometrics and is described below. It is a dynamic *ex ante* simulation of the longer-run equation, based upon Table 2.8, where *previously predicted values* of the dependent variable are used as the lagged dependent variable.

[16] This is why the monetary models of the nominal exchange rate have been so disappointing.

The second set of questions Q2 concerns the extent of international capital mobility and the determinants of the current account. Figure 2.8 shows that the NATREX model explains the evolution of the current account/GNP on the basis of the fundamentals Z above. The plot CAGNP is the ratio of the current account/GNP. The plot FCAGNP is the forecast from the NATREX model using the fundamentals Z. There is considerable mobility of capital internationally. The variation in the current account is sensitive to variations in investment and social saving, which depend upon the fundamentals in the NATREX model. The growth in the US reduces the current account, the growth abroad increases the current account, and the US index of time preference reduces the current account. In the longer run, a unit rise in social consumption/GNP, say due to a rise in the cyclically adjusted government budget deficit, will increase the foreign debt. The rise in the foreign debt will decrease private consumption, increase private saving. Hence a unit rise in government consumption will reduce the current account/GNP by 0.5. The other half will be reflected in an increased private saving and a crowding out of private investment. The value of one half for the change in the current account is the same numerical value found by Helliwell (1991). The ratio of the current account/GNP is not stationary because investment less saving relative to GNP is not stationary. This completes the intuitive exposition and summary of the chapter.

2. THE THEORETICAL STRUCTURE OF THE NATREX MODEL

2.1 *The Feedback Control (Dynamic Programming) Intertemporal Optimization*

The Investment Function. — The future is unpredictable: the fundamentals are not stationary (Table 2.4). It is impossible to know what disturbances are permanent and what are temporary. The uncertainty is embodied in our structural equations. Our analysis is based upon an intertemporal optimization with a robust feedback control, based upon dynamic programming, to guarantee that the system will converge to the perfect-foresight steady state, which is unknowable at any time. In the text, we describe in literary terms how our investment and saving functions are based upon rational and stable optimization processes, and the reader is referred to Infante and Stein (1973) for the derivations.[17]

As a rule, economists have used the Maximum Principle of Pontryagin to derive optimal-control laws. This is an open-loop type of optimization in that it yields an entire sequence of controls to be followed from initial conditions. The solution for the optimal control for the rate of change of the capital intensity, or for the consumption function, is derived by knowing the steady-state value of the capital intensity k^* where the marginal product of capital $y'(k^*; u)$ is equal to the sum of the discount and growth rates; and the differential equations are solved backwards from that value. Thereby a unique trajectory to the steady state is derived. There is saddle-point instability: only if the economy travels along the stable arm will the system converge to the steady state.

There must be perfect knowledge of both the steady-state capital intensity, the production and utility function to implement this procedure: *there is no room for error*. If the slightest error is made, the system will not converge to the unknown optimal steady state, but the economy will follow an errant trajectory, which will diverge from the unknown optimal steady state. Such a procedure is neither feasible nor sensible in economics. First: we do not have perfect knowledge of the production function $y(k;u)$, hence the steady-state value of k^* is unknowable. Hence the optimal control derivable from the Maximum Principle is not implementable. Second: the unknown optimal steady state may be changing over time in an unpredictable manner.

For this reason, Infante and Stein used dynamic programming to derive a suboptimal feedback control (SOFC). This is a closed-loop control, where all that is necessary are *current measurements* of a variable, not perfect foresight. No use is made of the ambiguous distinction between permanent/temporary or anticipated/unanticipated changes, for they are not operational concepts. Using our equations, the SOFC will drive the economy to the unknown optimal steady state. *The trajectory of the SOFC is asymptotic to the unknown perfect foresight trajectory, is implementable and guarantees*

---

[17] The subsequent discussion is based upon Ettore F. Infante and Jerome L. Stein 1973. Infante at the time was professor of Applied Mathematics at the Center for Dynamical Systems at Brown University. The proofs, based upon dynamic programming, are contained in that paper.

that the system will converge to the unknown and changing steady state. This is not true for the optimal controls derived from the Maximum Principle.

We contrast the Infante and Stein stable-feedback control law derived from dynamic programming with the non-implementable open-loop control which has been used in the standard intertemporal models. After showing the difference, we explain our investment equation.

Suppose that the decision-making unit attempts to maximize social utility U^*, from time 0 to infinity, defined by equation (*IS*-1) subject to constraints (*IS*-2), relating consumption per capita c, output per capita $f(k;u)$ and the rate of change of the capital intensity Dk, where $D = d/dt$. The social discount rate is δ and λ is the sum of the growth rate of labour plus the depreciation rate. The utility function U has the usual properties. Consumption is non-negative and Dk is given by (*IS*-2). In this optimization, no dichotomy exists between the saving and investment decisions.

$$U^*(t) = \int_0^T U(c)e^{-\delta t}\,dt \quad T \Rightarrow \text{infinity} \qquad (IS\text{-}1)$$

$$Dk = f(k; u) - \lambda k - c \qquad (IS\text{-}2)$$

The solution is as follows. At the steady state (the origin) $k = k^*$ when no control is used, the marginal net product of capital $f'(k^*; u)$ must be equal to the sum of the growth rate and discount rate (*IS*-3).

$$f'(k^*; u) = \lambda + \delta. \qquad (IS\text{-}3)$$

In the neighbourhood of the steady state, the optimal control is (*IS*-4). The rate of investment is proportional at rate $-A(k^*)$ to the gap between the actual and steady-state capital intensity. The value of $A(k^*)$ is (*IS*-5). *The implementation depends upon knowing the value of* k*. The term c^* is the steady-state value of c.

$$Dk = V(k) = -A(k^*)(k - k^*) \qquad (IS\text{-}4)$$

$$A(k^*) = (\delta/2)[(1 + 4U'(c^*)f''(k^*)/\delta^2 U''(c^*))\cdot{}^5 - 1] > 0 \qquad (IS\text{-}5)$$

The system is solved backwards by knowing the value of k^*, the transversality condition. However, these equations are simply not implementable unless one knows exactly what is the transversality condition k^*. Neither the production function f nor the parameter of productivity u is knowable in economics. If one made the slightest mistake, the system would diverge: be unstable. Hence, we took a different approach.

By approaching everything through dynamic programming, we were able to develop suboptimal feedback control laws (SOFC). We present one of them, which is easily implementable (*IS*-6). This SOFC, which we designate as V_1, is asymptotic to the optimal control, is easy to compute and is guaranteed to drive the system to the unknown and changing k^*, depending upon u. It is robust to perturbations and leads to stability. It requires only *current measurements* of the marginal product of capital, and does not require the utopian perfect foresight.

$$Dk = V_1(k) = [A(k)/-f''(k)][f'(k; u) - (\lambda + \delta)] \qquad (IS\text{-}6)$$

Equation (*IS*-6) states that optimal investment is positively related to the net marginal product of capital less the discount rate, in a closed economy. When the *current* net marginal product of capital exceeds (is below) the discount rate, the rate of change of the capital intensity dk/dt should be positive (negative). This control is a non-linear, stable, robust feedback control, which is asymptotic in time to optimal control $V(k)$, and looks very similar[18] to the optimal control $V(k)$. In the neighbourhood of the origin, the slopes $V'(k)$ and $V_1'(k)$ are identical.

We may relate SOFC law (*IS*-6) to an open decentralized economy with financial assets where there is a dichotomy between the investment and saving decisions, to derive our investment equations (2.4) and (2.5) in Box 2.1. The rate of net investment per unit of effective labour is:

$$I = nk + dk/dt = nk + V_1(k),$$

where n is the growth rate of effective labour, k is the capital intensity (capital/effective labour). Let the real long-term rate of interest substitute for the discount rate. The SOFC law states that one should focus upon the current marginal product of capital $f'(k; u)$ less the real long term rate of interest.

The Keynes–Tobin q-ratio is equation (2.4b). The value of q is the ratio of the present value of the stream of returns to an increment of capital, relative to its supply price, equation (2.4b). The current marginal physical product of capital is $f'(k; u)$, where u is a parameter of the marginal product function. Equation (IS-6)

---

[18] Infante and Stein, 1973: Table 1.

can be related to the Keynes–Tobin q-ratio where the discount rate substitutes for the real interest rate, and the expected marginal product of capital is taken as the current level. The SOFC law states that one should act as if the current rate $f'(k; u)$ will continue; but when $f'(k; u)$ changes, change dk/dt. This means that we can put $f'(k; u)$ in front of the integral sign. We derive equation (2.4) in Box 2.1.

$$dk/dt = I = I(q); \; I(1) = 0, \; I' > 0 \tag{2.4a}$$

$$q = \int_0^T f'(k; u)\exp(-rt)\,dt = f'(k; u)\int_0^T \exp(-rt)\,dt = f'(k; u)/r \tag{2.4b}$$

$$dk/dt = I(k, r; u) \tag{2.4}$$

The investment equation (2.4) is predicated on the condition that the agents optimize subject to the condition that they are aware that they do not know what the production function is or will be in the future. By using the SOFC they know that equation (2.4) will lead them to the unknown and changing optimal steady state with little social loss.

The Independent Saving Function.   In reality, saving and investment decisions are made independently. We shall use as our social (public plus private) consumption function a stabilizing function, derived from a dynamic programming approach, which guarantees that the foreign debt will converge, without requiring perfect foresight. The optimization process behind the consumption function is based upon dynamic programming as developed by Merton (1990: 101–17). Here there is a dichotomy between saving and investment and the marginal return on capital is taken as a parameter by the decision-making micro unit.

Merton's representative agent attempts to maximize the expected value of U^* in (*IS*-1) by choosing an optimal pattern of consumption and portfolio composition. The portfolio (in the simple case) consists of a safe asset and a risky asset. The return to the risky asset follows a Wiener process. The agent knows the mean and variance of the return on the risky asset.

The solution for the optimal consumption $C(t)$ is that it is proportional to *current* wealth $W(t)$. The factor of proportionality is a complicated term. A priori, one does not know if a rise in the mean rate of return will raise or lower consumption. To derive any useful results, one must arbitrarily specify the instantaneous utility function. If the instantaneous utility function is Bernoulli, $U(c(t)) = \ln c(t)$, then the factor of proportionality is the discount rate δ. The consumption function is $C(t) = \delta W(t)$, proportional at rate δ to current wealth. It states that consumption depends upon wealth or permanent income. Wealth is capital $k(t)$ less the real foreign debt $F(t)$, where a negative F is claims on foreigners. A rise in time preference raises social consumption $C = C(k, F; Z)$ for the given amount of wealth. The exogenous rate of time preference is an element of vector Z. Since current wealth $W(t) = k(t) - F(t)$ our saving function (GNP less consumption) is equation

$$S = y(k; Z) - rF - C = y(k; Z) - rF - \delta(k - F) = S(k, F; Z) \qquad (2.7)$$

We refer to δ as social time preference, which includes the government as well as the private sector. For example, a tax cut or rise in government expenditures is associated with a rise in time preference. We shall write the consumption function as $C = C(k, F; g)$, where g reflects the rate of discount δ. We measure g as the ratio of private consumption plus government purchases to GNP. To guarantee that the real foreign debt will converge when there are changes in time preference, we require that a rise in debt raise saving. That is, a rise in the foreign debt must lower social consumption by more than it lowers GNP. This is $S_F > 0$ in equation (2.7).

To summarize: our model is characterized by endogenous stability without requiring perfect foresight. We do not assume that there is an intertemporal budget constraint, where the initial and terminal debts are equal. Countries change from creditors to debtors and vice versa. We permit this to occur. We show that the foreign debt is an endogenous variable whose steady-state value, like that of the capital stock, is determined by productivity and thrift at home and abroad. The consumption function will prevent the debt from exploding. When the debt stabilizes, the current account is zero. The trade balance must be sufficient to pay the interest on the debt. Our approach is more general than the standard intertemporal optimization models which require perfect foresight.

2.2 The Structural Equations

We have explained how our investment (eq. 2.5) and saving (eq. 2.7) functions are derived from our dynamic-programming approach to intertemporal optimization. The other equations are now discussed.

Equation (2.2) states that the goods market is in equilibrium at capacity output, and ignores the cyclical elements.

$$y(k; u) = C(k, F, r; Z) + (dk/dt + nk) + B(R, k, F, k'; Z) \qquad (2.2)$$

The left-hand side of equation (2.2) is GDP per unit of effective labour $y(k; u)$, where k is the capital intensity (capital per unit of effective labour) and u is a measure of productivity. The components of aggregate demand are consumption C, investment $I = dk/dt + nk$ and the trade balance B. The corresponding goods market balance for the rest of the world is equation (2.3).

$$GDP' = C' + I' - B(R, k, F, k', Z) \qquad (2.3)$$

Foreign variables are denoted by a prime. We take the foreign-investment and saving functions as given, in deriving our theoretical model. Otherwise, the order of the dynamic system would be raised even further; and analytic tractability would be lost.

The rate of change of the foreign debt per effective worker dF/dt is investment (I) less saving (S) per unit of effective labour less nF, equation (2.6).

$$dF/dt = I - S - nF = -(CA + nF) \qquad (2.6)$$

Using equations (2.2), (2.5), and (2.7), we may also state (2.6) as saying that the rate of change of the foreign-debt intensity is the current-account deficit per effective worker $(-CA)$ less nF.

In the perfect-foresight intertemporal optimization models there is an intertemporal budget constraint which states that the present value of the sum of future trade-balance surpluses must be equal to the present level of foreign indebtedness. A country that begins the period t with an initial foreign debt $F(t)$ must run future trade surpluses to completely service the debt. The object is to prevent the debt from exploding. This prevents the theory from explaining how countries change from debtors to creditors or vice versa. Our model allows for such changes. The model implies (see the next section) that the dynamic system must lead to an endogenous steady-state value of the debt $F^*(Z)$ such that the trade balance in the steady state B^* is equal to the interest payments rF^* on the debt.[19] It is clear that since the debt stabilizes at $F^*(Z(T))$, the present value of the debt at time T, as T goes to infinity, is $F^*(Z)/(1 + r)^T = 0$. Our model

---

[19] The text implicitly assumes that $n = 0$. In fact, the steady-state condition that $dF/dt = 0$ means that the trade balance $B^* = (r^* - n) F^*(Z)$, where r^* is the real rate of interest in the steady state.

prevents the debt from exploding since it requires that the debt stabilize at the level of $F^*(Z)$, which depends upon $Z = \{$productivity and thrift at home and abroad$\}$.

The trade-balance equation $B(R, k, F; k', Z)$ includes capacity and debt variables as well as the real exchange rate R which is an inverse measure of competitiveness. To a large extent it is consistent with the estimates of Hooper[20] (1989: Table 3). The trade-balance in equation (2.2) is $B(R, k, F; k', Z)$.

$$B = \text{exports} - \text{imports} = X(R, k' + F; Z) - M(R, k - F; Z)$$

$$= B(R, k, F; k', Z)$$

The trade balance is (a) negatively related to the real exchange rate, which is the ratio of US to foreign prices in a common currency ($B_R < 0$); (b) negatively related to the capital stock k, a rise in k increases wealth and desired imports ($B_k < 0$); (c) positively related to the foreign capital stock k', a rise in k' increasing foreign wealth and demand for US exports ($B'_k > 0$); (d) positively related to foreign debt F which redistributes wealth from the home to the foreign country, raising foreign demand for US exports and lowering US demand for imports ($B_F > 0$). Of the exogenous fundamentals Z of productivity and time preference, only time preference influences the desired trade balance, under the assumption that trade is in the consumption goods. A rise in domestic time preference g (an element in Z) raises demand for imports and worsens the trade balance, with the reverse for a rise in foreign time preference.

Box 2.1   The NATREX model for the US/G-10
Goods market

$$y(k; u) = C(k, F, r; Z) + (dk/dt + nk) + B(R, k, F, k'; Z) \quad (2.2)$$

$$GDP' = C' + I' - B(R, k, F, k'; Z) \quad (2.3)$$

Capital formation

$$dk/dt = I(k, r; Z) \quad I_k < 0, \quad I_r < 0 \quad (2.4)$$

$$I = dk/dt + nk \quad (2.5)$$

---

[20] Hooper's results (1989: Table 3) were that an appreciation of the real exchange rate reduces the trade balance, a rise in US to foreign capital increases the trade balance. A rise in actual to capacity output in a given country increases its imports.

Rate of change of the debt

$$dF/dt = I - S - nF = -(CA + nF) \qquad (2.6)$$

Saving

$$S = y(k; Z) - rF - C(k, F, r; Z)$$
$$= S(k, F, r, Z), \quad \text{where } S_k > 0, \ S_F > 0 \qquad (2.7)$$

Portfolio equation

$$d(r - r')/dt = -a(r - r') \qquad (2.8)$$

Note: y = GDP per effective worker; k = capital intensity; F = real foreign-debt intensity (+), net claims upon foreigners (−); r = real long-term interest rate; B = real trade balance per effective worker; CA = current account per effective worker, C = real social consumption per effective worker; rF = real interest payments (+) per effective worker; S = real saving per effective worker; Z = vector of exogenous disturbances = (g, u, g', u', n) where g = parameter of time preference which raises the social consumption ratio; u=parameter of the productivity of capital which raises the q-ratio; n=growth of effective labour; a prime indicates the corresponding foreign variable.

Finally, equation (2.8) concerns portfolio balance or the relation between the US and the G-10 real rates of interest. Figure 2.3a plots the US and the G-10 real long-term interest rates. These data were used in the Federal Reserve studies by Hooper and Mann. They measured the real long-term bond yields by subtracting from the nominal US and G-10 long-term government bond yields a three-year centred moving average of CPI inflation rates ranging from six quarters in the past to six quarters in the future. They denote r = RLTUSQ, real long-term US quarterly and r' = *RLTFQ* real long-term foreign quarterly. Denote the real long-term US less G-10 interest-rate differential as UNFINT = $r - r'$. The evidence concerning real long-term interest-rate convergence is from the period 1973.3–1989.1. A further analysis of real interest-rate convergence focused upon the US and German real long-term interest rates, for which more recent data are available. The measure of inflation used here to obtain the real long-term rate from the long-term nominal interest rate was the inflation of the CPI over the previous year. Figure 2.3b plots the real long-term US rate (RUSLT) and real German long-term rates (RGERLT). From 1980.1–1992.3 there is convergence.

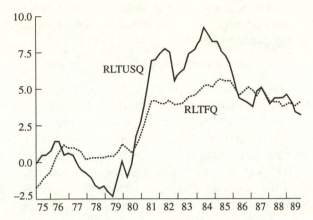

FIG. 2.3a   *Real long-term US (RLTUSQ) and G-10 (RLTFQ) interest rates*

We know that there will be portfolio substitution when the expected returns on domestic and comparable foreign assets differ, and there are no capital controls. The NATREX model focuses upon long-term investment and ignores short-term speculative capital flows. The expected return on domestic assets is the expected real long-term rate of interest r plus the expected real appreciation of the domestic currency over the investment horizon $E(DR)$.

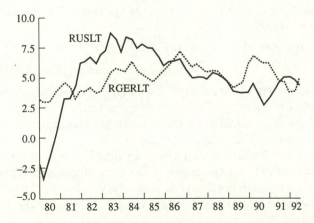

FIG. 2.3b   *Real long-term US (RUSLT) and German (RGERLT) interest rates*

The expected appreciation of the dollar is derived as follows. The expected real exchange rate to prevail at time $t+h$ is denoted $ER(t+h)$, in equation (2.8a).

$$ER(t+h) = bR^*(Z(t)) + (1-b)R(t) \qquad (2.8a)$$

There is a prior estimate, based upon the steady state (denoted by an asterisk) corresponding to the current fundamentals $R^*(Z(t))$. The weight attached to the prior is b, which reflects the belief that the fundamentals $Z(t)$ will persist. There is a sample based upon current information, which is the current real exchange rate, whose weight is $(1-b)$. The expected change in the exchange rate $E(DR) = ER(t+h) - R(t)$, equation (2.8b), is derived by substracting $R(t)$ from both sides of (2.8a).

$$E(DR) = ER(t+h) - R(t) = b[R^*(Z(t)) - R(t)] \qquad (2.8b)$$

Portfolio equilibrium is:

$$r + E(DR) = r + b[R^*(Z(t)) - R(t)] = r' \qquad (2.8c)$$

where r' is the expected real long-term foreign rate of interest. Coefficient b reflects the weight given to the belief that the steady-state real exchange rate associated with the current fundamentals $Z(t)$ will persist over the life of the investment.

We require that investors use all available information concerning the stationarity of $Z(t)$ or $R^*(Z(t))$. From equation (2.9a) we know that the change in the real exchange rate DR is stationary at a value of zero:[21]

$$D(DR) = -0.197 - 0.69 DR(-1) \quad \text{UROOT}(C, 0) = -5.7^{**} \qquad (2.9a)$$

$$(t=) \quad (-0.38) \qquad (-5.7) \qquad \text{MacKinnon } 1\% = -3.5$$

Moreover we know that, during the floating-rate period, the level of real exchange rate R(t) follows a random walk, is not stationary, because the fundamentals $Z = \{$time preference and growth$\}$ have not been stationary. This means that the steady-state value of the real exchange rate $R^*[Z(t)]$ is changing over time in a way that becomes ever less predictable as the length of the horizon increases. Therefore, in making long-term portfolio decisions, the weight b in (2.8b) is close to zero. The expected appreciation or depreciation of the real ex-

---

[21] The regression coefficient of $DR(-1)$ is significantly different from zero and hence stationary. The constant is not significant, hence $E(DR)$ is equal to zero.

change rate between the $US and G-10 is taken to be zero.[22] Since $E(DR) = 0$, the real interest rates should converge. This convergence occurs.

To test the hypothesis of real long-term interest rate convergence on more recent data, we examined the unit root properties of the real long-term interest-rate differential $(r - r') =$ RUSGER = RUSLT – RGERLT between the US and Germany, for the period 1980.1–1992.3. The constant in the equation[23] for the test of the unit root was not significant. The UROOT$(N, 1)$ test of RUSGER = $(r - r')$ gave an ADF statistic -2.285 (MacKinnon 5% = -1.9, 1% = -2.6) , which is significant at the 5 per cent level.

From these statistics (see also figures 2.3a, 2.3b) we obtain several empirical results. (a) The real long-term interest rates in the US and G-10, and US and Germany, converge to each other. (b) Half of the initial deviation in $(r - r')$ from zero is eliminated in a year and a half, in both cases. (c) There is no evidence that previous rates of changes of the real exchange rate have any effect upon the process whereby real long-term interest rates converge. (d) There is no evidence of a risk premium between the US and G-10. The differential $(r - r')$ is independent of the net creditor or debtor position of the US. (e) During this period, the Granger causality ran from the US real long-term rate to the G-10, but not the reverse. There was no Granger causality between US and German real long-term rates. For these reasons, we use the simplified equation (2.8) for the modelling: the real rates of interest converge to zero with a half-life of six quarters.

We focus upon seven endogenous variables in the seven equations in Box 2.1: the capital intensity k, the real exchange rate R, the real foreign-debt intensity F, the domestic real rate of interest r, the

---

[22] We performed a VAR on R and $r - r' =$ USFINT to determine (i) if the interest-rate differential is related to previous exchange rates, which would be the case if the expected change in the exchange rate were related to its previous history; (ii) the speed of convergence of the USFINT to a constant; (iii) if this constant is zero. Again the period is 1973.3–1989.1. Neither the lagged exchange rates nor the constant is significant.

[23] The test if variable x has a unit root involves the regression: $Dx = c + ax(-1) + b(i)Dx(-i)$, where $Dx(i)$ is a vector of lags corresponding to $b(i)$ a vector of coefficients. The test is whether coefficient a is significantly different from zero. If the variable x is stationary, it converges to $x^* = c/(-a)$. The constant referred to in the text is c. If c is not significantly different from zero, and a is significantly different from zero, then x^* converges to zero. In our case, x is the real interest-rate differential.

foreign real rate of interest r', saving S and investment I. The exogenous parameters Z are productivity and thrift/time preference at home and abroad.

2.3 Analytic Solution of the Model

The solution of the model can be viewed in several ways. The *medium run* is defined as the period where the capital stocks and foreign debt are taken as predetermined variables. Goods-market equilibrium equations (2.2) and (2.3) for the US and G-10 can be written as (2.10) and (2.11) respectively where we solve for the real exchange rate R. They are graphed in Figure 2.4 as the *IS* curve (in the space Rxr) for the US and *IS'* curve for the G-10 in the space (Rxr'). The *IS* curve, relating R and r and describing goods-market equilibrium, is negatively sloped for the following reason. A rise in the US real rate of interest reduces aggregate demand relative to capacity GDP. To equilibrate the goods market the ratio $R = Np/p'$ of US to foreign prices must decline: the real exchange rate must depreciate. The decline in relative prices will increase US competitiveness and restore goods-market equilibrium. No distinction is made in the NATREX model between changes in nominal exchange rates and in relative prices. In point of fact, the speeds of response differ and the NATREX model provides a better explana-

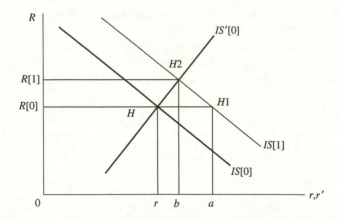

FIG. 2.4   *Determination of the real exchange rate (R) and real rates of interest, domestic r and foreign r'*

tion of a free exchange-rate regime than a fixed-rate regime. The foreign IS' curve is positively sloped in the Rxr' space because an appreciation of the US dollar is a depreciation of the G-10 currency. Equation (2.8), repeated here, is the portfolio adjustment. *Medium-run subsystem:*

$$R(t) = H(r(t), k(t), F(t); Z) \qquad \text{IS curve (2.10)}$$

$$R(t) = h(r'(t), k'(t), F(t); Z') \qquad \text{IS' curve (2.11)}$$

$$d(r(t) - r'(t))/dt = -a(r(t) - r'(t)) \quad \text{interest-rate convergence (2.8)}$$

The dynamics of this system can be described in Figure 2.4. Let the IS and IS' curves initially be $IS(0)$ and $IS'(0)$ respectively, when the fundamentals $Z = Z(0)$. The medium-run equilibrium occurs when real interest-rate convergence has occurred $r = r'$. This would be at a point like H where the real exchange rate is $R(0)$, equation 2.12 and real interest rates are equal equation, (2.13).

$$R(t) = R[k(t), F(t); k'(t), Z] \qquad (2.12)$$

$$r(t) = r' = r[k(t); k'(t), Z] \qquad (2.13)$$

Suppose that there is a change in fundamentals to $Z(1)$: either a decline in social saving or a rise in the investment demand in the home country. The scenario in Figure 2.4 corresponds to the scenario in Table 2.1. The IS curve shifts to $IS(1)$. To maintain goods-market equilibrium when investment rises relative to saving, the real interest rate would rise. Given the real exchange rate $R(0)$, the domestic real interest rate will rise to $0a$ or point $H1$. The interest-rate differential $H - H1$ will induce investors to purchase US, and sell foreign, long-term securities. The excess demand for goods in the US, and the redirection of portfolio investment to the US, will appreciate the US dollar and also lead to a convergence of real long-term interests rates: from $H1$ to $H2$ in the US and from H to $H2$ abroad. The medium-run equilibrium $H2$ is again described by equations (2.12) for $R(t)$ and (2.13) for $r(t) = r'(t)$, with $Z = Z(1)$. The real rate of interest (equation 2.13) is independent of the foreign debt, because the debt just re-allocates wealth between the two countries and does not affect world saving.

A medium-run equilibrium point H or $H2$ does not remain fixed, because capital and debt change. The general movement of the exchange rate is described by equation (2.14) derived from (2.10),

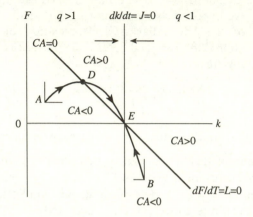

F<small>IG</small>. 2.5   *Trajectories of capital and debt to steady state, point E. Productivity effect ADE; decline in thrift BE*

(2.11), and (2.8). Given capital and debt, the movement from H to $H2$ is basically caused by the change in the fundamentals Z, but the lagged interest-rate adjustment, the term in (2.14), slows the real appreciation, giving the real long-term interest differential an important role in the speed of adjustment of R. In so far as the domestic real interest rate is greater than the foreign rate, the real exchange rate is below its medium-run equilibrium value at $H2$. Since R is below the medium-run equilibrium, the exchange rate appreciates.

$$dR/dt = [b_1 \, dk/dt + b_2 \, dk'/dt - b_3 \, dF/dt] + b_4(r - r') + c \cdot dZ/dt \quad (2.14)$$

The trajectory of the real exchange rate to the *longer run* involves endogenous movements of capital and debt as described by equations (2.4) and (2.6) in Box 2.1 and (2.12), and graphed as the phase diagram Figure 2.5. This will correspond to the lower half of Table 2.1 describing the scenarios.

The longer-run movement of capital and debt is described when there is interest-rate convergence: the movement of points like H or $H2$. Substitute the real interest rate equation (2.13) into the equation (2.4) for investment and (2.7) for saving and (2.6) for the capital inflow to derive: equation (2.15) for the rate of change of the capital intensity dk/dt and equation (2.16) for rate of change of the foreign debt (current account deficit, capital inflow).[24]

The locus of points where $dk/dt=0$ is graphed as the $J=0$ curve in Figure 2.5. This curve is independent of the foreign debt, because the foreign debt does not affect world saving and hence does not affect the world interest rate.[25] The rate of change of the capital intensity will be zero at $k=k^*$, when the marginal product of capital is equal to the world rate of interest, equation (2.15a), which is the $J=0$ curve. To the left of the curve $k < k^*$ the q-ratio exceeds unity and the capital intensity rises; and to the right where $k > k^*$, the q-ratio is less than unity and the capital intensity declines. The horizontal vectors describe the movement.

$$dk/dt = J(k; k', Z). \quad J_k < 0; \quad (2.15)$$

$$y'(k^*; u) = r(k^*, k'; Z) \quad (2.15a)$$

The rate of change of the foreign debt dF/dt is the capital inflow equal to investment less saving. This is the current account deficit.[26] The equation for $dF/dt = 0$ is graphed as the $L = 0$ curve. It is the set of capital and debt where there is no capital flow: saving is equal to investment, and the current account (equal to saving less investment) is zero.

$$dF/dt = J - S = L(k, F; k', Z) \quad L_k < 0, L_F < 0. \quad (2.16)$$

The curve $L = 0$ is negatively sloped because a rise in capital raises saving relative to investment and reduces the debt.[27] Along $L = 0$,

---

[24] The equations (2.15) (2.16) are derived as follows;

$$dk/dt = I[\, y'(k; u) - r(k; k', Z)] = J(k; k', Z) \quad (2.15)$$

$$dF/dt = J(k; k', Z) - S; \quad \text{and} \quad S = y(k; u) - r(k; k', Z)F -$$
$$C(k, F, r(k; k', Z)) = S(k, F; k', Z)$$

$$dF/dt = J(k; k', Z) - S(k, F; k', Z) = L(k, F; k', Z) \quad (2.16)$$

The stability conditions are $(J_k + L_F) < 0$ and $(J_k L_F - J_F L_k) > 0$. The structural equations imply that these conditions are met. The curves $J = 0$ and $L = 0$ and the vectors, in Figure 2.5, describe the stable case. The signs of J_Z and the values of dk^*/dZ and dF^*/dZ are given in Table 2.5.

[25] In Figure 2.4, a rise in the foreign debt shifts both IS and IS' curves downwards. That is, it lowers aggregate demand in the US and raises it abroad. It depreciates the dollar but has no effect upon the real interest rate.

[26] When $dF/dt = -(CA + nF) = 0$ then the current account deficit equals nF. To avoid cumbersome phrases in the description in the text, we describe the $n = 0$ case.

[27] It is also possible that a rise in capital lowers saving relative to investment and produces an upward-sloping $L=0$ curve. As long as a rise in debt raises saving, and a rise in capital lowers investment, the system will be stable. We work with what we believe to be the relevant case, where a rise in capital raises $S - I$.

$S = I$ or $CA = 0$. A rise in debt raises saving less investment, because it reduces wealth and hence consumption, in the stable case which we consider. This means that above the $L = 0$ curve, saving exceeds investment, there are current-account surpluses, and the debt declines towards $L = 0$. Below the curve, saving is less than investment, there are current-account deficits, and the debt rises to the curve. The vertical vectors describe the movement.

Table 2.3 and equations (2.17) and (2.18) describe the theoretical effects of changes in the fundamentals Z upon the steady-state values of the capital and debt intensities, dk^*/dZ and dF^*/dZ.

$$dk^*/dZ = J_Z/(-J_k); \quad (-J_k) > 0 \tag{2.17}$$

$$dF^*/dZ = [1/(-L_F)][L_k J_Z/(-J_k) + L_Z]; \quad (-L_F) > 0 \tag{2.18}$$

The meaning of J_z and L_z is as follows. J_z is the effect of a rise in Z upon the rate of investment. Thus a rise in productivity parameter u raises investment and $J_u > 0$. Similarly L_z is the effect of a rise in Z upon investment less saving, the capital inflow. A rise in u raises investment less saving and $L_z > 0$. A rise in time preference g raises interest rates and discourages investment $J_g < 0$. The major effect is to lower saving $L_g > 0$. The trajectories in Figure 2.5 describe the movements to the steady state. Table 2.2 above described these scenarios, so we may be terse here.

A rise in US time preference g corresponds to a movement from H to $H1$ to $H2$ in Figure 2.4 and the movement of capital and debt along trajectory BE in Figure 2.5. The initial effect is to raise the world rate of interest, and produce current-account deficits which increase the debt. The steady-state debt rises ($dF^*/dg > 0$), and capital declines ($dk^*/dg < 0$) due to the rise in the world rate of interest, as the economy moves along trajectory BE in Figure 2.5.

A rise in the US productivity of capital[28] *u* raises the capital intensity ($dk^*/du > 0$) and lowers the steady-state debt ($dF^*/du < 0$), because the rise in capital eventually raises output, and hence saving less investment. The initial effect is the movement in Figure 2.4 from H to $H1$ to $H2$. The trajectory of capital and debt is ADE in Figure 2.5. Initially, the rise in investment less saving leads to capital inflows. The current account $S - I$ is in deficit. The debt rises along with capital along AD. As the capital is put into place, average productivity rises, hence saving rises relative to investment

---

[28] A rise in the foreign u' is treated symmetrically.

TABLE 2.3 *The relation between disturbances to productivity and thrift in the US and G-10 and the steady-state comparative statics of the NATREX model*

disturbance	J_z	$L_z = (J - S)_z$	dk^*/dZ	dF^*/dZ	R_z
Rise in US mei (u)	+	+	+	−	+
Rise in G-10 mei (u')	−	−	−	+	−
Rise in US time preference (g)	−	+	−	+	+
Rise G-10 time preference (g')	−	−	−	−	−

even as capital continues to rise. Along trajectory DE, saving exceeds investment, there are current account surpluses, and the debt declines to F^* below its initial level.

The steady-state real exchange rate R^* is affected by the fundamentals directly by R_Z and indirectly via the effects upon capital $R_k dk^*/dZ$, $R_{k'} dk'/dZ$ and debt $R_F dF^*/dZ$. This follows from equations (2.12) for $R(k, F; Z)$, and (2.17) and (2.18) for the effects of the fundamentals upon capital and debt. The change in foreign capital is treated as exogenous and disregarded here.

$$dR^*/dZ = R_Z + R_k dk^*/dZ + R_{k'} dk'/dz + R_F dF^*/dZ;$$

$$R_k < 0, \ R_F < 0, \ R_{k'} > 0. \tag{2.19}$$

The effect of a change in fundamentals upon the steady-state real exchange rate in equation (2.19) can be summarized as follows, in terms of Figure 2.4. We have already discussed the direct effects R_Z, the first term. The induced effects are as follows. A rise in the domestic capital stock k will lower investment less saving, causing the IS curve in Figure 2.4 to shift down, $R_k < 0$. This depreciates R. Conversely, a rise in the foreign capital stock k' will lower foreign investment less saving, and the foreign current account $(-CA)$, causing the foreign IS' curve to shift up $R_{k'} > 0$. This appreciates R. A rise in debt F by the home country lowers domestic wealth and increases saving in the home country, shifting the IS curve down and depreciating R. At the same time the rise in F raises wealth in the foreign country and lowers foreign saving. This shifts the foreign IS' down by the same amount. Because the increased debt simply redistributes wealth, it depreciates the dollar $R_F < 0$ but has no effect upon the world real interest rate. The total effect dR^*/dZ is the sum of the direct effect and the three indirect effects.

For changes in time preference $dR^*/dg < 0$ and $dR^*/dg' > 0$. An increase in US borrowing to finance consumption depreciates R, while an increase in foreign borrowing to finance consumption appreciates R. As explained earlier, the effect of productivity changes on the long-run NATREX are ambiguous, since the long-run changes in capital and debt put opposite pressures upon R^*, the steady-state value of the real exchange rate.

We have finished describing the theoretical structure and analytic solution of the NATREX model.

3 THE EMPIRICAL RELATIONS BETWEEN THE ENDOGENOUS AND EXOGENOUS VARIABLES

In order to answer the questions posed at the beginning of this paper, we must obtain quantitative estimates of the basic equations in the model. We proceed in several steps. No single econometric test by itself is free from econometric problems. We adduce several different econometric equations which are directly related to the theory. We show that the results are robust to different ways of looking at the problem.

The crucial *endogenous* variables are $X =$ (real exchange rate, foreign debt intensity, capital intensity), when real interest-rate convergence has already occurred. In this section we relate X to the longer-run *fundamentals*. Theoretically the *exogenous* variables vector $Z = (u, u', g, g')$ are the *fundamentals*: productivity at home u and abroad u' and time preference at home g and abroad g'. Empirically we consider two measurable *endogenous* variables in vector X: the real exchange rate R = REXR and the ratio of the current account/GNP, denoted CAGNP, which reflects the rate of change of the foreign-debt intensity dF/dt. We have confidence in the measures of the real exchange rate and the flow variable, the current account. The real foreign-debt intensity variable F in the model makes no distinction between equity and debt, direct or indirect investment, and does not vary when the exchange rate changes. Thus the stock F in the model is not the same as the accounting measure of net liabilities to foreigners. For this reason, instead of the stock F we use the flow dF/dt and measure $(-dF/dt)$ by the ratio of the current account/GNP, and denoted CAGNP. The cyclical elements will be in both the numerator and denominator, so that the ratio is less cyclical than the current account. The flow CAGNP deficit proxies dF/dt in the model.

Our empirical estimates of Z are closely related to the theoretical concepts. We measure the US index of the time preference or *dis*count *ra*te $g = \text{DISRAT} = (C + G)/\text{GNP}$ by the ratio of consumption plus government purchases to GNP. For the US, we make no distinction between private and government consumption, and assume that government expenditures are primarily consumption rather than investment. To abstract from the cyclical elements,[29] we divide social consumption $(C + G)$ by GNP. Exogenous parameters DISRAT is the *average social propensity to consume*.

We do not have comparable data for the foreign country, which would require a weighted average (corresponding to the weights in REXR) of the G-10 DISRAT. Hence we have an omitted variable g' which we know is an important determinant in the growth process.

Our focus in the empirical analysis is on the trajectories (e.g., *ADE* or *BE* in Figure 2.5) rather than upon comparative steady-state effects. The reason is that to analyse comparative steady states involving capital and debt, we must have many observations along many steady states. The evolution of capital to the steady state takes a long time relative to our sample period of less than twenty years. It is doubtful that regression analysis is capable of estimating comparative steady-state effects under these conditions.[30]

Table 2.4 presents the Dickey–Fuller and Adjusted Dickey–Fuller statistics concerning the stationarity or non-stationarity of the basic variables. The significance level depends upon whether there is or is not a constant and also the lag structure. The real exchange rate, the ratio of the current account/GNP, and the fundamentals used:

---

[29] A 12-quarter moving average of DISRAT was not a useful variable in the regressions.

[30] Formally, suppose that the dynamic system were $dx/dt + ax = aBZ$, in expectation. The expected steady state is $x^* = BZ$. The solution of the differential equation is $x(t) = BZ + [x(0) - BZ]e^{-at}$. Unless t is large, a regression of $x(t)$ on Z will not yield the slope B. This mathematical point explains the advice of Campbell and Perron (1991: 153), which is worth quoting. 'For tests of the unit root hypothesis versus stationary alternatives the power depends very little on the number of observations *per se* but is influenced in an important way by the span of the data. . . . In most applications of interest, a data set containing fewer annual data over a long time period will lead to tests having higher power than if use was made of a data set containing more observations over a short time period.' To be sure, in the Australian chapter below we try to estimate something closer to the steady state.

TABLE 2.4 *Tests of stationarity of basic variables: ADF/DF statistics; sample period Jan. 1973 to April 1989; order of Integration* $I(1) = non\text{-}stationary$; $I(0) = stationary$ (**)

Variable	Value
I(1):	
Nominal exchange rate (C, 1)	-1.795
Real exchange rate (C, 1)	-1.8
Current account/GNP (N, 0)	0.3
Real long-term US interest rate (C, 1)	-1.4
Real long-term G-10 interest rate (C, 1)	-1.6
DISRAT ($C+G$)/GNP (C, 1)	-2.4
Trade balance/GNP (C, 1)	-1.6
Moving-average US real growth (C, 1)	-1.9
Moving-average G-10 real growth (C, 1)	-1.7
I(0):	
US-foreign real long-term interest (N, 1)	-1.8^*
US-German real long-term interest (N, 1)	-2.3^{**} Jan. 1980 to Mar. 1992
Investment income/GNP (C, 1)	-2.8^{**}
Per cent change real exchange rate (N, 0)	-5.7^{**}

Sources: Federal Reserve, OECD. In the ADF or DF statistics (C = constant, N = no constant, integer = lags). Significant at $^* = 10\%$, $^{**} = 5\%$ level, using the MacKinnon critical values. If the ADF or DF for the variable is significant,[31] then the variable is stationary = reject the hypothesis of unit root.

Z = {DISRAT, USGROWTH, FGROWTH} are not stationary. Their means are not independent of time. That is why we know that a PPP approach to real exchange-rate determination is inadequate. We shall be able to use a cointegration analysis. The change in the exchange rate, not shown, is stationary.

There is no way to measure directly the productivity variables (u, u') in the marginal productivity of capital function $y'(k; u)$. However, given time preference (g, g'), a rise in productivity stimulates capital formation and growth along trajectory ADE in

---

[31] We test whether or not the constant C is significant and what order of lags (j) greater than unity is significant. We continue the UROOT tests until we have an equation where all of the regressors (exclusive of the first lag term) are significant. The notation (C, j) or (N, j) indicates whether the constant C is significant (or not N), and the j indicates the lags greater than one that are significant. The significance level depends on whether or not there is a constant (C or N) and the number of lags.

Figure 2.5. Given (u, u'), changes in time preference affect growth only in so far as they affect the world real rate of interest. This is trajectory *BE* in Figure 2.5. Consequently, instead of the unobservable (u, u'), we proxy u by the growth rates. We measure the *capacity growth* of real GDP as a twelve-quarter moving average of the growth of real GDP, denoted USGROWTH in the US and as FGROWTH abroad. Given DISRAT, the USGROWTH variable, should reflect the productivity variable u; and given the growth variables, DISRAT reflects time preference.

The correlation matrix in Table 2.5 indicates that the regressors are not completely independent of each other. (a) The US-GROWTH and foreign FGROWTH growth rates are correlated, $r = 0.568$. I conclude that there is a common shock which affects productivity in the US and abroad, but the *R*-SQ between them is only 32 per cent. Therefore, both growth rates must be taken into consideration. (b) There is a weak negative relation between DISRAT and the effects of the two growth rates. Presumably this results from a change in social saving upon the world real rate of interest (a shift of the *IS* curve from *IS*(0) to *IS*(1) in Figure 2.4 raises the world rate of interest from point *H* to point *H*2), which affects investment and growth.

TABLE 2.5 *Correlation matrix Jan. 1975 to Apr. 1989*

	DISRAT	USGROWTH	FGROWTH
DISRAT	1	− .166	− .237
USGROWTH		1	.568
FGROWTH			1

Our longer-run system attempts to capture the movements of points like *H* or *H*2 (Figure 2.4) where real long-term interest-rate convergence has already occurred, and where the growth of the debt is endogenous along the trajectories *ADE* or *BE* in Figure 2.5. However, we proxy the productivity parameters (u, u') by moving averages of the growth rates of real GDP, which reflects the growth of capacity output. Hence the growth of capital and GDP are treated as predetermined variables in Tables 2.7 to 2.10.

Our predetermined variables are $Z = $ (USGROWTH, FGROWTH, DISRAT), we have an omitted variable, the weighted foreign

TABLE 2.6 *Johansen maximum likelihood procedure (trended case), cointegration LR test based on trace of the stochastic matrix; 50 observations, maximum lag in VAR = 2. Variables included in the cointegrating vector: REXR, DISRAT, USGROWTH, FGROWTH; list of eigenvalues in descending order: 0.416, 0.347, 0.137, 0.066*

Null	Alternative	Statistic	95% critical value	90% critical value
$r = 0$	$r >= 1$	58.99	47.2	43.9
$r <= 1$	$r >= 2$	32.09	29.68	26.79
$r <= 2$	$r >= 3$	10.78	15.41	13.3
$r <= 3$	$r = 4$	3.4	3.76	2.69

DISRAT, and there is some correlation among the variables in Z. The object is to determine to what extent the fundamentals Z can explain the evolution of $X = $ (REXR, CAGNP), in a manner consistent with the NATREX model. Then we can provide quantitative answers to questions [Q] above. However, since we expect that there is more than one cointegrating equation and there is an omitted variable, no single econometric technique by itself will provide a satisfactory answer to these questions. Therefore, we use several techniques and show that we obtain the same answers with each technique.

Our empirical research strategy is as follows. *First*: Table 2.6 shows that there are two cointegrating vectors.[32] This means that (as expected) there are two combinations of the variables (X, Z) which produce stationary residuals. *Second*: we exhibit several different possible estimating equations. Some are estimated by OLS (Tables 2.8, 2.10) and others by non-linear least-squares NLS (Tables 2.7, 2.9). *Third*: we compare the results of the different techniques and show explicitly in Table 2.11 (corresponding to Table 2.3) that the same results are obtained with each method.

We exhibit several different estimating equations based upon the basic dynamic system equation (2.20) relating the endogenous $X = $ (REXR, CAGNP) to the exogenous variables. Variables X and Z are integrated of order $I(1)$ as seen in Table 2.6. Subtract $X(t-1)$ from both sides and obtain (2.21). Variable e is an iid term with a zero expectation. As a first procedure, we shall use OLS to estimate (2.20) for the endogenous variables.

---

[32] I am indebted to Guay C. Lim for this table and econometric advice, which was always weighed carefully but not always followed.

$$X(t) = a X(t-1) + bZ(t) + cZ(t-1) + e \qquad (2.20)$$

$$DX = X(t) - X(t-1) = -(1-a)X(t-1) + bZ(t) + cZ(t-1) + e \quad (2.21)$$

The second prodedure uses NLS. Suppose that when $Z(t) = Z(t-1)$, the expectation of the change in the exogenous variable is zero $E(DX) = 0$. Hence the expected steady-state equation is (2.22), and the expected steady-state value of X is $X^* = BZ(t-1)$, equation (2.23). This 'steady-state' $X^* = BZ$ is what we would like to capture as a cointegrating equation.

$$X^* = aX^* + bZ(t-1) + cZ(t-1) \qquad (2.22)$$

$$X^* = [(b+c)/(1-a)]Z(t-1) = B \cdot Z(t-1) \qquad (2.23)$$

Subtract (2.22) from both sides of (2.20) and derive (2.24):

$$X(t) = BZ(t-1) + a[X(t-1) - BZ(t-1)] + b[Z(t) - Z(t-1)] + e \quad (2.24)$$

Subtract $X(t-1)$ from both sides of (2.24) to derive (2.25):

$$DX = X(t) - X(t-1) = -(1-a)[X(t-1) - BZ(t-1)]$$
$$+ b[Z(t) - Z(t-1)] + e. \qquad (2.25)$$

There are several components of the endogenous variable in equation (2.24). The *first* is the value of B associated with the steady state in $X^* = BZ(t-1)$. This is our sought-for cointegrating equation. Second is the error correction component $a[X(t-1) - BZ(t-1)]$. The third part $b[Z(t) - Z(t-1)]$ is the reaction to innovations. The last two components are in equation (2.25) for DX.

The *changes* in the exogenous variables $DZ = [Z(t) - Z(t-1)]$ in equation (2.24) and (2.25) should be D(DISRAT, USGROWTH, FGROWTH). However, they do not show up very significantly in the estimation. We therefore use a market measure of DZ. In Figure 2.4, changes in the fundamentals DZ shift the IS and IS' curves and produce interest-rate differentials $(r - r')$, such as $H - H1$, which lead to portfolio adjustments and capital flows which then produce a convergence. To avoid a simultaneous equation problem, we measure DZ by USFINT (-1), the real long-term interest differential lagged by one quarter. This measure of DZ as well as Z is significant in our estimating equations below.

Tables 2.8 and 2.10 use OLS to estimate equation (2.20). Tables 2.7 and 2.9 use NLS non-linear least squares in (2.24) to check the robustness of our results to the estimation method utilized. In (2.24), the NLS technique estimates B which is simultaneously in both the first and second terms, so the estimation is *constrained* by the requirement that the same B should be obtained.

An alternative method of estimating the relationship between the cointegrated variables is the Phillips–Loretan technique, which is (2.26) not (2.24), where the set $[X(t), Z(t)]$ are matched with no lags (Campbell and Perron 1991: 190).

$$X(t) = BZ(t) + a[X(t-1) - BZ(t-1)] + b[Z(t) - Z(t-1)] + e \quad (2.26)$$

When we used (2.24) in Table 2.7 we obtained significant and economically sensible results for vector B. When we used (2.26), the only significant result in vector B was the coefficient of DISRAT, which was not economically sensible.[33] The rationale for cointegration tests is the avoidance of spurious correlation. Phillips showed (Campbell and Perron 1991: 176) that in the case of spurious correlation the following occur as the sample size increases. (a) The Durbin–Watson statistic converges to zero; (b) the R^2 converges to a random variable; (c) the t-statistics of the coefficients diverge. We do not observe any of these warning signals.

We obtain the same results whether we use OLS or NLS estimation.[34] The results of Tables 2.7 to 2.10 are summarized in Table 2.11, which corresponds to Table 2.2 above. *US growth* (a) appreciates the real exchange rate R but not significantly; and (b) significantly reduces the US current account/GNP. This corresponds to the movement along trajectory AD in Figure 2.5. *Foreign growth* (a) depreciates the US dollar significantly and (b) significantly increases the US current account to GNP. This corresponds to the foreign country moving along its trajectory AD in Figure 2.5. A rise in the index of *US time preference* DISRAT (a) significantly depreciates the long-run value of the dollar and (b) significantly reduces the current account. The DISRAT variable captures the movement along trajectory BE in Figure 2.5. The *shorter-run effect* of a rise in

---

[33] It stated that a rise in the social consumption ratio appreciates the steady-state real value of the dollar.

[34] For the real exchange rate, the residuals in the OLS equation are stationary and pass all of the usual diagnostic tests, cited at the foot of Table 2.9. In the NLS equation Table 2.8 for the real exchange rate, the residuals from the entire equation are stationary. However, the residuals from the hypothesized cointegrating part $R - BZ$ do not pass the stationarity test at the 5% level. This is a reason why the estimates are compared using different methods: NLS and OLS, summarized in Table 2.12. In the equation for the ratio of the current account/GNP, the residuals from the OLS equation are stationary and pass the usual diagnostic tests, cited below Table 2.11. In the NLS equation for the ratio of the current account/GNP, the residuals are stationary both from the entire equation and from the cointegrating equation CAGNP $- BZ$. Hence, we do seem to have a cointegrating equation.

TABLE 2.7 *Non-linear least-squares (NLS) estimates of the determinants of the real exchange rate, sample Feb. 1975 to Apr. 1989, number of observations 59.* REXR = $[C(1) + C(2)^*$USGROWTH$(-1) + C(3)^*$FGROWTH$(-1) + C(4)^*$DISRAT$(-1)] + C(5)^*$[REXR$(-1) - C(2)^*$USGROWTH$(-1) - C(3)^*$FGROWTH$(-1) - C(4)^*$DISRAT$(-1)] + C(6)^*$USFINT$(-1) + e$

Variable	Coeff.	Std. error	t-stat	2-tail sig.
Constant	422.7	148	2.86	0.006
USGROWTH	1.17	1.79	0.65	0.52
FGROWTH	− 8.12	3.26	− 2.49	0.016
DISRAT	− 3.4	1.72	− 1.99	0.05
$C(5)$	0.74	0.055	13.3	0.00
USFINT(-1)	2.5	0.62	4.05	0.00

Note: Adj. $R - SQ = 0.96$; DF stat. for residual from equation is UROOT$(N, 0) = -6.5$; DF stat. for $R - BZ$ is UROOT$(N, 0) = -1.27$.

the US less G-10 real long-term rates of interest (a) appreciates the US dollar significantly, but (b) does not significantly affect the US current account. The reason may be that there is a lag between changes in real long-term interest rates and investment less saving equal to the current account.

TABLE 2.8 *Determinants of the real exchange rate. OLS estimates sample period Jan. 1975 to Apr. 1989, observations 60.* REXR = $C(1) + C(2)^*$REXR$(-1) + C(3)^*$USGROWTH $+ C(4)^*$FGROWTH $+ C(5)^*$DISRAT $+ C(6)^*$USFINT$(-1) + e$

Variable	Coeff.	Std-error	t-stat	2-tail sig.
Constant	114.8	28.7	4.00	0.002
REXR(-1)	0.75	0.055	13.49	0.00
USGROWTH	0.55	0.49	1.13	0.26
DISRAT	− 0.98	0.365	− 2.7	0.009
FGROWTH	− 1.825	0.88	− 2.1	0.04
USFINT(-1)	2.77	0.62	4.4	0.00

Note: Adj. $R - SQ = 0.96$; Durbin–Watson stat. = 1.76; LM test, 4 lags, prob. = 0.25; ARCH test, 4 lags, prob. = 0.98; heteroskedasticity test, prob. = 0.26; ADF stat. on res., UROOT$(N, 1) = -5.2$; prob. of null hypothesis $[C(3) = 0, C(4) = 0, C(5) = 0]$ = 0.005.

TABLE 2.9 *Non-linear estimation NLS of CAGNP the ratio of the current account/GNP. Sample Feb. 1975 to Mar. 1989, number of observations 58.*
CAGNP=$[C(1)+C(2)^*\text{USGROWTH}(-1)+C(3)^*\text{FGROWTH}(-1)+C(4)^*$
DISRAT$(-1)] + C(5)^*[\text{CAGNP}(-1) - C(1) - C(2)^*\text{USGROWTH}(-1) -$
$C(3)^*\text{FGROWTH}(-1) - C(4)^*\text{DISRAT}(-1)] + C(6)^*\text{USFINT}(-1) + e$

Variable	Coeff.	Std. error	t-stat	2-tail sig.
$C(1)$	9.4	3.7	2.5	0.01
MAGROWTH	− 0.15	0.06	− 2.5	0.015
MAFGROW	0.29	0.12	2.4	0.019
DISRAT	− 0.12	0.04	− 2.8	0.00
$C(5)$	0.84	0.06	13.2	0.00
USFINT(-1)	− 0.0076	0.0097	− 0.78	0.43

Note: Adj. $R - SQ = 0.96$; DF stat. on res. $= \text{CAGNP} - BZ$ gives UROOT(N, 0) − 2.2.

The explanatory power of the NATREX, as the fundamental equilibrium exchange rate, is high. We show this in several ways. First is the structural stability of the estimates. Instead of selecting an arbitrary breakpoint, we use the recursive residuals which generalize the Chow test. If the maintained model is valid, and not changing over time, the recursive residuals will lie about the zero

TABLE 2.10 *OLS estimate of CAGNP, the ratio of the current account/GNP, sample Jan. 1975 to Mar. 1989, observations 59.* CAGNP = $C(1)$ + $C(2)^*\text{CAGNP}(-1)$ + $C(3)^*\text{USGROWTH}$ + $C(4)^*$ FGROWTH + $C(5)^*\text{DISRAT} + e$

VARIABLE	COEFF.	STD.ERROR	T-STAT	2-TAIL SIG
CONSTANT	1.76	0.85	2.1	0.04
CAGNP(-1)	0.83	0.06	13.4	0.00
USGROWTH	− 0.034	0.016	− 2.1	0.04
FGROWTH	0.06	0.019	3.24	0.002
DISRAT	− 0.023	0.01	− 2.25	0.029

Note: Adj. $R - SQ = 0.95$; Durbin–Watson stat. = 1.97; LM test, serial correlation, 4 lags, prob. = 0.97; ARCH test, 4 lags, prob. = 0.37; heteroskedasticity test, prob. = 0.15; ADF test res. UROOT (N, 1) − 5.6; prob $[C(3) + C(4) = 0] = 0.02$; prob. $[C(3) = 0, \quad C(4) = 0, \quad C(5) = 0] = 0.005$; Jarque–Bera normality test stat. 2.86, prob. = 0.24.

TABLE 2.11 *Summary of effects of the fundamentals upon the real exchange rate and ratio of current account/GNP [two-tail significance]*

Z	dR/dZ		d(CAGNP)/dZ	
	NLS	OLS*	NLS	OLS**
USGROWTH	1.17 [0.52]	2.2[0.26]	− 0.15[0.015]	− 0.2[0.04]
FGROWTH	− 8.12[0.016]	− 7.3[0.04]	0.29[0.019]	0.35[0.002]
DISRAT	− 3.4[0.05]	− 3.92[0.009]	− 0.12[0.00]	− 0.14[0.029]

Notes: *OLS estimate $dR/dZ = c/(1 − a) = c/(1 − 0.75) = 4$ times the co- efficient c in Table 2.8; **OLS estimate $d(CAGNP)/dZ = c/(1 − a) = c/(1 − 0.83) = 5.88$ times the coefficient c in Table 2.10.

point and within the plus or minus two standard-error bands. Figure 2.7 describes the recursive residuals from the real exchange-rate Table 2.8; and Figure 2.9 from the current account/GNP in Table 2.11. The recursive residuals almost always lie within the standard-error bands, except for the real exchange rate for a short period in 1981 and 1984.

Second, is the explanatory power. Figure 2.6 compares the actual real exchange rate REXR(*t*) with a dynamic *ex ante* simulation of the NATREX. The NATREX is derived by using the coefficients in Table 2.8 and actual values of Z and dZ. However, instead of using

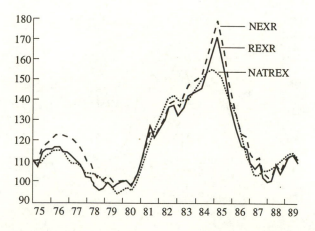

FIG. 2.6 *Real exchange rate (REXR), NATREX (dynamic ex ante forecast), nominal exchange rate (NEXR)*

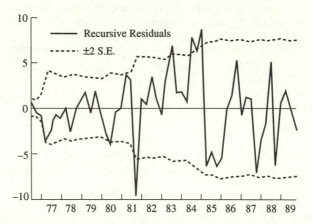

FIG. 2.7   *Real exchange rate (Table 2.9), recursive residuals*

the lagged dependent variable $R(t-1)$, we use the *previously predicted value* $R'(t-1)$ of the real exchange rate (denoted by a prime). The graph of NATREX is:

$$R'(t) = C(1) + C(2)^* R'(t-1) + \sum C(i) Z(i) + C(6)^* \text{USFINT}(-1).$$

It is seen that the real exchange rate converges to the NATREX, but there are some significant short-period deviations, resulting

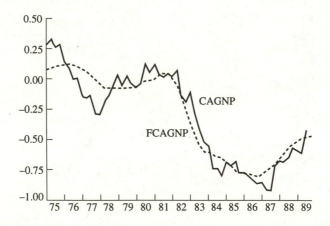

FIG. 2.8   *Current account/GNP (CAGNP), dynamic ex ante forecast (Table 2.11)*

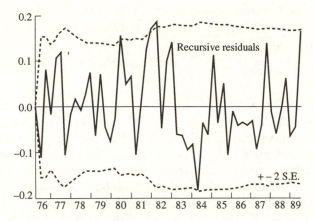

FIG. 2.9   *Current account/GNP, recursive residuals*

from the non-fundamentals. This deviation is the first term in equation (2.1). We attribute these deviations of the real exchange rate from the 'equilibrium exchange rate' to the speculative factors, related to anticipated short-term nominal interest rates at home and abroad, and possibly to cyclical factors. The model is quite stable as shown in the recursive residuals Figure 2.7.

The fundamentals Z significantly explain capital flows measured by the ratio of the current account[35] to GNP (to abstract from cyclical factors). Foreign growth significantly increases the current account, domestic growth decreases the current account, and time preference (DISRAT) significantly decreases the current account. The *growth variables* reflect movements along trajectory *AD* in Figure 2.5, where capital is rising and is partially financed by capital inflows which raise the debt for a while. The *time-preference variable* reflects movements along trajectory *BE* in Figure 2.5 where the capital intensity is declining but the debt is rising.

The explanatory power of the fundamentals Z is high. Figure 2.8 is a dynamic *ex ante* simulation of the capital flow, based upon Table 2.10. The *previously predicted* value of the CAGNP is used as the *lagged dependent* variable. The fundamentals track the evolution

---

[35] The current account is measured on a quarterly basis and GNP on an annual basis. Therefore, multiply each coefficient in Tables 2.9 and 2.10 by 4 to obtain comparable annual figures.

of the current account/GNP very well. The recursive residuals (Figure 2.9) indicate that the model is quite stable.

4. CONCLUSION

The NATREX model focuses upon the real and not the nominal exchange rate. It answered question Q1 concerning the fundamental determinants of the real exchange rate. Equation (2.1) above relates the nominal exchange rate $N(t)$ to the real exchange rate, the fundamentals, and relative prices. We have both identified the fundamentals and shown that, over time but not in the very short run, the real exchange rate converges to its equilibrium as defined by the NATREX. *There is long, but not short, period rationality.*

The real exchange rate $R = Np/p'$ is the ratio of relative prices at home and abroad in a common currency. This endogenous variable produces external equilibrium. We did not separate the roles of the nominal exchange rate N and relative prices p/p' because there is no consensus at present concerning the determinants of the rate of inflation in the medium run. The role of monetary aggregates as indicators or intermediate targets of the rate of inflation is the subject of controversy and inquiry.[36] For the US/G-10, the role of relative prices in the nominal exchange rate is quite small relative to the real exchange rate. This is seen in Figure 2.6, where the nominal (NEXR) and real exchange rate (REXR = NEXR(p/p')) practically coincide. The reason why the PPP theory is not valid is precisely because the fundamentals Z have been changing. Table 2.4 shows that the fundamentals are not stationary. The evolution of the real exchange rate concerns the evolution of the second and third terms in equation (2.1) above.

There has been an active debate concerning the sensitivity of capital flows to disturbances of saving and investment.[37] On the basis of Tables 2.9, 2.10, and summary Table 2.11, we now show

---

[36] There is great disillusionment among monetarists about the use of monetary aggregates as indicators or intermediate targets for the rate of inflation. See Federal Reserve Bank of St Louis, *Review*, spring 1994, which discusses these issues. This is another reason why the conventional monetary models in international finance are disappointing. See appendix chapter below.

[37] See the survey paper by Obstfeld (1993), Polly Allen's discussion (1993), McKibbin and Sachs (1991), and Niehans (1994).

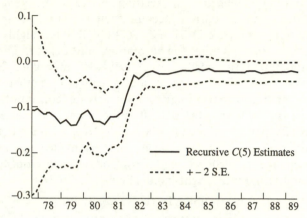

FIG. 2.10 *Recursive estimate coefficient of DISRAT in current account/ GNP equation*

how we answer questions Q2 and Q3 at the beginning of this paper, and why we believe that there is a high degree of capital mobility. Capital flows are saving less investment, equal to the current account, and are not necessarily reflected by interest-rate differentials.[38] The NATREX theory states that the fundamentals Z, productivity, and thrift, determine saving less investment and hence capital flows. The phase diagram Figure 2.5 indicates the trajectory of the current account as a response to the fundamentals.

The Feldstein–Horioka view that there is no capital mobility means that $d(CAGNP)/dZ = 0$, disturbances to productivity and thrift in the longer run do not affect capital flows. This means that we should not find that the vector B of coefficients in Tables 2.9, 2.10, and summary Table 2.11 columns 3 and 4 are significant. That is not the case. We find that each element in these tables is highly significant, both separately and jointly.[39] The high explanatory power of the results in Tables 2.9 and 2.10 are summarized in Figures 2.8–2.10.

---

[38] See Niehans (1994) for an excellent discussion of this issue.

[39] At the foot of Table 2.10 are test statistics. The probability that the coefficients of USGROWTH, FGROWTH, and DISRAT are zero is 0.005. The residuals are normal (Jarque–Bera test statistic), are not serially correlated, and there is no heteroskedasticity.

Question Q3 concerns the relation between the government expenditures and the current account. The social consumption or index of time preference DISRAT $= (C + G)/$GNP is a highly significant variable in explaining the current-account deficits. The recursive estimates of the coefficient of DISRAT in Figure 2.10 are highly stable. In this measure, it does not matter whether government expenditures have increased or private consumption has increased (say, due to a tax cut). It is their sum that matters. The basic goods market balance $(1 = (C + G)/$GNP $+ I/$GNP $+ CA/$GNP) equation is (2.27a). The change in the current account resulting from a change in DISRAT is (2.27b). The 'crowding out effect' is the second term on the right-hand side of (2.27b).

$$1 = \text{DISRAT} + (I/Y) + \text{CAGNP} \qquad (2.27a)$$

$$d(\text{CAGNP})/d(\text{DISRAT}) = -1 - d(I/Y)/d(\text{DISRAT}) \qquad (2.27b)$$

We do not ask what is the effect of Z upon the current account, given the real exchange rate. Our system jointly determines the real exchange rate and current-account deficit. Thus $B = dX/dZ$ is the total effect of a change in a fundamental upon an endogenous variable.

The current account is measured quarterly and GNP is at an annual rate; therefore we shall multiply coefficients by 4. Table 2.11 column 3 gives the NLS estimate of the effect of DISRAT upon CAGNP as -0.12 or -0.48 on an annual basis. This is the estimate of the movement along the trajectory. Table 2.11 column 4 gives the longer-run OLS estimate of the effect of DISRAT upon CAGNP as -0.14 times 4 to put it on an annual basis as -0.56. We obtain the same estimate -0.5 both ways. Our analysis is that for the US in the longer run (trajectory) half of the disturbances to I-S are financed abroad and half crowd out private investment. The stability of the recursive estimate of the coefficient of DISRAT as the sample size increases (Figure 2.10) indicates that no significant changes have occurred since 1982.

We conclude that in the longer run along the trajectory BE in Figure 2.5 a unit rise in government consumption will increase the steady-state debt. The rise in the debt will reduce wealth and raise private saving. There will be a rise in the world rate of interest which will reduce investment. The crowding out of private investment occurs because the decline in social saving shifts the IS curve to the right in Figure 2.4 and raises the world real rate of interest from *H* to *H*1. The net effect is that the current-account deficit will rise by one half and the other half will be met by a rise in private saving less investment. Similarly, if the government expenditures/GNP declined by 1 point with no change in private consumption, the current-account/GNP deficit would decrease by 0.5. This is the same number obtained by John Helliwell (1991: 31) in his study.[40] The current account deficits in the 1980s cannot be explained without using the effects of DISRAT.

Foreign growth generated by the rise in investment demand will lead to a capital outflow, a rise in the US current account, and a depreciation of the US dollar along the early part of the trajectory. From the viewpoint of the foreign country, this is a movement along trajectory *AD* in Figure 2.5, where the capital and debt are rising.

We have shown how the evolution of the real exchange rate and foreign debt are jointly determined, and that the fundamentals productivity and thrift generate significant capital mobility for the US. Market-determined real exchange rates are 'equilibrium rates' as trends but not as short-run movements.[41]

REFERENCES

Allen, Polly Reynolds. 1993. 'Comments on Obstfeld's paper' [see below]. International Finance Section, Princeton University.

Boothe, Paul, Kevin Clinton, Agathe Côté, and David Longworth. 1985. 'International asset substitutability: theory and evidence for Canada'. Bank of Canada, Ottawa, Canada.

Campbell, John Y. and Pierre Perron. 1991. 'Pitfalls and opportunities: what macroeconomists should know about unit roots'. In National Bureau of Economic Research, Macroeconomics Annual 1991, MIT Press.

Corbae, Dean and Sam Ouliaris. 1991. 'A test of long-run purchasing power parity allowing for structural breaks'. *Economic Record*, Mar. 26–33.

---

[40] Helliwell wrote: 'the ratio of the induced external deficit to the induced fiscal deficit . . . returns to . . . between .45 and .49 for the rest of the six year period'.

[41] This is our response to the issues raised by John Williamson (1994).

Helliwell, John F. 1991. 'The fiscal deficit and the external deficit: siblings but not twins'. In Rudolph G. Penner (ed.) *The Great Fiscal Experiment.* Washington, DC, The Urban Institute.

Hooper, Peter. 1989. 'Exchange rates and the US external adjustment in the short and the long run'. Washington, DC, Board of Governors of the Federal Reserve System, Discussion Paper 346.

Infante, Ettore and Jerome L. Stein. 1973. 'Optimal Growth with Robust Feedback Control'. *Review of Economic Studies,* 40 (1), 47–60.

Lothian, James R. and Mark P. Taylor. 1992. 'Real exchange rate behavior: the recent float from the perspective of the past two centuries'. Fordham University, Graduate School of Business, Working Paper.

McKibbin, Warwick and Jeffrey Sachs. 1991. *Global Linkages.* Washington, DC, Brookings Institute.

Merton, Robert C. 1990. *Continuous Time Finance.* Cambridge, Mass., Basil Blackwell.

Niehans, Jurg. 1994. 'Elusive capital flows: recent literature in perspective'. *Journal of International and Comparative Economics,* 3(1), 21–44.

Nurkse, Ragnar. 1945. *Conditions of International Monetary Equilibrium: Essays in International Finance.* Princeton University, International Finance Section, spring.

Obstfeld, Maurice. 1993. 'International capital mobility in the 1990s'. Conference on the International Monetary System, International Finance Section, Princeton University.

Pontryagin, L. S., *et al.* 1964. *The Mathematical Theory of Optimal Processes.* New York, Macmillan.

Williamson, John. 1994. 'On the calculation of equilibrium exchange rates'. In John Williamson (ed.) *Equilibrium Exchange Rates.* Washington, DC, Institute for International Economics.

3

The Dynamics of the Real Exchange Rate and Current Account in a Small Open Economy: Australia

GUAY C. LIM AND JEROME L. STEIN

1. AIMS OF THE CHAPTER

1.1 Historical Background[1]

The Australian dollar was floated in December 1983 in order to gain monetary independence. At the same time, capital controls were abolished and there was free mobility of capital. Since then, there have been large variations in the nominal exchange rate ($N = \$US/\$Australian$) and the real exchange rate (R), where a rise in either signifies an appreciation of the Australian dollar. The real exchange rate is the amount of goods one $A can purchase abroad relative to what it can purchase at home. The relation between the real and nominal rate is equation (3.1), where p is the Australian and p' is the foreign (in our study, the US) GDP deflator.

$$N = Rp'/p \tag{3.1}$$

During the floating-rate period, the nominal (N) and real (R) rates have moved together (Figure 3.1). Although the nominal exchange rate and relative prices have common trends, these two variables are not cointegrated. A stationary variable is one whose mean and variance are independent of time. Neither the real exchange rate nor the fundamentals discussed below is stationary. In the floating-rate period, it is necessary to explain movements in both the real exchange rate and in relative prices to explain movements in the nominal exchange rate.

---

[1] This narrative section draws upon: Blundell-Wignall *et al.* (1993), referred to as the RBA (Reserve Bank of Australia) study; Macfarlane (1990); and Macfarlane and Tease (1990).

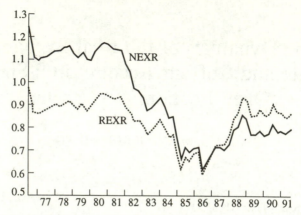

FIG. 3.1   *Real (REXR), nominal (NEXR) = $US/$Australian, exchange rates*

There is little disagreement that a major influence on the real exchange rate has been the exogenous terms of trade.[2] The arithmetic relation between them is equation (3.2), based upon equations (3.1), (a)–(c). Equation (a) states that the Australian price deflator is a geometric average of the prices of the goods produced. Good 1 is the export good, and good n is non-tradable. Equation (b) is the comparable relation in the US where the export good is good 2. The terms of trade T is equation (c), the ratio of the price of export good 1 to import good 2 measured in a common currency.

$$p = p_n^a p_1^{(1-a)} \tag{a}$$

$$p' = (p_n')^b (p_2')^{(1-b)} \tag{b}$$

$$T = N p_1 / p_2' \tag{c}$$

$$Rn = p_n / p_1 \tag{d}$$

The real exchange rate R is arithmetically related to both the exogenous terms of trade T and to $Rn = p_n / p_1$ the ratio of the price of the Australian non-tradable good to the price of its export good, as stated in equation (3.2). Since the terms of trade T and the relative prices (p_n'/p_2') in the US are exogenous for Australia, endogenous variations in the real exchange rate correspond to endogenous variations in the ratio of the price of non-tradables to

---

[2] Blundell-Wignall and Gregory (1990).

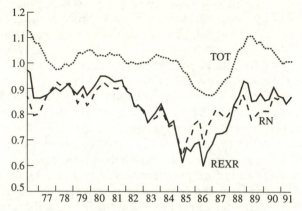

FIG. 3.2   *Real exchange rate (REXR), terms of trade (TOT), ratio of real exchange rate/terms of trade (Rn)*

export goods. Normalize the mean of the exogenous term $c = (p_2'/p_n')^b$ in the US at unity, to obtain the last term in (3.2). Variable R is the real exchange rate, and R_n is the relative price of non-tradables. Equation (3.2a) expresses the real exchange rate in logarithms; and e is the log of the random exogenous term $c = (p_2'/p_n')^b$.

$$R = T(R_n)^a (p_2'/p_n')^b = T(R_n)^a c \sim T(R_n)^a \qquad (3.2)$$

$$\log R = \log T + a \log R_n + e \qquad (3.2a)$$

The weight given to the non-tradable sector in the GDP deflator is exponent a. The smaller is a, the closer are the real exchange rate and the terms of trade. It is then *arithmetically true* that R is determined by exogenous T. What is important and interesting is to explain the fundamentals which determine the endogenous component of the real exchange rate: variable R_n, the relative price of non-tradables.

Figure 3.2 plots the real exchange rate R, the terms of trade T and the ratio $RN = R/T = (R_n)^a c$ of the real exchange rate to the terms of trade. This is a function of the relative price of non-tradables.[3] If the

---

[3] The relative price of non-tradables cannot be measured unambiguously, since it is not clear just what is or is not non-tradable. For example, traditionally services have been classified as non-tradable. However, a major portion of US exports consists of services: insurance, financial services, education. Therefore, the indirect measure RN above was used to find the relative price of non-tradables.

weight given to the non-tradable sector were negligible, this ratio would be unity. Figure 3.2 shows the importance of the endogenous relative price of non-tradables as a component of the real exchange rate.

There have been large real trade deficits relative to real GDP in Australia during the period of the 1980s. Prior to the float, the deficit was financed by equity capital; and since the float, by portfolio investment.[4] As a result of the trade deficits, the foreign debt has been rising. Net foreign debt as a share of GDP rose from 5 per cent at the beginning of the 1980s to about 14 per cent in 1984, as a result of current-account imbalances. Much of the debt was denominated in foreign currency. Partly driven by the depreci-ation of the currency, the debt rose to over 36 per cent in 1986. The size and growth of the foreign debt and the debt-service ratio led the Treasurer in May 1986 to make an analogy between Australia and a 'banana republic'. The credit-worthiness of Australian debt was ques-tioned, the debt was downgraded, and the value of the currency fell.

The aims of this chapter are: to identify the fundamental determi-nants of the equilibrium real exchange rate (NATREX), examine whether the actual rate converges to the NATREX, explain the evolution of the foreign debt, and explain when it should or should not be a cause for concern. Part 1.2 discusses what we know about the Australian exchange rates and associated fundamentals. What theories are or are not consistent with the evidence? We draw upon the existing studies, primarily that of the Reserve Bank of Australia, as well as on our own calculations. Part 1.3 summarizes the work of Edwards and Balassa, so that the reader can place our work into the context of the literature.

1.2 What do we Know? Quantitative Results

There are certain basic phenomena concerning the Australian economy that are not consistent with the current state of theory. Hence, in attempting to apply a theory to the Australian economy, one must be aware of the cognitive dissonances and avoid making improper theoretical assumptions.

The standard theoretical models generally assume[5] the following. (a) The real exchange rate is stationary (its mean and variance are

---

[4] Macfarlane and Tease 1990: Table 1.

[5] Since all of these issues are discussed in detail in the appendix chapter our discussion here will be brief and just focused upon Australia.

independent of time), such that it will converge relatively quickly[6] to a constant mean. (b) The appreciation of nominal exchange rate is equal to the differential between the foreign and the domestic nominal rates of interest, plus an iid term with a zero expectation and possibly a constant which reflects a country (political) risk premium. (c) Temporary changes in the government budget deficit are matched by equal changes in the current-account deficit, whereas permanent changes in the government budget deficit have no effect upon the current account.

Each one of the assumptions (a), (b), and (c) is inconsistent with the Australian experience. First: the real value of the Australian dollar relative to the $US during the period 1975.3–1991.3 was not stationary, as shown in Table 3.1. The Reserve Bank of Australia study obtains the same results for the real-trade weighted value of the Australian dollar during the period[7] 1969.3–1992.3. The non-stationarity of the real exchange rate is not peculiar to the recent period, but also applies over a long-run horizon. Corbae and Ouliaris examined the real exchange rate from 1890–1984, and also permitted structural breaks. They concluded that 'the real exchange rate cannot be modelled as a stationary process and therefore reject the absolute version of PPP'. This suggests that 'the real exchange rate was affected by a series of permanent real shocks', and its mean is not a constant. An important implication of the non-stationarity of the real exchange rate is that one cannot explain the variations in the equilibrium nominal exchange rate (equation 3.1) primarily by variations in relative prices, assuming that the real exchange rate converges to a constant independent of time.

Second: the uncovered interest-rate parity/rational-expectations hypothesis which assumes perfect foresight plus an iid term is rejected.[8] The uncovered interest-rate parity with rational expectations (UIRP/RE) assumption is that the percentage nominal appreciation of the Australian dollar is equal to the US less Australian nominal interest rates (on comparable assets) plus an iid term and possibly a constant. This is equation (3.3), with the hypothesis that

---

[6] If the convergence is very slow (say a century), then to all intents and purposes, there is no convergence during the sample period of say 25 years.

[7] The notation for dates is that the quarter is denoted by one digit after the decimal and the month by two digits: first quarter of 1991 is 1991.1, January 1991 is 1991.01.

[8] We are drawing upon the RBA study, equations (B4), (B8), (B10), using our notation.

$b = 1$ and e is iid with a zero expectation. The constant a may be a political-risk premium. The (log of the) nominal value of the Australian dollar is $N(t)$, the Australian h-monthly period nominal treasury interest rate is $i(t)$ and the US counterpart is $i'(t)$, all evaluated at time t. The logarithm of the nominal exchange rate at month $t + h$ is $N(t + h)$. The logarithm of the h-period forward rate is $F(t + h; t)$.

$$N(t + h) - N(t) = a + b[i'(t) - i(t)] + e \quad H: b = 1, E(e) = 0, e = \text{iid} \quad (3.3)$$

The period examined was 1984.01–1993.01, where there were no capital controls and the exchange rate was free. The freedom of capital movements is seen by examining the covered interest-rate parity (CIRP) condition (3.4): the forward premium at time t on a contract maturing at $t + h$, $F(t + h; t) - N(t)$, is equal to the interest-rate differential $i'(t) - i(t)$. If there is a political-risk premium, it would appear in the constant a'. The hypothesis is that $b' = 1$ and $a' = 0$.

$$F(t + h; t) - N(t) = a' + b'[i'(t) - i(t)] + e'.$$
$$H: a' = 0, b' = 1, E(e) = 0, e' = \text{iid} \quad (3.4)$$

Regression equation (3.4a) shows that we cannot reject the (CIRP) *covered* interest-rate parity. There is no political-risk premium on short-term treasury securities and the forward premium is essentially equal to the interest-rate differential. The standard errors are in parentheses.

$$F(t + 3; t) - N(t) = 0.0005 + 0.9856(i'(t) - i(t)) \quad (3.4a)$$

(st. error) $\quad$ (0.0004) (0.0264),

RBAR-SQ = 0.96, Chi-sq $(a = 0, b = 1) = 9.4$

Regression (3.5a) corresponds to equation (3.3). We reject the UIRP/RE hypothesis. The slope b is negative and significantly different from its hypothesized value of unity.

$$[N(t + 3) - N(t)] = -0.0426 - 2.397[i'(t) - i(t)] \quad (3.5a)$$

(st. error) $\quad$ (0.0192) (0.9772), $\quad$ RBAR-SQ = 0.06

Alternatively, since CIRP holds, we may substitute the forward premium for the interest-rate differential and examine (3.5b) to see if the uncovered interest-rate/rational expectations hypothesis is valid. The UIRP/RE hypothesis is that the coefficient of the forward premium is unity. This hypothesis is rejected. The negative slope is significantly different than its hypothesized value of plus one.

$$[N(t+3) - N(t)] = -0.0357 - 1.9285[F(t+3; t) - N(t)] \qquad (3.5b)$$

(st. error)   (0.0189) (1.1433),   RBAR-SQ = 0.05

Equations (3.5a) and (3.5b) contain the same result. There is no informational content in the forward premium or current interest-rate differential concerning subsequent movements of the exchange rate. The adjusted R-SQ is essentially zero. Blundell-Wignall *et al.* in the Reserve Bank of Australia study correctly state (1994: 49) that:

This result is commonplace in the literature on testing for uncovered interest rate parity. No economic hypothesis has been rejected more decisively, over more time periods, and for more countries than UIP [UIRP/RE]. . . . Many researchers interpret rejection of UIP as evidence of a time varying risk premium, while still maintaining the assumption of rational expectations. However, as the risk premium is then typically defined to be the deviation from UIP, this interpretation is merely a tautology.

The third hypothesis is that *temporary* changes in the government budget deficit are matched by equal changes in the current-account deficit, whereas *permanent* changes in the government budget deficit have no effect upon the current account. This issue is discussed in the appendix chapter, Table A4, and relies upon the study by Andersen. For Australia, Andersen found that the long-run (permanent) effect of a unit change in the government deficit is to change the current-account deficit by 0.5, and there is no short-run (temporary) change effect upon the current-account deficit, contrary to the hypothesis. The lesson so far is that it is inadmissible to try to model the Australian economy on the basis of the monetary models with rational expectations or by assuming that agents optimize on the basis of perfect foresight plus an iid term with a zero expectation.

Figure 3.3 plots the real long-term interest rates in Australia and the US. The real long-term interest-rate differential Australia less US, denoted $(r - r')$ in the model, is not entirely exogenous. We know from the study by the Reserve Bank of Australia that: the real long-term interest rate differential between Australian and US ten-year bonds is stationary or very close to it (Table 3.1), and not significantly different from zero. We believe that there is some tendency for the real rates to converge. On long-term investments there is also the influence of a risk premium, which is to some extent

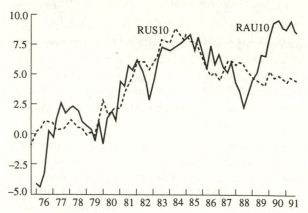

FIG. 3.3   *Real long-term Australian (RAU10) and US (RUS10) interest rates*

related to the foreign indebtedness $F(t)$ of Australia. The path and level of foreign debt may be a measure of the belief that there will be a depreciation in the future. The form of the relation is described in equation (3.5c). There is a dynamic adjustment such that $(r - r')$ converges to zero, but the path of the foreign debt affects the convergence.

$$d(r - r')/dt = -a(r - r') + h(F, t). \tag{5c}$$

Regression equation (3.5d) below is consistent with the modelling described. The dependent variable is $(r - r')$ (t) the real long-term interest rate differential at time t. The real long-term rate is the nominal yield on ten-year bonds less the rate of inflation of the GDP deflator from $(t - 4)$ to time t, measured in quarters. The dynamic system involves the lagged dependent variable $(r - r')(t - 1)$ and a measure of indebtedness: the cumulative sum[9] of the real trade deficit/real GDP, denoted CUMDEF. The period is 1975. 4–1991.3.

$$(r - r')(t) = -0.239 + 0.76(r - r')(t - 1) + 0.00166 \text{ CUMDEF} \tag{5d}$$

$$(t\text{-stat}) \quad (-0.89) \quad (8.98) \qquad\qquad (1.6)$$

Adjusted R-SQ = 0.65; Durbin–Watson stat. = 2.2

The constant term is not significant. The coefficient (0.76) is significant. The convergence of real long-term interest rates follows $(.76)^t$. The cumulative deficit has some significance but only at the

---

[9] This is taken from the Reserve Bank of Australia.

11 per cent level. We believe that the risk permium $h(F, t)$ is significant, but that the risk factor is not a constant. Moreover, we performed a unit root test on $(r - r')$. The differential was stationary at the 10 per cent level. The ADF statistic UROOT[10] $(r - r') =$ -2.6 (10% level $= -2.5$). Therefore, as suggested in Figure 3.3, there is a relation between the real long-term interest rates in the US and Australia, but it is not tight.

The Reserve Bank of Australia (RBA) study focuses upon the equilibrium real exchange rate, as we do in our NATREX model. Both ignore the role of short-term speculative capital flows because, as shown in equations 3.5a and 3.5b above, they are noise, not reflections of rational expectations. The Reserve Bank of Australia study covers the entire period 1973.1–1992.3 and the floating-rate period 1984.1–1992.3. The determinants of the equilibrium real exchange rate in the RBA study are presented in Table 3.1. Using a cointegration analysis, they relate the real exchange rate R to the following exogenous variables: the terms of trade, the real long-term interest differential Australia less US, and net foreign assets as a per cent of GDP. The entry in the Table is the regression coefficient and the t-statistics are in parentheses.

Their equilibrium real exchange rate tracks the movement in the real exchange rate (RBA 1994: Figures 17, 18), but there are sustained periods of deviation from the equilibrium. The major influence upon the real exchange rate in their study is the terms of trade. This is to be expected from equation (3.2a) above, since $\log R = \log T + a \log R_n + e$. They did not consider the determinants of the endogenous relative price of non-tradables Rn. The real long-term interest-rate differential is the second significant factor in their study. The net foreign-asset position was significant only during the adjustable-peg period, not during the period of floating. The RBA study also shows that the real long interest-rate differential between Australian and US ten-year bonds is stationary at the 10 per-cent level (RBA 1994: Table 2).[11] The ratio of the current account/GDP is not stationary, since the coefficient of the lagged term is positive (RBA, table 2).

---

[10] A constant and one lag were used.
[11] This is the same result cited above. The RBA used the CPI measure of inflation. The series graphed in Figure 3.3 uses GDP deflators. Similar results concerning stationarity are obtained with both measures.

TABLE 3.1   *Summary of the Reserve Bank of Australia study*

A. *Unit Root Tests*[12] *(the critical value at the 5% level for stationarity is − 1.95)*

	t-statistic
Non-stationary variables	
log real exchange rate $US	− 0.288
log real exchange rate, traded wgt.	0.443
log terms of trade	− 0.204
current account/GDP	2.754
Stationary variables	
real Australia–world interest rate	− 2.001
real Australia–US interest rate	− 1.981

B. *Regressors of the real exchange rate against the US Dollar ($US/$A)*[13]

exogenous variable	1973.1–1992.3	1984.1–1992.3
Terms of trade	0.619	0.8
	(2.9)	(3.2)
Real interest differential	0.013	0.025
	(2.5)	(2.5)
Net foreign assets/GDP	1.18	0.211
	(3.8)	(0.36)
Error correction, restricted	− 0.22	− 0.36
	(− 2.2)	(− 1.9)

Source: Reserve Bank of Australia, Table B2.

1.3 The Analyses of Edwards and Balassa

We are concerned with the role of the fundamentals in determining the longer-run evolution of the real exchange rate and current account for the small open Australian economy. We have shown that the primary source of variation in the nominal exchange rate

---

[12] The unit root test equation for variable y used by the RBA is: $\Delta y(t) = \alpha + \beta t + (\rho - 1)y(t - 1) + \Sigma c(i)\Delta y(t - i) + e$. If the variable is stationary we must reject the hypothesis that $(\rho - 1)$ is 0. For stationarity, $(\rho - 1)$ must be negative.
[13] Long-run coefficients were estimated with the Phillips–Hansen procedure. The restricted error correction results exclude insignificant lagged innovation terms. The t-statistics are in parentheses.

during the floating-rate period was the real exchange rate; and that the PPP hypothesis has at most limited explanatory power. Moreover, the variable of importance for resource allocation and growth is the real exchange rate. We relate our NATREX model to the work of Sebastian Edwards, which has been applied to Latin America, and to Balassa's framework. Edwards wrote (1988) that:

> In spite of the importance that real exchange rates have attained in recent policy discussions there have been basically no attempts to empirically analyze the forces behind real exchange-rate behaviour. . . . In many ways the issue of real exchange rate determination . . . has remained in a murky state. . . . in reviewing the literature on the subject it is surprising to find virtually no studies that formally attempt to explain the distinction between the equilibrium and disequilibrium (misaligned) real exchange rates.

Edwards considers (1988: 313–17) a small economy which produces both a tradable and a non-tradable good, and offers an explanation of the determination of the real exchange rate. In the short run, both nominal and real factors are important determinants. In the long run, only real factors are relevant. His steady state is attained when the following four conditions hold simultaneously:

> (1) the non-tradables market clears; (2) the external sector is in equilibrium... [current account] $CA = 0$...; (3) fiscal policy is sustainable... (4) portfolio equilibrium holds. The real exchange rate prevailing under these steady state conditions is the long run equilibrium real exchange rate (1988: 316)

The economy produces exportable good 1 and non-tradable good n, and consumes importable good 2 and non-traded good n. If we ignore the dichotomy between the private and government sector, two equations characterize his steady state. First: there is the clearing of the market for non-tradables (n), where q_n is the supply function and c_n is the demand function. Production depends upon the relative price of non-tradables to exportables $R_n = (p_n/p_1)$ and demand depends upon the relative price of non-tradable to importables $p_n/p_2 = (p_n/p_1)(p_1/p_2) = R_n T$ and wealth. This is equation (E1).

Second: his trade balance, or clearing of the market for tradables, is equation (E2). The quantity of exports supplied q_1 depends negatively upon $R_n = p_n/p_1$ the relative price of non-tradables, and the quantity of imports demanded c_2 depends positively upon the relative price of non-tradables (p_n/p_2) = TR_n. Let the numeraire be

p_1 the price of the exported good. The value of exports in terms of the numeraire is $Q_1 = q_1$. T is the terms of trade, and the value of imports is C_2. The trade–balance equation is (E2). In his steady state the trade balance is zero. His real wealth a is the sum of real domestic and foreign money, and adjusts through changes in reserves and the price of foreign money.

Using the definitions $Rn = (p_n/p_1)$ and the terms of trade $T = (p_1/p_2)$, we write Edwards' demand and supply in terms of relative price of non-tradables R_n and the terms of trade. The quantities are in lower case and values in terms of the export good are in upper case.

$$C_n(TR_n, a) = Q_n(R_n); \qquad C_n' < 0, \ Q_n' > 0. \qquad \text{(E1)}$$

$$B = q_1(R_n) - c_2(TR_n, a)/T = 0 \quad c_2' > 0, \ q_1' < 0 \qquad \text{(E2)}$$

$$= Q_1(R_n) - C_2(R_n, T, a) = 0$$

$$Rn = (p_n/p_1), \ TR_n = p_n/p_2$$

In his model capital flows[14] are assumed to be zero, due to capital controls. He does not have an investment function. The inherited stocks of real capital and foreign debt are fixed. His endogenous variable is the relative price of non-tradables and the *exogenous* variables are the terms of trade, the level and composition of government consumption, and import tariffs. Theoretically, the effects of changes in the terms of trade and import tariffs upon the relative price of non-tradables are ambiguous.[15]. Formally, these two equations can be solved for the relative price of non-tradables R_n and wealth a as functions of the terms of trade T and any tariffs.

$$R_n = R_n(T), \ a = a(T) \qquad \text{(E3)}$$

He wrote that:

given the relative simplicity of that model some other possible real determinants of the equilibrium RER that were not explicitly derived from the model were also included in some of the equations estimated. For example, the variable technical progress was included in order to capture the possible role of the so-called Ricardo–Balassa effect . . . According to this hypothesis countries experiencing a faster rate of technological progress will experience an equilibrium RER appreciation. (1988: 333).

---

[14] In his model, capital flows are ignored, but in the empirical work capital flows are exogenous.

[15] See the chapter by Connolly and Devereux later in this volume.

His empirical analysis based upon OLS is as follows. He uses a proxy for the relative price of non-tradables. (1) The only fundamentals for which he had reliable data are the external terms of trade, and capital flows. The ratio of government consumption to GDP was used as a proxy for government consumption of non-tradables. Technological progress was proxied by the rate of growth of real GDP. (2a) In the OLS regressions, an improvement in the terms of trade appreciated the proxy[16] for the relative price of non-tradables. (2b) The coefficient of the government expenditure variable was not significant. (2c) A rise in real growth depreciated the proxy for the relative price of non-tradables, contrary to the Ricardo–Balassa hypothesis.

Balassa hypothesized that there would be a trend of appreciation of the real exchange rate for developing countries on the basis of the argument that an increase in productivity in traded goods sold at world prices will raise the relative price of non-traded goods. The Balassa framework is extremely simple. It consists of adding to equations (3.1), (a), (b), (c) and (3.2) above the equation that price equals marginal cost in each sector, and the assumption that there is wage equality between sectors of a given country. The marginal cost is the nominal wage W divided by the marginal productivity of labour H. Therefore the relative price of non-tradables to tradables denoted p_n/p_t is (B1) at home, and similarly for the foreign country. It follows that the relative price of non-tradables R_n is equal to the ratio of productivity in the tradables relative to the non-tradables.

$$p_n/p_t = R_n = (W/H_n)/(W/H_t) = H_t/H_n. \tag{B1}$$

The real exchange rate R in equation (3.2) becomes (B2):

$$R = T(H_t/H_n)^a/(H't/H'n)^b \tag{B2}$$

In the Balassa framwork, the real exchange rate R is positively related to the terms of trade T and the ratio of productivity in the tradables (t) relative to the non-tradables (n). The problem with the Balassa framework is that the marginal productivity of labour $H_i(k_i, u_i)$, $i = t, n$ in the two sectors is not explained. The productivity of labour depends upon the capital–labour ratio (capital intensity) k_i and the level of overall productivity u_i in tradables and

---

[16] His proxy for the relative price of non-tradables RER = E. WPI (US)/CPI, where E = domestic currency/$US, WPI(US) is the US wholesale price index, and CPI is the domestic price index.

non-tradables. The capital intensity in each of the two sectors is an endogenous variable which is not explained in the Balassa framework.

The way to view equation (B1) is to realize that capital and labour will be allocated between tradable and non-tradable goods such that the value of the marginal products of labour and capital will be equal in the two sectors. The value of the marginal product of labour is $p_t H_t(k_t; u_t)$ in tradables and $p_n H_n(k_n; u_n)$ in non-tradables. The value of the marginal product of capital is $p_t h_t(k_t; u_t)$ in tradables and $p_n h_n(k_n; u_n)$ in non-tradables. The u_i is the level of total factor productivity. These equations can be written as (B3) and (B4), though they were ignored by Balassa. That is, (B1) cannot state simply that the relative price of non-tradables R_n is determined by relative labour productivity H_t/H_n because the latter is an endogenous variable.

$$H_t(k_t; u_t) = R_n H_n(k_n; u_n) \text{ wage equality} \qquad \text{(B3)}$$

$$h_t(k_t; u_t) = R_n h_n(k_n; u_n) \text{ rent equality} \qquad \text{(B4)}$$

$$Rn = p_n/p_t$$

There is a third equation which relates the capital intensities to the total capital labour ratio k and the allocation of labour L_t/L between the two sectors, (B5).

$$k = k_t(L_t/L) + k_n(1 - L_t/L) \qquad \text{(B5)}$$

We now have three equations (B3)–(B5) to determine the capital intensities k_t, k_n, and allocation of labour L_t/L in terms of the relative price of non-tradables Rn and total capital intensity k. Call these equations (B6)–(B8).

$$k_t = a_t(R_n, k; u) \qquad \text{(B6)}$$

$$k_n = a_n(R_n, k; u) \qquad \text{(B7)}$$

$$L_t/L = e(R_n, k; u) \qquad \text{(B8)}$$

The Balassa analysis does not explain the real exchange rate. Equations (B6)–(B8) are three equations in four unknowns: R_n, k_n, k_t and L_t/L. A more general theory is required to determine the relative price of non-tradables. We shall explain this in our model which combines the elements of both the Edwards and Balassa frameworks.

2   A DYNAMIC MODEL OF THE FUNDAMENTAL DETERMINANTS OF THE NATURAL REAL EXCHANGE RATE IN A SMALL OPEN ECONOMY

Our study is in the same spirit as that of the Reserve Bank of Australia. It concerns the role of the fundamentals in determining the longer-run equilibrium relative price of non-tradables and capital flows, which determine the foreign debt. Equation (3.2) would then explain the real exchange rate. We use the NATREX growth model of the real exchange rate which accords an important role to the fundamentals in the medium to long run, and where capital and debt are endogenous variables. We specifically consider the effects of real shocks denoted by vector $Z = (T, u, s, r')$ associated with the terms of trade (T), productivity $(u = u_t, u_n)$, thrift (s) and the world real rate of interest (r') on the dynamic path of the real exchange rate, current account, capital, and debt. Thereby we show what will be the trajectories of the endogenous foreign debt and the relative price of non-tradables. Will the real foreign debt converge and at what level? What has produced the foreign debt, is it a problem, and what can policy do to affect the trajectory of the foreign debt?

2.1   The Structural Equations for the Small Open Economy Model

Chapter 1 explained that there are several versions of the NATREX model which depend upon several characteristics: the size of the economy relative to its trading partners in tradable goods and assets, and substitutabilities among goods and assets between countries and within the home country. The Australian version in this chapter differs from the one used in Chapter 2 concerning the US dollar/G-10 real exchange rate. Australia is small in the tradable-goods market and faces perfectly elastic world demand for and supply of tradable goods. Thus the terms of trade are exogenous. The relative price of non-tradables $R_n = p_n/p_1$ is the only endogenous relative price, and the real exchange rate $R = T(R_n)^a$, where a is the weight of non-traded goods in the GDP deflator. We assume that: (a) the economy produces export good 1, and non-traded good n; (b) the economy consumes imported good 2 and the non-traded good; (c) fraction m of the investment good consists of imported good 2 and fraction $(1 - m)$ of the non-traded good.

There are two aspects to our NATREX: the hypothetical medium run where the stocks of capital $k(t)$ and debt $F(t)$ are taken as given, and the longer-run trajectory where capital and debt are endogenous. The endogenous relative price of non-tradables which produces goods-market equilibrium is $R_n(t) = R_n[k(t), F(t); Z(t)]$. Thus the NATREX is $R = T(R_n)^a = R[k(t), F(t); Z(t)]$. Capital and debt evolve over time with investment and saving, thus producing a trajectory of the NATREX and current-account deficits or surpluses. We are able to explain the reasons why current-account deficits or surpluses have occurred and hence when the foreign debt is or is not a problem.

The steady-state values of capital and sustainable debt associated with given fundamentals are $k^*(Z)$ and $F^*(Z)$. Thus the NATREX will converge to $R^*[Z(t)]$. However, as shown below, the fundamentals $Z(t)$ are not stationary, i.e., are not independent of time. Consequently, the steady-state NATREX evolves over time. That is the reason why we find that the real exchange rate is not stationary. Our NATREX, which replaces purchasing-power parity, is the *moving equilibrium real exchange rate*. By focusing upon the real exchange rate, our framework is applicable both to the free and stabilized exchange-rate periods, but there will be a difference of the speed of convergence of the real exchange rate to the NATREX between these periods because prices are not as flexible as the nominal exchange rate. The empirical analysis is presented in part 3.

The rationale for the equations of the NATREX model and their relation to the theories of intertemporal optimization have been explained in Chapter 2 concerning the $US, and need not be repeated here. The difference between the NATREX model used in Chapter 2 for a large economy, and the version used for a small economy was described in Chapter 1. We can therefore present the model relevant for Australia rather tersely.

In the analysis, all quantity variables are measured per unit of effective labour in the entire economy. Equation (3.6) states that the aggregate excess demand for all goods, traded plus non-traded, equal to $(I - S) + CA$ is equal to zero. In a small open economy where the terms of trade are exogenous, the world will buy all of the export supply and provide all of the import demand of the traded good. The markets for the traded goods always clear at the world prices. Market disequilibrium must therefore be reflected in the non-traded good. Thus the excess demand for goods is equal to (3.6a) the excess demand for non-traded goods measured in terms of the export good 1. Equation (3.6) and (3.6a) are equivalent in a small open economy.[17] The excess demand for non-traded goods can be related to the Edwards and our extension of the Balassa analyses in the following way.

Box 3.1   The NATREX model for a small open economy

Goods market clearing = balance in non-tradables:

$$(I - S) + CA = 0 \qquad (3.6)$$

$$C_n(R_n, k - F; s, T) + (1 - m)I(q) - Q_n(R_n, k; u) = 0 \qquad (3.6a)$$

Current account:

$$CA = Q_1(R_n, k; u) - mI(q) - C_2(R_n, k - F; s, T) - r'F \qquad (3.7)$$

Real exchange rates:

$$R = T(R_n)^a \qquad (3.2)$$

Investment equation:

$$dk/dt = I(q) \qquad (3.8)$$

$$I = I(q) + nk = I(k, R_n, r; T, u)$$

$$I_k < 0, I_T > 0, \quad I_r < 0, I_u > 0, I_{Rn} < 0 \qquad (3.9)$$

Capital inflow:

$$dF/dt = I - S - nF \qquad (3.10)$$

Saving equation:

$$S = S(k, F; Z) \quad S_F > 0, S_k > 0 \qquad (3.11)$$

Portfolio balance:

$$r = r' + h(F, t) \qquad (3.12)$$

Symbols: all quantity variables are measured per unit of effective labour in the entire economy; k capital per worker; $y(k;u)$ real GDP per worker; F real foreign debt (+) per worker; R real exchange rate (rise is appreciation); $Rn = pn/p1$ = relative price of non-tradable to export good, I = investment per worker; S = saving per worker; $r(r')$ real domestic (world) interest rate; B real trade balance per worker; T terms of trade = $p1/p2$; s thrift parameter; u productivity parameter; $Z = (T, s, u, r')$.

---

[17] Equations (3.6) and (3.6a) here correspond to (1.7) and (1.7b) in Chapter 1.

The demand for the non-traded good consists of consumption C_n and investment $(1-m)I$. The consumption function is similar to what was described in Edwards' model above, with a change. Wealth equal to capital less foreign debt $k - F$, appears in our consumption function and not in Edwards'. Parameter 's', discussed below, is an index of thrift. Fraction $(1-m)$ of investment consists of the non-traded good. Hence $(1-m)I$ is the demand for non-traded goods used for investment. The supply of the non-traded good Q_n is similar to (E1) but also depends upon the capital and labour in that sector. We showed in equations (B6)–(B8) above that the capital intensity k_n and the fraction of the total labour force L_n/L allocated to the non-tradable sector depends upon the relative price of non-traded goods $R_n = p_n/p_1$, the overall capital intensity k and the vector u of total factor productivity.[18] Equation (3.2), repeated in Box 3.1, relates the relative price of non-traded goods $R_n = p_n/p_1$ to the real exchange rate R, given the terms of trade T. The term (p_n'/p_2') is exogenous to Australia and has been normalized at unity. Thus instead of Edwards' (E1) for market clearing of the non-tradables, we have equation (3.6a) in Box 3.1.

The current account CA, equation (3.7), generalizes (E2). It is the trade balance B less interest payments $r'F$ on the real foreign debt at the foreign real rate of interest. The trade balance is the value of good 1, the export good less the value of import good 2, which consists of consumption and fraction m of total investment. The quantity of export good 1 supplied q_1 depends upon the relative price of non-tradables, the capital intensity k_t, and labour L_t/L allocated to the tradable sectors. These variables are determined by allocation equations (B6)–(B8) above, so that k_t and L_t/L depend

---

[18] Equation (3.6a) measures expenditures in terms of the numeraire good 1. Let quantities be written in lower-case and values in upper-case letters. The excess demand for the non-traded good is:

$$R_n c_n + (1-m)I - R_n q_n = 0. \tag{a}$$

Using (E1) in (a), modified by using $k - F$ as wealth, obtain:

$$R_n c_n(TR_n, k - F; s) + (1-m)I(F) - R_n q_n(R_n, k; u) = 0. \tag{b}$$

Equation (3.6a) in the text is (b), and we assume that the consumption demand for non-tradables is elastic.

The supply of the non-traded good divided by the total labour force in the economy is: $Q_n/L = q_n(k_n, 1; u_n)(L_n/L)$. The term kn is the capital intensity in the non-traded goods sector. Using (B7) and (B8), we derive (3.6a), the total quantity of the non-traded good supplied (divided by the total labour force L in the economy).

upon R_n, k and vector u. If the traded good sector is capital (labour) intensive then a rise in capital will increase (decrease) the export supply.[19] The value of exports (using, as does Edwards, the price of exported good 1 as the numeraire) is $Q_1(R_n, k; u)$.

The value of imports of consumer goods consists of good 2 and is similar to that in (E2), but our wealth is capital less debt $k - F$. The variable $TRn = pn/p_2$ is the relative price of the non-tradable to the price of the import good. Hence consumption of the import good $C_2 = c_2(TR_n, k - F; s)/T = C_2(R_n, k - F; s, T)$. Parameter s reflects thrift. Fraction m of investment consists of the imported good. The trade balance is $B = Q_1(R_n, k; u) - mI(q) - C_2(R_n, k - F; s, T)$ and the current account is $B - r'F$ in equation (3.7).

The uncertainty in the model concerns the evolution of the exogenous variables Z, the terms of trade, total factor productivity, and social time preference. Our investment function and intertemporal optimization follows the logic of suboptimal feedback control using dynamic programming, described in Chapter 2 concerning the US dollar. The conclusion is that the rate of change of the capital intensity should be positively related to the the current Keynes–Tobin q-ratio: the capital value of an asset relative to its supply price. This is obtained, using current measurements, by capitalizing the *current observable* value of the marginal product of capital $pf'(k; u)$ by the current real rate of interest $r(t)$. Investment (3.8a) is positively related to q. When $q = 1$, then the capital intensity is kept constant.

Capital is used to produce export good 1 and the non-traded good; and the capital good consists of both imported good 2 and the non-traded good n. Capital is allocated between the tradable and non-tradable sector to equalize the rents per unit of capital, as stated in equation (B4) above. The common value of the marginal physical product of capital (measured in terms of good 1) in the two sectors is $f'(k; R_n, u)$, where vector $u = (u, u_n)$ is a parameter of the marginal product function. This is based upon (B4), (B6), and (B7).

The investment good is a composite of import good 2 and non-traded good n in the form $dk = I_2^m I_n^{(1-m)}$. The price of the capital

---

[19] Let the trade balance measured in good 1 be: $B = q_1(K_1, L_1; u_1) - c_2(TR_n, k - F)/T - mI$. Using (B6)–(B8), k_1 and L_1/L in the supply function depend upon Rn, k and vector u. Hence the trade balance is $B = Q_1(R_n, k; u) - C_2(R_n, k - F; s, T) - mI(q) = B(R_n, k, F; u, s, T)$.

good is $p_k = (p_2)^m (p_n)^{1-m}$. Fraction m of the supply price of a capital good consists of imported good 2 and fraction $1 - m$ of the non-traded good. The relative price $p = p_1/p_k = T^m/Rn^{1-m}$, a function of the relative price of non-tradables $R_n = p_n/p_1$ and the terms of trade T. The q ratio is (3.8b): the expected value of the ratio of the stream of returns relative to the supply price. The terms of trade T and the vector of productivity $u = (u_1, u_n)$ increases investment, the real rate of interest decreases investment. The relative price of non-tradables has an ambiguous effect. A rise in R_n stimulates investment in non-tradables, since only a fraction of the capital goods is imported. The rise in R_n discourages investment in the export sector. It is expected that R_n has a negligible effect upon investment but its main effect is to allocate capital between the two sectors.

The investment equation[20] is (3.8) above, which is based upon the logic of the suboptimal feedback control in an open economy with financial assets. Since Australia is a small country, T is exogenous.

$$dk/dt = I = I(q); \ I(1) = 0, \ I' > 0 \tag{3.8a}$$

$$q = E \int pf'(k; u)\exp(-rt)\,dt = [T^m/(R_n)^{1-m}]\,f'(k; u)/r$$

$$= q(k, T, R_n, u, r) \tag{3.8b}$$

Our consumption (saving) is social: public plus private. We do not make any assumptions about Ricardian equivalence. We take the same approach as we did in Chapter 2 concerning the social consumption function, based upon Merton's model of intertemporal stochastic optimizing using dynamic programming. Consumption is proportional to *current* wealth. Using a Bernoulli utility function, the factor of proportionality is the rate of time preference, which is the discount rate.[21] As in Chapter 2, our consumption function is $C = C(k - F; 1 - s)$, $C' > 0$. Social consumption depends upon wealth, capital less foreign debt, and is parameterized by a measure of social thrift s which is an inverse measure of the social discount rate.

We do not believe that a country has an 'intertemporal budget constraint' where the initial and terminal values of the debt must be equal, or that the terminal debt be zero. We permit a country to

---

[20] Fraction m of total investment expenditure is spent on the imported good and $(1 - m)$ on the non-traded good. Total investment expenditure, measured in terms of export good 1, is a function of the q-ratio. See Allen and Stein (1990: 913–14).
[21] See the discussion in Chapter 2.

change from a debtor to a creditor and vice versa. Instead, we require that the equilibrium value of the debt be a dynamically stable endogenous variable, which is a function of the fundamentals Z. A rise in debt lowers wealth and lowers consumption. For example, in face of the rising foreign debt, the government may raise consumption taxes or the households may lower their private consumption. Thus there is a built-in element of stability. We know that s the national saving ratio of private plus government saving to GDP is not stationary, the mean is not independent of time. Saving is GNP less consumption, which is $S = y(k; u) - rF - C(k - F; 1 - s) = S(k, F; Z)$. A rise in debt will lower wealth and increase saving $S_F > 0$, in the stable case which leads to an endogenous sustainable debt, which we require. A rise in capital will raise saving for low values of capital (where y' is high) and lower it for low values of capital (where y' is low). We refer to $s = S/\text{GNP}$ as a measure of social thrift. Thus a general saving function is (3.11) above, where all derivatives are positive, except possibly S_k for high values of capital. The parameters in Z are productivity, terms of trade, the real foreign interest rate, and social thrift.

Our portfolio balance equation linking Australian and US real long-term interest rates follows the discussion in Chapter 2. We know several things. (1) The uncovered interest-rate parity hypothesis is not valid. This means that nominal (real) short-term interest-rate differentials are not predictors of changes in nominal (real) exchange rates. (2) There is no political-risk premium on covered short-term investment. These are based upon equations (3.4a), (3.5a), and (3.5b) above. (3) The real long-term interest-rate differential on Australian less US ten-year bonds (graphed in Figure 3.3) is stationary. See equation (3.5c) and the related discussion above. This result occurs whether the inflation is measured by the GDP or CPI deflators. Although we find evidence of stationarity, there are some significant deviations, particularly in recent years. The differential is related to the foreign debt, but the relation is not strong.

We model the relation between the Australian and US real long-term interest rates with portfolio balance equation (3.12) in Box 3.1. This is an algebraic approximation to equation (3.5c). It is derived on the basis of the reasoning in Chapter 2. The Australian real long-term rate of interest converges to the US real long-term rate, but the convergence speed is negatively related to the foreign debt which is a risk premium for long-term portfolio investment, and reflects the probability of a devaluation.

2.2 The Mathematical Structure

The mathematical structure of the model is described by equations (3.13)–(3.15) below.[22] The economic scenarios will be explained, using this analysis, after we present the empirical results. The *relative price of non-tradables* $R_n = p_n/p_1$ equilibrates the market for non-tradables in equation (3.6) or (3.6a). Relative price R_n is a function of both the exogenous variables Z, and capital and debt which are endogenous over a longer period. Changes in the parameters $Z = (T, s, u, r')$ have both 'medium-run' impacts and long-run impacts upon the real exchange rate because they affect the evolution of capital and debt, which evolve according to equations (3.14) and (3.15) below. The evolving values of capital and debt produce new solutions for R_n in equation (3.13). The medium-run effects of changes in Z, when capital and debt are relatively constant, are conventional. Our contribution is to examine the evolution of the medium effects, of changes in Z when capital and debt are changing endogenously along the trajectory to the steady state.

2.3 The Relative Price of Non-tradables Clears the Goods Market

The relative price of non-tradables R_n, equilibrates the market for non-tradables $D_n - Q_n = 0$. In a small open economy, the terms of trade are exogenous. Since the market for tradables is always in equilibrium at the exogenous terms of trade, equilibrium in the goods market, $I - S + CA = 0$, follows when the market for non-tradables is in equilibrium. Using equations (3.6a) and (3.2), the equilibrium in the market for non-tradables (3.13a) is graphed in Figure 3.4. Equation (3.13) solves explicitly for Rn, the relative price of non-tradables.

The demand for non-tradables $D_n = C_n + (1 - m)I$ is the left-hand side of (3.13a). It is based upon (3.6) using the investment function (3.9) and portfolio balance equation (3.12). The demand Dn is

---

[22] The logical structure is similar to that in Chapter 2, but is applied here to the case where the terms of trade are exogenous, so that given the terms of trade, the real exchange rate is positively related to the ratio of the price of non-tradables to the price of the export good.

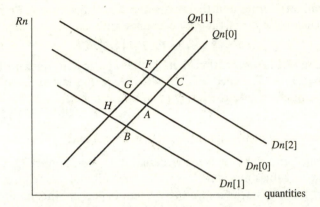

FIG. 3.4 *The relative price of non-tradables Rn = pn/p1, equations (3.13a) and (3.13)*

negatively related to R_n, because a rise in the relative price of non-tradables decreases the quantity demanded both of non-tradable consumption and investment. This is the family of curves D_n in Figure 3.4.

$$C_n(R_n, k - F; s, T) + (1 - m)I(k, R_n, F; r', u) = Q_n(R_n, k; u) \quad (3.13a)$$

The supply of non-tradables Q_n, on the right-hand side of (3.13a), is positively related to R_n, because a rise in the relative price of non-tradables increases the quantity supplied. This is the family of curves Q_n in Figure 3.4. Both the demand and the supply of non-tradables (Figure 3.4) depend upon the exogenous variables Z and the evolving endogenous variables capital and debt.

Solve (3.13a) for the relative price of non-tradables and obtain (3.13). The relative price R_n is a function of capital, debt, and the exogenous variables Z. We shall explain the partial derivatives, which reflect how the D_n and Q_n curves shift, when we explain the empirical results.

$$R_n(t) = R_n(k(t), F(t); Z(t)). \quad Z = [T, u, r'], u = (u_t, u_n) \quad (3.13)$$

The real exchange rate $R(t)$ is (3.14), based upon (3.13) and (3.2).

$$R(t) = T[R_n(k(t), F(t); Z(t))]^a = R(k(t), F(t); Z) \quad (3.14)$$

This is a general formulation, which describes what Edwards would call the 'steady state', and contains the Balassa analysis. The evolution of capital and debt shift the demand and supply of non-tradable curves and thereby generate a trajectory of $Rn(t)$ and $R(t)$. The evolution of the real exchange rate is (3.14a).

$$dR/dt = [R_k dk/dt + R_F dF/dt] + R_z dZ/dt. \tag{3.14a}$$

Equation (3.14a) shows that there are two basic determinants of the exchange rate. The medium-run effects are the last term and the longer-run effects are the terms in square brackets.

2.4 The Evolution of Capital and Debt Over Time

As capital and debt evolve, the demand D_n and supply Q_n curves for non-tradables in Figure 3.4 shift. The value of the relative price of non-tradables which produces equilibrium in the market for non-traded goods changes. The evolution of capital dk/dt is equation (3.15), obtained by using (3.9), (3.12), and (3.13). The evolution of the foreign debt dF/dt, which is the capital inflow, is equation (3.16), obtained by using (3.15) and (3.11).

Function $L = J - S$, is investment less saving. Hence the evolution of the real exchange rate (3.14a) is (3.17).

$$dk/dt = J(k, F; Z) \quad J_k < 0,\ J_F < 0 \tag{3.15}$$

$$dF/dt = (J - S) = L(k, F; Z) \quad L_k < 0,\ L_F < 0,\ G = J_k L_F - J_F L_k > 0 \tag{3.16}$$

$$dR/dt = R_k J(k, F; Z) + R_F L(k, F; Z) + R_z dZ/dt \tag{3.17}$$

We now have the complete dynamical system concerning the evolution of the real exchange rate, capital, and the foreign debt. The current-account deficit is $dF/dt + nF$. In the steady state $dk/dt = J = 0$ and $dF/dt = L = 0$, as described by (3.18) and (3.19).

Figure 3.5 describes the trajectories of capital and debt to the steady state, which is the origin. The curve $J = 0$ in Figure 3.5 describes (3.18): it is the set of capital and debt at which the rate of net investment is zero. It is negatively sloped because a rise in k lowers the marginal product of capital and tends to make net investment negative. A decline in the debt F reduces the risk premium $h(F)$ in the portfolio balance equation, and lowers the real rate of interest to restore the rate of net investment to zero. To the left (right) of $J = 0$, net investment is positive (negative), as indicated by the vectors. The $L = 0$ curve in equation (3.19) is the set of capital and debt at which the capital flow $dF/dt = I - S = -CA$ is zero.[23] It

---

[23] For expositional simplicity only, the discussion assumes that the growth rate $n = 0$ so that $dF/dt + nF = I - S$ is written as $dF/dt = I - S = -CA$.

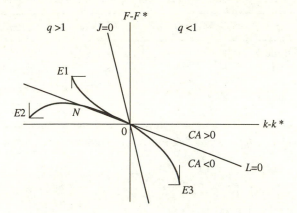

FIG. 3.5 *Trajectories of capital and debt to steady state, the origin. Productivity produces trajectory E2–N–0; saving produces E1–0; terms of trade produces E1–0 or E2–N–0; world rate of interest produces E3–0*

is also negatively sloped if $(S - J)_k > 0$. A rise in capital raises saving less investment, produces a capital outflow, and decreases the debt. Instead of the 'intertemporal budget constraint', we require that the real debt converge to a sustainable constant F^* such that the $CA = B^* - rF^* = 0$.

For stability, several conditions must be satisfied. (i) A rise in the capital intensity lowers the marginal product of capital and adversely affects investment. (ii) A rise in the debt, given capital, must raise saving relative to investment, produce a capital outflow, and reduce the debt back to the $L = 0$ curve. (iii) The $L = 0$ curve must have an algebraically greater slope than the $J = 0$ curve in Figure 3.5. This is stability condition $G > 0$. Above (below) the $L = 0$ curve, there are current-account surpluses (deficits) and the debt declines (rises).

The simultaneous solution of (3.18) and (3.19) implies (3.20) and (3.21), that the steady-state values are functions of Z. The steady-state relative price of non-tradables is (3.22a) and the real exchange rate is (3.22b). Vector $Z = (T, s, u, r')$ of the fundamentals is exogenous.

$$J(k^*, F^*; Z) = 0 \quad J_k < 0 \quad J_F < 0 \tag{3.18}$$

$$L(k^*, F^*; Z) = 0 \quad L_k < 0 \quad L_F < 0, \, G = J_k L_F - J_F L_k > 0 \tag{3.19}$$

TABLE 3.2　*Steady-state effects upon capital and debt of changes in Z*

Z	dk^*/dZ	dF^*/dZ	J_z	$L_z = (J - S)_z$	$\delta Rn/\delta Z$
Terms of trade T	+	−	+	+	?
Productivity u	+	−	+	+	$u_n < 0, u_t > 0$
Thrift s	+	−	0	−	−
Real US interest rate r'	−	+	−	−	−

Notes: $G = (J_K L_F - J_F L_K) > 0$; $dk^*/dZ = (J_z S_F - J_F S_z)/G$; $dF^*/dZ = (J_k S_Z - J_Z S_k)/G$

$$k^* = K(Z) \tag{3.20}$$

$$F^* = F(Z) \tag{3.21}$$

$$R_n^* = R_n[K(Z), F(Z); Z] = R_n^*(Z) \tag{3.22a}$$

$$R^* = T(R_n^*)^a = R^*(Z) \tag{3.22b}$$

The steady-state effects of changes in Z upon capital and debt, in equations (3.20) and (3.21), are summarized in Table 3.2. The steady-state effects depend upon the partial derivatives J_z and L_z, and will be discussed when we explain the econometric results.

The effects J_z and L_z refer to the effect of a rise in Z upon the investment function and upon the capital inflow, investment less saving, respectively. The effect $\delta Rn/\delta Z$ is the direct effect of a rise in Z upon the relative price of non-tradables, given capital and debt.

Our procedure is to first look at the econometric results. In Part 4, we interpret the the econometric results, Part 3, in the context of the dynamic model.

3. EMPIRICAL ANALYSIS

We use the NATREX model to explain the evolution of the relative price of non-tradables (R_n) and the real exchange rate (R). The fundamentals Z: thrift, productivity, the world real rate of interest, and the terms of trade, determine the relative price of non-tradables. The real exchange rate is arithmetically the terms of trade times a function of the relative price of non-tradables (equation 3.2). Hence we can explain the evolution of the real exchange rate as a function of fundamentals Z. The evolution of R_n and R is decomposed into three parts, as seen in equations (3.22a) and (3.22b). The first part is how Z affects R_n and R, given capital and debt. The second part is how capital and debt evolve in response to the fundamentals. The third part is how the evolution of capital and debt affect the evolution of R_n and R.

3.1 The Real Exchange Rate Cointegrating Equations

A description of all the data used in our study and their unit root properties is in appendix Table 3.A1. The sample period is 1974.1 to 1993.3. The long-run relationships are estimated according to the principles of cointegration developed by Engle and Granger (1987). Before we estimate the cointegrating equation we first must examine the order of integration of the data series, and test for the number of cointegrating vectors. From appendix Table 3.A1 we note that all of the fundamental variables have the same order of integration as R, the real exchange rate of the Australian dollar, so a cointegration regression can potentially be formed. The appendix Table 3.A2 contains the Johansen (1988) tests for the number of cointegrating vectors. The Johansen maximum-likelihood procedure which tests for the number of cointegrating vectors in Table 3.A2, shows that we have one cointegrating vector. In Part 4 we explain how the empirical results can be explained within the context of the NATREX model.

The dynamic econometric model describes the behaviour of the relative price of non-tradables R_n and the real exchange rate R, as a function of vector Z and, for simplicity, lagged terms $Z(t-1)$ of order one. These are all measurable variables. The error term is e. Equation (3.23a) is the econometric equation for R_n; and (3.23b) for the real exchange rate.

$$R_n(t) = a_1 + a_2 R_n(t-1) + b_1 Z(t) + b_2 Z(t-1) + e(t). \qquad (3.23a)$$

$$R(t) = a_1' + a_2' R(t-1) + b_1' Z(t) + b_2' Z(t-1) + e'(t). \qquad (3.23b)$$

The steady-state value of the relative price of non-tradables is (3.22a) and for the real exchange rate it is (3.22b). These are the *cointegrating equations*.[24] The steady-state effect of a change in Z is $dR^*/dZ = A'$ and $dR_n^*/dZ = A$.

---

[24] See Lim (1992) for the rationale for applying the cointegration technique to estimate such types of dynamic models.

$$R_n^* = R_n^*(Z) = AZ \qquad (3.22a)$$

$$R^* = T[Rn^*(Z)]^a = R^*(Z) = A'Z \qquad (3.22b)$$

The relation between the real exchange rate R and the relative price of non-tradables R_n is $R = Np/p' = TR_n{}^a$. That is, $RN = R/T = R_n{}^a$. We cannot measure Rn directly, so we measure Rn by the ratio R/T of the real exchange rate to the terms of trade. Variable RN is plotted in Figure 3.2 above. Theoretically, vector Z contains: the exogenous terms of trade T, social thrift, the parameter of productivity u, and the world real rate of interest r'. As our measure of social thrift (s), we use both $s' =$ household saving/disposable income, and $s'' =$ the government budget surplus/real GDP. We use the US real long-term interest rate as our measure of the world real rate of interest r'.

It is impossible to have a direct estimate of productivity parameter u in the production function, so an indirect approach is taken. The productivity vector $u = (u_n, u_t)$ in the non-tradable and tradable sectors affects the marginal products of capital, equation (B4). GDP per worker is $y = y(k; u_n, u_t)$. As our proxy for the measure of productivity $u = (u_n, u_t)$, we use the average product of labour $y(k; u) =$ GDP per employed worker, which depends upon both endogenous capital k and exogenous parameters $u = (u_n, u_t)$. This means that GDP per worker reflects both the total capital intensity in the economy and the parameters of productivity in both the traded and non-traded sectors. The investment equation states that the rate of capital formation is generated by parameters $u = (u_n, u_t)$ and the world rate of interest. For this reason, variations in productivity $y = y(k; u_n, u_t)$ arise from both u_n and u_t.

Our steady state $R_n^*(Z)$ and $R^*(Z)$ are evaluated in terms of exogenous variables T, s', s'', r' as well as y, which is a combination of the endogenous capital and productivity vector u. This formulation allows us to see if the Balassa hypothesis, concerning the positive relation between productivity and the real exchange rate, is valid for Australia.[25]

The estimates of the cointegrating equation (3.24) in Tables 3.3 and 3.4, for the relative price of non-tradables and the real exchange rate respectively, are done through NLS non-linear least

---

[25] As noted above, Edwards found that the Balassa hypothesis is inconsistent with his Latin American data. Connolly and Devereux (Chapter 5 below) found just the opposite.

squares following the approach advocated by Phillips and Loretan (1991). The first term is the cointegrating equation and the second term is the error correction. The estimates of A are constrained to be the same in both parts, and are printed in bold letters. As we did in chapter 2, the term $[Z - Z(-1)]$ was measured indirectly as the lagged real long-term interest-rate differential between Australia and the US, which is $(r - r')$. The logic is that when the disturbances change, an excess demand for or supply of goods is produced which changes the real long-term Australian less US interest-rate differential. This leads to a portfolio adjustment which drives the differential back towards equality.

$$R = \mathbf{A}Z + b[R(-1) - \mathbf{A}Z(-1)] + c[Z - Z(-1)] + e \qquad (3.24)$$

$$Z = [T, s', s'', y, r']; \quad [Z - Z(-1)] \sim (r - r')(-1)$$

Table 3.3, based upon non-linear least squares (NLS), contains the estimates for the relative price of non-tradables R_n corresponding to equation (3.24). Table 3.4 does the same thing for the real exchange rate $R = TR_n{}^a$. The results from Tables 3.3 and 3.4 are that we have cointegrating equations, whereby the relative price of non-tradables and the real exchange rate are explained by the fundamentals Z. The terms of trade variable was not a statistically significant factor[26] in explaining the relative price of non-tradables, so Table 3.3 reports the results when T was not in Z.

In the cointegrating equation in Table 3.3 for the *relative price of non-tradables*, $R_n = AZ$ (a) both the household (s') and government (s'') saving ratios appreciate R_n; (b) GDP per worker (y) depreciates the relative price of non-tradables; (c) The US real long-term interest rate (r') was negative but not significant. The error-correction term is highly significant. The shorter-run term DZ measured by the real Australian less US long-term interest rates appreciated the relative price of non-tradables.

Figure 3.6 plots the relative price of non-tradables Rn denoted as RN and the value from the cointegration equation part of Table 3.3, denoted $RNEQ = AZ$. It is clear that the fundamentals Z, other than the terms of trade, significantly affect the relative price of non-tradables.

---

[26] The economic analysis below shows how the terms of trade affects the demand for non-tradables, in an ambiguous way.

TABLE 3.3 *The relative price of non-tradables (ratio of real exchange rate/terms of trade) 1975.4–1991.3, number observations 64.* $R_n = [c(1) + c(2)^* s' + c(3)^* s'' + c(4)^* r' + c(5)^* y] + c(6)^* [R_n(-1) - c(1) - c(2)^* s'(-1) - c(3)^* s''(-1) - c(4)^* r'(-1) - c(5)^* y(-1)] + c(7)^* (r - r')(-1)$

Variable	Coeff.	t-stat	2-tail sig.
Constant	1.46	4.79	0.00
Household s'	0.008	2.44	0.017
Gov't s''	0.047	2.55	0.013
US Interest	−0.005	−1.03	0.30
Productivity	−0.71	−2.17	0.03
Error Correct.	0.64	6.6	0.00
Int. diff.	0.005	2.49	0.0154

Notes: Adjusted R-square = 0.77; Durbin–Watson = 1.9; DF $(N, 0)$ of $(R_n - AZ)$ residuals – 3.26

The real exchange rate $R = T(Rn)^a$ is the terms of trade times a function of the relative price of non-tradables. We examine the equation (3.24) for the real exchange rate, and present the results in Table 3.4 using non-linear least squares. The results are that in the cointegrating equation $R = A'Z$, (a) the terms of trade appreciate the real exchange rate; (b) both the household s' and the government

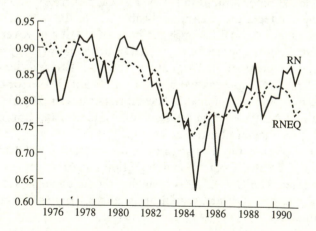

FIG. 3.6 *Relative price of non-tradables (RN), NATREX value of RN (RNEQ)*

TABLE 3.4 *Equation for the real exchange rate: 1975.1–1991.3, number of observations: 64.* $R = [c(1) + c(2)^* T + c(3)^* s' + c(4)^* s'' + c(5)^* r' + c(6)^* y] + c(7)^* [R(-1) - c(1) - c(2)^* T(-1) - c(3)^* s'(-1) - c(4)^* s''(-1) - c(5)^* r'(-1) - c(6)^* y(-1)] + c(8)^* (r - r')(-1)$

Variable	Coeff.	Std-err.	t-stat	2-tail sig.
Constant	0.599	0.35	1.7	0.09
Terms of trade	0.84	0.17	5.1	0.00
Household s'	0.008	0.003	2.4	0.018
Gov't s''	0.0449	0.018	2.4	0.0197
Real US interest	− 0.005	0.005	− 1.05	0.29
Productivity	− 0.688	0.325	− 2.1	0.039
Error corr.	0.637	0.09	6.4	0.00
Int. diff.	0.005	0.002	2.3	0.025

Notes: Adjusted R-squared 0.89; Durbin–Watson = 1.95; ADF $(R - AZ)$: UROOT $(N, 0) = -3.2$.

s'' saving ratios appreciate the real exchange rate; (c) productivity depreciates the real exchange rate;[27] (d) the US real interest rate is not significant. The error-correction term is significant. The shorter-run term, which is the lagged Australian less US real long-term interest rate, appreciates the real exchange rate.

The results are consistent with Table 3.3. Obviously the terms of trade is an important determinant of the real exchange rate since $R = TR_n{}^a$. The fundamentals which significantly affect the relative price of non-tradables affect the real exchange rate in a similar way, as stated above.

Figure 3.7 plots the real exchange rate R and the NATREX = $A'Z$ which is the cointegrating part of the real exchange rate equation in Table 3.4. The real exchange rate does indeed converge to its equilibrium value, the NATREX. However, there are shorter-period deviations due to the disequilibrium factors of speculation and cyclical movements.

---

[27] We also used a moving average of the growth of real GDP as a measure of productivity MAGROWTH, as we did in Chapter 2, instead of GDP per worker. The MAGROWTH variable was not significant and it reduced the significance of the government saving ratio and the innovation term $(r - r')$.

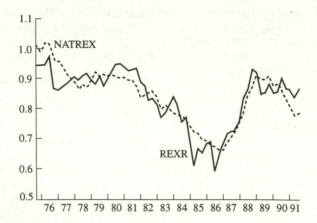

FIG. 3.7   *Real exchange rate (REXR), NATREX = A'Z (Table 3.4)*

4. EXPLANATION OF EMPIRICAL RESULTS

We now explain the empirical results concerning the relative price of non-tradables in Table 3.3 and the real exchange rate in Table 3.4 in terms of the NATREX model. The relative price of non-tradables in (3.22a) $Rn = R_n(K(Z), F(Z); Z(t))$ equilibrates the demand for with the supply of non-tradables, Figure 3.4. Each disturbance Z has a *direct effect* upon the relative price of non-tradables, $\delta Rn/\delta z$ which is the first term in (3.25) and the last column in Table 3.2. There is also an *indirect effect* operating upon the subsequent changes in capital and debt, the first two columns in Table 3.2, which correspond to the dk^*/dZ and dF^*/dZ terms in (3.25). The cointegrating equation $R_n = AZ$ captures something close to the total effects. The direct effects may be quite different from the indirect effects.

$$dR_n^*/dZ = \delta R_n/\delta Z + (\delta R_n/\delta k)\,dk^*/dZ + (\delta R_n/\delta F)\,dF^*/dZ \qquad (3.25)$$

4.1 The Appreciation due to Rises in the Saving Ratios

The direct effects upon the relative price of non-tradables Rn can be understood from equation (3.13a) repeated here and Figure 3.4.

$$C_n(R_n, k-F; s, T) + (1-m)I(k, R_n, F; r', u) = Q_n(R_n, k; u) \qquad (3.13a)$$

Start at point A in Figure 3.4 where the demand $Dn(O)$ for and supply of $Qn(O)$ non-tradables are equal. Let there be a rise in the saving ratio s' or s''. The rise in the saving ratio decreases the demand for consumption of non-tradables. Hence the demand for non-tradables declines from $Dn(0)$ to $Dn(1)$ in Figure 3.4, and the relative price of non-tradables declines to point B. Since the real exchange rate $R = T(Rn)^a$, the real exchange rate also depreciates initially. A rise in the saving ratio initially depreciates the real exchange rate. This is $\delta Rn/\delta s$ in (3.25a) below. In the econometric Tables 3.3 and 3.4, the impact effect of a rise in the saving ratio $\delta Rn/\delta s$ is reflected in a lower Australian real interest rate relative to the US rate, which depreciates the real exchange rate. Thus $\delta R/\delta s$ corresponds to a decline in $(r - r')$.

The long-run effect (Table 3.2) is to decrease debt and increase capital. The rise in saving less investment produces a depreciated exchange rate, current-account surpluses, and capital outflows. The initial rise in saving which lowers the real rate of interest may stimulate some capital formation. The economy is initially at a point $E1$ in Figure 3.5 where there are trade surpluses and capital outflows. The capital outflow reduces the debt which, in turn, reduces the risk premium and stimulates capital formation. The decline in the debt lowers saving which offsets the initial rise in the saving ratio. The endogenous steady-state debt stabilizes at a lower level. The trajectory is $E1$–0 in Figure 3.5, leading to lower debt and higher capital ($dk^*/ds > 0$, $dF^*/ds < 0$ in Table 3.2).

The decline in debt and rise in capital further affect the market for non-tradables. Wealth unambiguously raises the demand for non-tradables, and appreciates the relative price of non-tradables and the real exchange rate. Thus $(\delta R_n/\delta F)\ dF^*/ds > 0$ in equation (3.25a) below. This may raise the demand above $Dn(1)$, say back to $Dn(0)$.

The rise in capital has an ambiguous effect upon the supply of non-tradables, depending upon which sector is capital intensive. If the non-tradable sector is labour intensive, as we believe, the rise in capital decreases the supply of non-tradables from $Qn(0)$, to $Qn(1)$. In equation (3.25a) below $(\delta R_n/\delta k)\ dk^*/ds > 0$. Thus the relative price rises to point G.

In that case, both of the indirect effects raise the relative price of non-tradables from B to point G in Figure 3.4.

$$dRn^*/ds = \delta R_n/\delta s + [(\delta R_n/\delta k)dk^*/ds + (\delta R_n/\delta F)dF^*/ds] > 0 \quad (3.25a)$$

$$\quad\quad\quad (-) \quad\quad\quad (+) \quad\quad\quad\quad\quad (+)$$

As observed in Table 3.3 and 3.4 above, in the cointegrating equations $dR_n/ds > 0$ and $dR/ds > 0$ for both saving ratios. We conclude that the indirect effects of a rise in the saving ratio upon capital and debt (the terms in brackets) appreciate the relative price of non-tradables and real exchange rate by more than the impact effect depreciates them, thereby raising the relative price of non-tradables to G from initial point A.

4.2 *The Effect of a Rise in Productivity*

Our theoretical measure of productivity is vector $u = (u_n, u_t)$ in the non-tradable and tradable sectors respectively. We cannot measure these directly but use GDP per worker $y = y(k; u_n, u_t)$ as our proxy, and do not know which component of u was the cause of the rise in productivity. The cointegrating equations stated that a rise in productivity y depreciates the relative price of non-tradables (Table 3.3), and also depreciates the real exchange rate (Table 3.4). We explain these results by hypothesizing that the productivity parameter u_n in the non-tradable sector has risen relative to that in the tradable sector. The capital intensity k_n and fraction of the labour force L_n/L in non-tradables rise (equations B6–B8). Start at point G in Figure 3.4, where the demand is $Dn(O)$ and the supply is $Qn(1)$. The supply of non-tradable goods rises from $Qn(1)$ to $Qn(O)$ and lowers the relative price of non-traded goods from G to A. This is a direct effect.

The rise in u_n raises the marginal product of capital in the non-tradable goods sector. The q-ratio rises and raises investment relative to saving. The rise in u_n shifts resources from the tradable sector to the non-tradable sector (equations B6–B8), and decreases the supply of export good. Hence the trade balance declines.

The economy is at a point similar to $E2$ in Figure 3.5. There is capital formation and a current-account deficit. The current-account deficits raise the debt which has been financing capital formation. As capital accumulates, the q-ratio declines and output gradually rises. The latter tends to raise saving relative to investment. When the economy reaches point N in Figure 3.5, the greater saving matches the declining investment. Capital continues to accumulate. From point N, saving exceeds investment and there are capital outflows. Along the trajectory N–0 capital rises and debt declines.

The rise in wealth increases the demand for non-tradables, but the rise in u_n was the cause of the rise in capital. Hence the capital invested in the non-tradable sector rises and further increases the supply of non-tradables. The indirect effects are to increase the demand for non-tradables, but the supply increases by even more. The total effect dR_n/du_n is to depreciate the relative price of non-tradables, equation (3.25b).

$$dR_n/du_n = (\delta R_n/\delta u_n) + [(\delta R_n/\delta k)dk/du_n + (\delta R_n/\delta F)dF/du_n] < 0 \quad (3.25b)$$

$$(-) \qquad\qquad (-) \qquad\qquad\qquad (+)$$

The real exchange rate $R = TR_n{}^a$. Hence the decline in the relative price of non-tradables also produces a depreciation in the real exchange rate. We explain the results in Tables 3.3 and 3.4 by suggesting that the productivity rise was primarily in the non-traded goods sector. Hence the rise in GDP per worker depreciates the relative price of non-tradables and the real exchange rate in the cointegrating equations.

4.3 The Terms of Trade and the Real Rate of Interest

The terms of trade did not have a significant longer-run effect upon the relative price of non-tradables Rn in Table 3.3, but significantly affects the real exchange rate $R = TR_n^a$ in Table 3.4. The real US long-term interest rate did not have a significant effect upon either Rn or R in these tables. We suggest the following explanation.

Let there be an improvement in the terms of trade. At the given relative price $R_n = p_n/p_1$ of non-tradables to the export good 1, a rise in the terms of trade $T = p_1/p_2$ means a rise in $p_n/p_2 = TR_n$, the relative price of the non-tradable to the import good. The rise in p_n/p_2 decreases the consumption of the non-traded good. At the same time, the rise in the terms of trade raises the q-ratio and increases investment demand. The non-traded component of investment increases. The net medium-run effect of a rise in the terms of trade upon the demand curve Dn (Fig. 3.4) and hence the relative price of non-tradables is ambiguous. However, we hypothesize that the consumption effect dominates. If the economy started at point A, the rise in the terms of trade reduces the demand to $Dn(1)$ and reduces the relative price of non-tradables to point B. This is the medium-run effect.

The current-account balance is also affected by the terms of trade. The price effect is to increase the current account. Hence the economy is at point $E1$ in Figure 3.5. There is capital accumulation and current-account surpluses. It is possible that the rise in investment generated by the terms of trade exceeds saving and produces a current-account deficit. Then the economy would be at point $E2$ in Figure 3.5. In either case, there is capital accumulation leading to a higher capital stock ($dk^*/dT > 0$ Table 3.2). The steady-state debt also declines ($dF^*/dT < 0$ Table 3.2). In one case, the movement is monotonic from $E1$ to the origin. In the other case, the debt first rises along $E2$–N and then declines along N–0. Thus the economy will have a higher capital and less debt.

The medium-run effect shifted the equilibrium in non-tradables from A to B. The rise in capital will affect both the supply of and demand for non-tradables. Since the non-tradable sector is labour intensive, the supply will decrease from $Qn(0)$ to $Qn(1)$ and shift the economy from point B to point H. The decline in debt raises wealth and increases the demand for non-tradables from $Dn(1)$ to $Dn(0)$. The net total effect of a rise in the terms of trade is to shift from point A to point G, with a negligible effect upon the relative price of non-tradables. That is our hypothesis for the result in Table 3.3. There is no significant long-run effect of the terms of trade upon the relative price of non-tradables, in the cointegrating equation. This means that Rn is independent of T in the longer run, so there is practically a one-to-one effect of the terms of trade upon the real exchange rate, as we see in Table 3.4. The coefficient of the terms of trade 0.84, with a standard error of 0.17, is not significantly different from unity.

We observe in Tables 3.3 and 3.4 that a rise in the US real long-term rate of interest r' depreciates the relative price of non-tradables and the real exchange rate, but the effects are not significant. Theoretically, a rise in r' should depreciate R_n and hence R. The scenario is as follows. A rise in the rate of interest r' reduces investment demand, since some of the capital goods are non-tradable. The demand for non-tradables declines from $Dn(0)$ to $Dn(1)$ in Figure 3.4 as a result of the decline in investment, and the relative price of non-tradables declines from A to B.

The economy is at point $E3$ in Figure 3.5. The capital intensity is declining due to the fall in the q-ratio. Since Australia is a debtor country, the rise in the rate of interest produces current-account deficits and the debt rises. The trajectory is $E3$–0 where capital declines and debt rises ($dk^*/dr' < 0$, $dF^*/dr' > 0$ in Table 3.2).

Since capital has diminished and the non-tradable sector is labour intensive, the supply of non-tradables increases, thereby further depreciating the relative price of non-tradables. Similarly, the decline in wealth k-F further reduces the demand for non-tradables. The sum of all of these effects is to reduce the long-run relative price of non-tradables and the real exchange rate. The results in Tables 3.3 and 3.4 show that these effects are negative but insignificant empirically.

5. CONCLUSIONS

The underlying movements in the equilibrium real exchange rate, which we call the NATREX, and in the relative price of non-tradables are explained by the evolution of the fundamentals. They are: the terms of trade, the saving ratio, productivity of capital in the tradable and non-tradable sectors, and world real interest rates. The crucial variable to be explained by the fundamentals is the relative price of non-tradables R_n since, *arithmetically*, the real exchange rate $R = TR_n{}^a$ where a is the weight of the non-tradables in the GDP deflator. Figures 3.6 and 3.7 show how well the fundamentals explain the underlying movements in these variables. The fundamentals cannot explain much of the short-term exchange-rate variations, which are due to speculative and cyclical factors.

There are several main implications for policy. First, we can answer the question: when is the foreign debt a cause for concern?[28] The answer is that real trade deficits and the growth of the debt are initially produced by a rise in the productivity of capital which stimulates investment or a decline in thrift. Both *initially* increase the debt. In the first case, the real debt will eventually decline as a result of a more productive economy. Both GDP and GNP will rise. In the second case, the real debt will rise to a higher steady-state

---

[28] Unlike the results in Chapter 2, where we explained the ratio of the current account/GNP, here we were not successful in finding a cointegrating equation to explain the real trade deficit, using the fundamentals. We were only able to find an equation for the real trade deficit/GDP which states that growth increases it and thrift decreases it. But that is a short-run type of Keynesian equation and not what we are seeking.

level and reduce real GNP. Hence, the debt is only a source of concern if it has resulted from a decline in the social saving ratio. *Social policies designed to reduce a trade deficit which adversely affect growth are counterproductive.*

Second: there is a faster convergence of the real exchange rate to the NATREX in the free-exchange period than in the stabilized period (Figures 3.6, 3.7). The reason is that the nominal exchange rate can adjust quickly, whereas prices are sticky. Hence the deviation $[Np/p' - \text{NATREX}]$ goes to zero faster when the nominal rate N is free.

REFERENCES

Allen, Polly Reynolds and Jerome L. Stein. 1990. 'Capital market integration'. *Journal of Banking and Finance*, Special Issue on Real and Nominal Exchange Rates, 14(5), 909–28.

Andersen, P. S. 1990. 'Developments in external and internal balances'. *BIS Economic Papers*, 29 Oct., Basle, Bank for International Settlements.

Balassa, B. 1964. 'The purchasing power parity doctrine: a reappraisal'. *Journal of Political Economy*, 72, 584–96.

Blundell-Wignall, A. and Gregory, R. G. 1989. 'Exchange rate policy in advanced commodity exporting countries: the case of Australia and New Zealand'. Paper presented at a conference on Exchange Rate Policy in Selected Countries, International Monetary Fund, Oct. 1989.

Blundell-Wignall, Adrian, Jerome Fahrer, and Alexandra Heath. 1994. [Referred to as RBA, Reserve Bank of Australia study] 'Major influences on the Australian dollar exchange rate'. In Blundell-Wignall, Adrian (ed.) *The Exchange Rate: International Trade and the Balance of Payments*, Reserve Bank of Australia.

Corbae, D. and Ouliaris, S. 1991. 'A test of long-run purchasing power parity allowing for structural breaks'. *Economic Record*, Mar., 26–33.

—— 1988. 'Cointegration and tests of purchasing power parity'. *Review of Economics and Statistics*, 70, 508–11.

Edwards, S. 1988. 'Real and monetary determinants of real exchange rate behavior'. *Journal of Development Economics*, 29, 311–41.

—— 1993. 'Commodity export prices and real exchange rate variability in developing countries: oil in Venezuela'. American Econ. Assoc., Anaheim, Calif., Jan.

Enders, W. 1988. 'ARIMA and cointegration tests of PPP under fixed and flexible exchange rate regimes'. *Review of Economics and Statistics*, 70, 504–8.

Engle, R. F. and C. W. J. Granger. 1987. 'Cointegration and error correction: representation, estimation and testing'. *Econometrica*, Mar., 251–76.

Gavin, Michael. 1990. 'Structural adjustment to a terms of trade disturbance'. *Journal of International Economics*, 28, 217–43.

Harrison, Glenn. 1992. 'Market dynamics, programmed traders and futures markets: beginning of the laboratory search for a smoking gun'. Special Issue, *Economic Record*.

Johansen, S. 1988. 'Statistical analysis of cointegrating vectors'. *Journal of Economic Dynamics and Control*, 12, 231–54.

Khan, M. S. and P. J. Montiel. 1987. 'Real exchange rate dynamics in a small, primary-exporting country'. IMF Staff Papers, 681–710.

Kim, Y. 1990. 'Purchasing power parity in the long run: a cointegration approach'. *Journal of Money, Credit and Banking*, Nov. 491–503.

Lim, G. C. 1992. 'Testing for the fundamental determinants of the real exchange rate'. *Journal of Banking and Finance*, 16, 625–42.

Macfarlane, I. J. 1990. 'International interest rate linkages and monetary policy: the case of Australia'. Bank for International Settlements, International Interest Rate Linkages and Monetary Policy, Basle.

—— and W. J. Tease. 1990. 'Capital flows and exchange rate determination'. Bank for International Settlements, International Capital Flows, Exchange Rate Determination and Consistent Current Account Imbalances, Basle.

Merton, Robert C. 1990. *Continuous Time Finance*. Cambridge, Mass., Blackwell.

Phillips, P. C. B. and M. Loretan. 1991. 'Estimating long-run economic equilibria'. *Review of Economic Studies*, 58, 407–36.

RBA: Reserve Bank of Australia. See Blundell-Wignall *et al.*

Stein, J. L. 1970. *Money and Capacity Growth*. New York, Columbia University Press.

—— 1987. *The Economics of Futures Markets*. Oxford, Blackwell.

—— 1990. 'The real exchange rate'. *Journal of Banking and Finance*, Special Issue, Nov., 1045–78

—— 1992a. 'Cobwebs, rational expectations and futures markets'. *Review of Economics and Statistics*, 74 (1)

—— 1992b. 'Price discovery processes'. Special Issue, *Economic Record*.

APPENDIX

TABLE 3.A1 *Tests for stationarity, augmented Dickey–Fuller statistics (ADF)*

Variable	ADF
Real exchange rate (C, 1)	− 1.7666
Terms of trade (C, 4)	− 2.1
GDP per worker (C, 1)	− 1.79
Thrift-households (C, 1)	− 2.4
Thrift-government (C, 1)	− 2.0
Real US interest rate (C, 1)	− 1.8

Notes: The C or N indicates whether a constant was or was not used in the unit root test, depending upon its significance. The integer indicates the number of lags used, depending upon their significance. All are $I(1)$, not stationary. Source for data is DX, a time series data base which includes data published in the Statistical Bulletins of the Reserve Bank of Australia and data published by the Australian Bureau of Statistics. Sample period is 1974.1–1993.3. The MacKinnon critical values are: $1\% = - 3.536$, $5\% = 2.907$, $10\% = - 2.591$. R is the real exchange rate, calculated as Np/p', where N is the nominal \$US/\$A exchange rate and p/p' is the ratio of the Australian (p) to the US (p') GDP deflator; T the terms of trade is the ratio of the implicit price deflator for exports of goods and services to the implicit price deflator for imports of goods and services; $s' =$ thrift-household is the ratio of household saving to household disposable income; $s'' =$ thrift-government is the real budget surplus/real GDP; productivity is GDP per person employed; the real US long-term interest rate is the difference between the nominal interest rate on ten-year treasury bonds less the rate of change of the US GNP deflator.

TABLE 3.A2   *Testing for the number of cointegrating vectors Johansen maximum likelihood procedure. The variable set is (R, T, y, s', s'', r')*

Null	Alternative	Max. eig. stat. [90% crit]	Trace stat. [95% crit]
$r = 0$	$r = 1$	37.85 [37.4]	103.2 [102.1]
$r <= 1$	$r = 2$	31.2 [31.7]	65.3 [76.0]
$r <= 2$	$r = 3$	12.2 [25.5]	34.0 [53.1]
$r <= 3$	$r = 4$	10.8 [19.7]	21.8 [34.9]
$r <= 4$	$r = 5$	5.9 [13.7]	10.9 [17.8]

Notes: Maximum eigenvalue statistics (max. eig.) and trace statistics (trace stat.), with [critical values].

4

The Natural Real Exchange Rate between the French Franc and the Deutschmark: Implications for Monetary Union

LILIANE L. CROUHY-VEYRAC AND MICHÈLE SAINT MARC[1]

Un jour viendra où il n'y aura d'autres champs de bataille que les marchés s'ouvrant au commerce, et les esprits aux idées.
Une monnaie continentale ... ayant pour point d'appui le capital Europe tout entier, et pour moteur l'activité libre de deux cents millions d'hommes.
Victor Hugo, *Discours d'ouverture du congrès de la Paix*, 21 août 1849

1. INTRODUCTION

In the wake of the Maastricht Treaty and the subsequent disruptions to the European Monetary System, some of the most important questions about the economic relations of France and Germany concern the conditions for successful joining of their currencies as members of a European Monetary Union and the optimal policies for the Second Stage of the transition. At first glance, the NATREX model appears to offer little to this debate, for several reasons. Only real variables are considered: real exchange rates and real interest rates. The starting-point of the NATREX model is a hypothetical medium-run equilibrium, assumed to be independent of the nominal exchange-rate regime. This medium run describes an economy in which speculative and cyclical factors have averaged out to zero. Yet most of the economic costs of pegging a nominal exchange rate

[1] We gratefully acknowledge the financial support of the: Ministère de la Recherche et de l'Enseignement Supèrieur, under grant no. 87.A.0640, CNRS Laboratoire Associé, Institut Orléanais de Finance, Université d'Orleans, Groupe HEC, Jouy-en-Josas, France, and the advice of Alain Montfort.

are found precisely in those cyclical deviations ignored by the NATREX approach.

In spite of these apparent limitations, estimation of the determinants of the bilateral NATREX between France and Germany should help answer some of the questions related to nominal exchange rates and the prospects for European Monetary Union. The real exchange rate between France and Germany has fluctuated by about 20 per cent over the last two decades (see Figure 4.1, the curve labelled Real Exchange Rate $R(t)$). In spite of the growing similarities and increasing integration between the two economies, the movements of the bilateral French/German real exchange rate have not diminished. Should these continuing movements in the real exchange rate throughout the period of EMS be taken as evidence of insufficient integration to justify fixed nominal exchange rates?

The NATREX is a *moving equilibrium real exchange rate*, responding to endogenous changes in capital and net foreign debt and to repeated real fundamental disturbances. If the real fundamentals can explain most of the variations in the French/German bilateral real exchange rate, then the real exchange-rate changes can be interpreted as necessary adjustments to the moving equilibrium NATREX, regardless of the nominal exchange-rate policy. More-

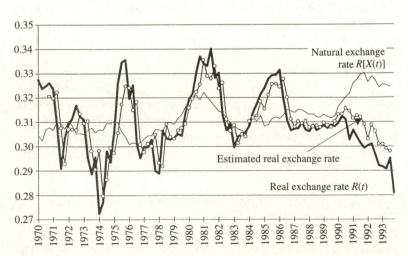

FIG. 4.1 *The Engle–Granger two-step linear least-square method: the natural, the real, and the estimated real exchange rate DM/FF*

over, we would expect such changes in the bilateral equilibrium real exchange rate between France and Germany to continue in the future, with or without a monetary union.

2. THE FRENCH AND GERMAN ECONOMIC RECORD, 1971–1989

Economic policies and priorities have differed in France and Germany during the last four decades. In France, industrial policy was the main priority and was conducted in 'Colbert's tradition of an administered mixed economy'. By contrast, West Germany promoted the 'social market economy', emphasizing the liberalization of markets and allowing relative prices to be determined by the markets. These policy differences contributed to the differences in price inflation between the two countries. During the 1970s Crouhy and Melitz (1976) and Pollin and Fitoussi (1977) argued that distortions in relative prices in France were contributing to French inflation.

After the 1974 oil shock, economic policy in France, more than in Germany, was aimed at protecting employment and raising the purchasing power of wage earners, even in the absence of productivity gains. Crouhy-Veyrac and Saint Marc (1991) showed that from 1974–85, growth of real wages exceeded the growth of productivity in France, driving down profit rates, while the opposite was occurring in Germany.

Through the 1980s, however, French and German economic policies and their economies began to converge. Just before German reunification, the two economies were similar in many respects. Each was the main trading partner of the other, GDP per capita was similar, and their economies had similar weights in the world economy, measured by national income and consumption. Government budget deficits of both countries were low. Yet many differences still remained.

Throughout the period before German reunification, the Deutschmark served as a reference for price stability, anchoring the other European currencies, and played a much larger role in international financial relations than did the French franc. The mark was used as a reserve currency by central banks, eventually making up 20 per cent of foreign-exchange reserves and challenging

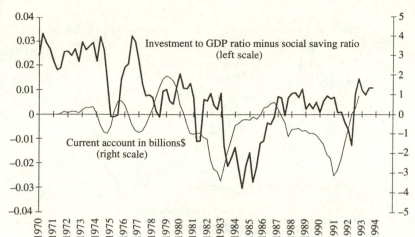

FIG. 4.2 *The current account and domestic financial capacity in France*
Source: OECD

the dollar. Germany is a more open economy than France. In 1990, German exports were 36 per cent of GDP compared to 17 per cent in France. The German economy was more competitive than the French economy in international goods markets, with a current-ac-

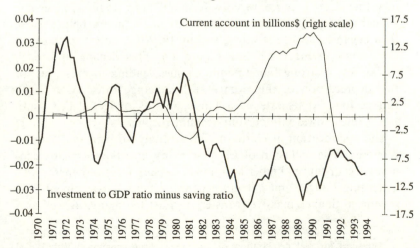

FIG. 4.3 *The current account and domestic financial capacity in Germany*
Source: OECD

FIG. 4.4   *Saving rates in France and Germany*
Source: OECD

count surplus for most years after 1970, whereas France had current-account deficits (Figures 4.2 and 4.3).

Compared to Germany, the French economy was characterized by greater changes. Starting at lower levels, French GDP and investment grew more rapidly from 1975 to 1980. Conversely, French saving/GDP ratio, higher than in Germany before 1980, then began to decline steadily, and by 1989 was only two-thirds of Germany's saving ratio. See Figure 4.4. This decline in French saving was a strong fundamental change, leading to pressures for real depreciation of the French real exchange rate.[2] After 1989, France lowered its rate of inflation and its budget deficit (until 1992), and moved into current-account surplus.

The reunification of Germany has strongly affected the German economy. The inclusion of East Germany into the Germany economy has produced higher inflation and rising unemployment, with increasing budget and current-account deficits. Government borrowing to finance massive transfers to East Germany, as well as a

---

[2] Pressures for real depreciation of the French franc, combined with lagged adjustment of prices in France, led the French authorities to intervene in the foreign-exchange markets to maintain the fixed nominal exchange rate in the EMS (*Cohen and Wyplosz 1989*).

lower rate of household saving in the East, has lowered the aggregate German saving rate. With the opening of some lower-cost investment opportunities in Eastern Europe, some German factories have begun to relocate.

The incorporation of East Germany has also created disruptions in German data series, leaving problems of both reliability and interpretation. It should be noted that the East German data remain incomplete and unreliable. For Germany as a whole, although household saving remains high, total social saving is down. Business-sector saving is down due to wage increases, and government borrowing to finance the building of the East German infrastructure absorbed 70 per cent of German household saving. Recently, Germany has moved from its usual role as a net international lender to one of net borrower.

3. MODELLING THE BILATERAL RELATIONSHIP BETWEEN FRANCE AND GERMANY

Theoretically, the evaluation of the bilateral natural real exchange rate (NATREX) between France and Germany presents a somewhat different situation from either the large US economy modelled in Chapter 2 or the small Australian economy modelled in Chapter 3. France and Germany trade in goods, services, and financial assets—with each other, but even more so with other countries. One way of describing this situation would be a model of three interacting countries: France, Germany, and the rest of the world. We have chosen an alternative, somewhat simpler approach.

France and Germany are each modelled separately relative to the outside world, represented by the United States. For each country we determine the influence of the exogenous fundamentals on the country's NATREX *vis-à-vis* the outside world. The NATREX of a given country $i =$ (France, Germany) is the real exchange rate which produces external balance *vis-à-vis the world*, represented by the US. External balance means that the sum of the current account plus the non-speculative capital account, is equal to zero, when output is at its equilibrium rate. Thus the NATREX ignores the speculative and cyclical factors and is the rate justified by the fundamentals, productivity and thrift, denoted by Z. Denote the

NATREX of country i as $R_i[Z]$. The deviation $R - R_i[Z]$ of the actual real exchange rate R from the NATREX is attributable to speculative and cyclical factors. We show throughout this book that this deviation is stationary at a mean of zero. That is, the cyclical and speculative forces average out to zero in their influence upon the real exchange rate.

We then look at the ratio of the NATREX of France relative to that of Germany to determine the bilateral NATREX between France and Germany. Each NATREX is associated with internal and *external balance in each country vis-à-vis the rest of the world* (US). This bilateral NATREX denoted $R[Z]$ equal to $Ri[Z]/Rj[Z]$ is a function of a vector of fundamental determinants primarily in the two countries—thrift and productivity. Fundamental disturbances from the outside world, such as the world real interest rate, influence the bilateral rate only to the extent that they have different effects on the French and German NATREXs.

The model for each country, France or Germany, is similar to the NATREX model used for the United States in Chapter 2, except that France and Germany are seen as too small in the world financial markets to influence the world real interest rate. In the goods market, the country is considered large enough to influence its terms of trade, and distinction between non-tradable and tradable goods is ignored. In the financial markets, the country is assumed to face a fixed exogenous real world interest rate, as in the Australian case. Less than perfect capital mobility produces lags in the adjustment of the domestic real interest rate to the world rate. The domestic real interest rate, although eventually adjusting to equal the world rate, responds in the medium run to changes in the exogenous fundamentals, reducing the *medium-run* response of the NATREX. An assumption that capital moves from the outside world more freely into and out of Germany than France makes the medium-run response of the German NATREX relatively larger, with the real interest rate providing more adjustment in France. Such differences in the degrees of financial integration of France and Germany with the outside world make the medium-run bilateral NATREX between France and Germany a function of changes in the world real interest rate. In the longer run, the real long-term rates of interest will both equal the US real long-term rate.

4. A THEORETICAL MODEL OF EACH COUNTRY, FRANCE AND GERMANY

The real exchange rate for country i is defined as the nominal value, $N_i = \$US/$units of currency i, divided by the (P'/P), where $P' = US$ GDP deflator and P_i is the GDP deflator of country i. An increase of N_i implies a nominal appreciation of currency i, while an increase in R_i is a real appreciation, in terms of the $US.

$$Ri = Ni/(P'/Pi) = N\,Pi/P'. \qquad (4.1)$$

The bilateral real rate R between country France and Germany is the ratio of R_F/R_G and is equation (4.2) $R = N_F P_F/N_G P_G = (\$US/franc)$ $P_F/(\$US/DM)P_G = (DM/\text{Franc})P_F/P_G$.

The model for country i incorporates the behavioural and optimization assumptions described by Stein in Chapter 2, the difference being that here the world interest rate is exogenous. We need not repeat Tables 2.3 and Box 2.1 of Chapter 2, but will use the graphic analysis of Figure 4.5 (which is Figure 4 in Chapter 2, making the appropriate modifications).

The *IS* curve is the set of real exchange rates R_i and real long-term interest rates r_i which are associated with external balance vis-à-vis the rest of the world, when the economy is at capacity output and cyclical and speculative forces average out to zero. It is negatively sloped because an appreciation in the real exchange rate

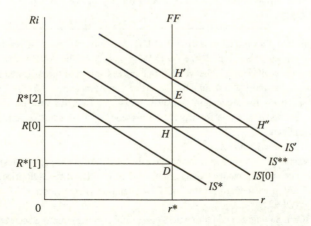

FIG. 4.5 *Modified version of Figure 2.4*

TABLE 4.1   *Tests of stationarity for exchange rates, relative prices and fundamentals. France–Germany (period 1971.1–1990.4)*

Variables	Stationarity test	ADF
Integrated of order 1		
Nominal Exchange Rate DM/FF	(T,0)	− 1.80
Relative price deflator	(C,1)	− 0.83
Real long-term US interest rate	(C,1)	− 1.01
Relative business capital labour ratio France/West Germany	(N,1)	0.74
Relative business capital stock ratio France/West Germany	(C,0)	2.28
Relative social saving France/Germany	(N,0)	− 1.29
Integrated of order 1 (*but cannot reject the hypothesis of stationarity at the 5% level*)		
Real exchange rate	(C,0)	− 2.90*
Real long-term interest rate differential France minus Germany	(N,1)	− 2.39*
Relations of Cointegration		
Nominal Exchange Rate & Relative Price Deflator France minus Germany: Constant and one lag (C,1)	ADF = − 2.68 (10% = − 3.10)	
Relative business capital stock France/Germany & real long-term interest rate differential France minus Germany: constant and one lag (C,1)	ADF = − 3.22 (5% = − 3.42, 10% = − 3.10)	

The *Augmented Dickey Fuller statistics* (ADF) for unit root tests of residuals are obtained from the regression: $DX_t = c + b_0 X_{t-1} + b_i DX_{t-i}$. The ADF statistic is the t-statistic of the coefficient b_0. The MacKinnon critical values of the Adjusted Dickey–Fuller statistics at the 1%, 5%, and 10% levels of significance are − 3.513, − 2.900 and − 2.586 respectively for a constant (− 2.592, − 1.944, and − 1.618 with no constant). The test presented is the one for which the presence of a constant or not, and the lag, are significant.

Definition of symbols, and sources:

Nominal exchange rate: Bilateral exchange rate DM/FF (OECD, spot rates)

Real Exchange rate: Nominal exchange rate adjusted with Relative GDP price deflator

Relative GDP price deflator=ratio of GDP deflator (France) on GNP deflator (Germany) (OECD)

Relative Social Saving: Social Domestic Saving ratio (France) minus Social Domestic Saving ratio (Germany)

Social Domestic Saving ratio=GDP-Private-Public Consumption/GDP (OECD)
Relative Productivity: Ratio of total business capital/total business employment (France) over Ratio of total business capital/total business employment (West Germany) (OECD)
Relative Capital Stock; Ratio of total business capital (France) over Ratio of total business capital (West Germany) (OECD)
i^*(measured as US): Nominal rate on long-term government bonds (IMF)
r^*(measured as US): Real long-term anticipated interest rate $=i^*$ minus inflation (percentage quarterly change of US GNP deflator a year ahead) (OECD)

reduces aggregate demand and a decline in the real rate of interest is required to offset the appreciation to keep aggregate demand equal to capacity output.

The *FF* curve is the real long-term rate of interest which produces portfolio balance. The latter occurs when the real rate of interest at home plus the expected real appreciation of the domestic currency is equal to the foreign long-term real rate of interest. This is the same as saying that portfolio balance occurs when the nominal long-term interest-rate differential between the foreign and domestic rates is equal to the average expected appreciation of the nominal exchange rate. Since investment is long term, the period considered is long term. Investors know that they cannot predict real exchange-rate movements, since the real exchange rate is not stationary. Its variance increases with distance from the present. Investors use all available information. The real exchange rate R is integrated $I(1)$ such that its first differences are stationary, with an expectation of the change in the real exchange rate equal zero. Therefore, portfolio balance involves the convergence of the real long-term interest rate to the US value. In Chapter 2 we showed that the German real long-term rate of interest converges to the US real long-term rate of interest and that the causation runs from the US real long-term rate to the German long-term rate.

A similar situation exists with France relative to the US. The French real long-term rate of interest converges to the US real long-term rate. That is, the differential is stationary at an expected value of zero. The speed of convergence of the French real long-term rate to the US counterpart is slower than the German. We observe in Table 4.1 that the real long-term interest-rate differential in France less Germany is stationary, and it has an expected value of zero. Hence the portfolio balance curve for both

France and Germany is vertical at the US real long-term rate of interest r', that is the real long-term interest rate in each country converges to the US rate, but at different speeds.

Figure 4.5 describes country i, in terms of the real exchange rate and real long-term interest rate, when speculative and cyclical factors average out to zero. We use this figure to describe the medium-run response to an increase in demand for goods, as a result of either increased investment due to higher productivity or decreased social saving due to a decline of thrift. In Figure 4.5, the *IS* curve depicts the goods market, and the *FF* curve, the portfolio balance in financial markets.

Start at point H where the real exchange rate is $R(0)$ and the domestic real long-term rate of interest is equal to the US rate r'. Increased demand for goods for any purpose—a rise in desired investment or desired consumption—will shift the *IS* curve to the right to *IS'*. To preserve equilibrium between aggregate demand and capacity output, either the real exchange rate must appreciate or the real rate of interest must rise. The greater the degree of capital mobility, the faster will the domestic real long-term rate of interest r_i converge to the US real rate r'. The greater the ability of the country to borrow from foreigners, the larger the capital inflow, the greater the appreciation of the NATREX, R_i, and the smaller the rise in the domestic real interest rate, r_i. In the case of great capital mobility the NATREX will rise to point H', where $r_i = r$. If there were little capital mobility, the real interest rate would rise towards point H'' to restore goods market equilibrium and then converge to H'. Thus the medium-run impact of a rise in productivity which induces a rise in investment or a decline in social thrift which decreases saving is to appreciate the real exchange rate. If the disturbance only occurred in country i, then the bilateral NATREX real exchange rate in country i would rise relative to that of country j.

Through time the resulting changes in stocks of capital and net debt to foreigners gradually influence excess demand for goods and desired borrowing which is investment less social saving. This is reflected in the subsequent shift of the *IS* curve. The trajectories of capital, debt, and the real exchange rate will depend on the reasons for borrowing. The domestic real interest rate eventually returns to the world rate, regardless of the reason for borrowing. There will be continuing capital flows when saving does not equal investment, even though portfolio balance has equalized real interest rates.

The purpose for the borrowing, whether for consumption or investment, through time affects the responses of the endogenous fundamentals, capital k_i and foreign debt F_i, and the size of the long-run real depreciation. Following the same reasoning described in Chapter 2, we claim that (a) borrowing for consumption first appreciates and then depreciates the real exchange rate; (b) borrowing to finance productive investment first appreciates the real exchange rate and the new steady-state real exchange rate will be above its initial level.

Borrowing for consumption produces current account deficits which raise the foreign debt but do not stimulate capital formation. Wealth declines. In a stable economy, saving will gradually rise in response to the declining wealth. The foreign debt (F) will stabilize at a higher level. The steady-state *IS* curve will be *IS**. The economy may even be converted from a creditor to a debtor. In the new steady state, the country's higher interest payments to foreigners must be matched by a move toward surplus in the trade balance, requiring a depreciation of the steady-state NATREX, $R^*(1)$. In Figure 4.5 the steady-state NATREX is at a point such as D, reflecting the gradual decline of demand for goods and the shift of the *IS* curve to *IS** in response to the changes in the capital stock and in the net debt to foreigners.

Borrowing for investment, due to an increase of productivity (denoted by u) also produces capital inflows and initially raises net debt to foreigners. However, the capital stock (k) rises even more than debt, gradually increasing the country's wealth, GDP, and saving, and reducing the rate of investment. As investment less saving, *I-S*, declines, the country borrows less and less and then becomes a net lender. The foreign debt (F) stabilizes at a lower level and the country may be converted from a debtor to a creditor. With interest payments coming from foreigners, in the new steady state produced by a rise in productivity the NATREX will have appreciated.[3] In Figure 4.5, the *IS* curve shifts to *IS***, and the economy moves to point E at a real exchange rate $R^*(2)$.

---

[3] The NATREX model of Australia in Chapter 3 shows that with two sectors—tradable and non-tradable goods—and an exogenous terms of trade, a rise in productivity in the tradable sector will produce an appreciation of the steady-state NATREX, whether or not the increases in output and saving are sufficient to move the country to net creditor status. While our chosen version of the NATREX model includes neither a non-tradable sector nor an exogenous terms of trade, these factors may also play a role in explaining the empirically observed long-run appreciation of the NATREX in France and Germany.

In summary, the NATREX for country i is a function in the medium run of the *exogenous fundamentals* $Z = (s_i, u_i, r')$ and of the endogenous fundamentals (k_i, F_i). s = saving ratio; u = productivity of capital; F = foreign debt; k = capital; r' = world real rate of interest. This NATREX is the real exchange rate associated with external and internal balance, when cyclical and speculative factors average out to zero.

$$R_i = R_i(s_i, u_i, r'; k_i, F_i). \tag{4.3}$$

In the steady state, capital and debt are functions of the exogenous fundamentals, so the NATREX then is a function only of the exogenous fundamentals,

$$R_i^* = R^*(s_i, u_i, r'). \tag{4.4}$$

Hence the bilateral NATREX between France (F) and Germany (G) is equation (4.5).

$$R = R_F(k_F, F_F; Z_F)/R_G(k_G, F_G; Z_G) = R(k_F, F_F, k_G, F_G; Z_F, Z_G) \tag{4.5}$$

An increase of saving in France relative to Germany (a rise in s) will induce in the medium run a real depreciation of the French franc relative to the DM, but in the long run, a real appreciation. An increase of productivity in France relative to Germany, raising the French/German investment ratio, will induce a real appreciation of the franc relative to the mark both in the medium run and in the new steady state.[4]

A rise in the world real rate of interest will depreciate both currencies in the medium run, but the franc less so, because there is a greater and faster mobility of capital between Germany and the US than between France and the US. In the long run, a rise in the US real rate of interest will tend to appreciate the DM because Germany is a creditor country, and depreciate the French franc because France is a debtor country.

5. DATA FOR THE EXOGENOUS FUNDAMENTALS

Our empirical analysis covers the period 1971.1 through 1990.4. We consider three exogenous fundamentals as influencing the bilateral

---

[4] If we used a two-sector model, as was done in Chapter 3, then a rise in productivity generally involves a greater growth of productivity in the tradable than in the non-tradable sector. The latter implies an appreciation of the real exchange rate.

French/German NATREX. The two exogenous fundamentals that influence both the medium-run and long-run bilateral French/German NATREX are relative thrift, $s = s_F - s_G$, and relative productivity, u is measured by u_F/u_G. The exogenous world real rate of interest, r', is expected to influence the bilateral NATREX mainly in the medium run.

5.1 Relative Productivity

As a proxy for productivity in each country, we use the ratio of business capital to employment. This capital/employment ratio is the value of capital equipment in the business sector, valued at constant (1985) prices per employed worker: $u_i = k_i = K_i/L_i$, where L_i refers to employed labour (Villa 1990). Relative productivity in France compared to Germany is proxied by the ratio of the French to German capital/employment ratios.

$$u \sim k = k_F/k_G = (K_F/L_F)/(K_G/L_G) \qquad (4.6)$$

From 1975 to 1980 the French capital/employment ratio rose more rapidly than the German, and afterward, until German reunification, remained fairly stable or decreased slightly. Our capital/employment ratio for Germany uses the West German data only, even for the four quarters after reunification. German reunification in 1990 changed the actual capital stock and labour force to be measured in Germany. The economic reality was one of disruption and transition, still continuing. Data for East Germany are not even available, and estimates of the East German capital stock are wholly unreliable. Even the West German capital/employment ratio is strongly affected by reunification, due to the large increase of migration into and employment in West Germany. West German employment increased by 2 million persons during 1988–91, producing a large decline in West German average productivity, having nothing to do with exogenous marginal productivity.

5.2 Relative Thrift

Relative French/German thrift is proxied by the difference in the ratios of social saving to GDP in the two countries,

$$s = s_F - s_G = (S/\text{GDP})_F - (S/\text{GNP})_G, \qquad (4.7)$$

where S is the difference between GDP (GNP in Germany) and consumption (private plus public) in the national income accounts (Saint Marc 1993).

The change in relative social saving over the period is substantial, as seen in Figure 4.4. While both countries reduced social saving sharply after the 1973 oil shock, due to increased government consumption, the saving ratio was higher in France than in Germany until 1982. But starting in 1980, the French saving ratio began a downward trend, reflecting increases in both private and public consumption, whereas the German social-saving ratio remained fairly stable. Since 1991, in spite of the consumption demands in Germany stemming from reunification, the French social saving ratio has continued to decline relative to the German ratio.

Further analysis is needed to assess the exogeneity of the relative social saving variable. Relative social saving, s, is highly correlated with the capital/employment ratio (correlation coefficient = 0.73 for 1971–90). The theoretical model claims that a higher capital stock raises GDP more than consumption and raises saving. A better proxy for relative exogenous thrift than the relative social saving ratio, s, would be a derived variable, the *exogenous relative social saving ratio*, s^e. We derive s^e by regressing the relative social saving ratio, s, on the relative capital/employment ratio, k, and defining the residual as s^e.

For the four quarters of 1990, after German reunification, we have reconstructed the data available on Germany, aggregating the West and the East, but we are most dubious about its value.

5.3 The World Real Rate of Interest

Because the United States dominates the international markets in financial assets, we use the US long-term government-bond rate as a proxy for the world nominal rate of interest faced by each of these countries. To capture the anticipated real long-term US rate of interest, we deflate the nominal interest rate on US long-term government bonds by the US GDP deflator, measured one year ahead. The GDP deflator one year ahead may be superior in this context to a current or lagged deflator, for we are trying to use rational expectations as much as is sensible or feasible.

6. EMPIRICAL EVIDENCE

6.1 Stationarity of the Variables

The NATREX approach hypothesizes that the NATREX is a function of the exogenous fundamentals. The NATREX will be stationary if the fundamentals are stationary, but when the fundamentals are non-stationary and co-integrated with the NATREX, we would expect the NATREX also to be non-stationary.

Table 4.1 summarizes the results of stationarity tests on the bilateral French/German real exchange rate, R, and proxies for the three exogenous fundamentals—the relative capital/employment ratio, k; the relative social saving ratio, s; and the US real long-term interest rate, r'. The relative capital/employment ratio and the relative social saving ratio, which are our fundamental determinants of the real exchange rate, are clearly non-stationary: they have unit roots. The stationarity is measured by the ADF (adjusted Dickey–Fuller statistic), where $ADF(C, j)$ indicates that a constant and j lagged terms are used.

The real exchange rate has several definitions. One is the real effective exchange rate, as reported in the International Monetary Fund International Financial Statistics. This is a measure of competitiveness in world markets. If we measure the real French–German bilateral exchange rate ($R1$) as the ratio of the French to the German *real effective exchange rates*, this variable is not stationary at the 10 per cent level, $(ADF(C, 1) = -1.27)$. Second: If the nominal French–German bilateral rate is adjusted by the ratio of French/German *CPI indexes*, then this real exchange rate ($R2$) is stationary. The $ADF(C, 1) = -3.01$. Third, if we adjust the nominal French/German bilateral rate by the ratio of French/German GDP deflators, ($R3$) is on the borderline with respect to stationarity. We can reject the hypothesis of stationarity at the 1 per cent level, but not at the 5 per cent level.

$R1$ = real effective French/real effective German exchange rate

$R2 = [(DM/\$US)/(FF/\$US)][French CPI/German CPI]$

$R3 = [(DM/\$US)/(FF/\$US)][French GDP deflator/German GDP deflator]$

We decided to use $R3$ as our measure of the real bilateral exchange rate between France and Germany. A look at the trajectory of the bilateral French/German real exchange rate from August 1971 to October 1990 shows that it has been surprisingly stable. Using price

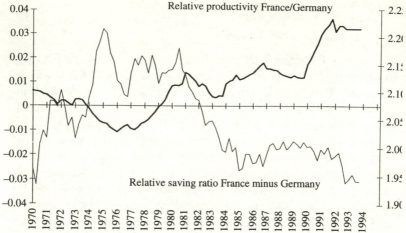

FIG. 4.6   The two fundamentals behind the natural exchange rate DM/FF
Source: OECD

deflators where $1985 = 100$, the real DM value of the $FF(R = (DM/FF)\ P_F/P_G)$ has fluctuated between 0.27 and 0.34, a variation of about 20 per cent, considerably smaller than the variations in the relative capital/employment and social-saving ratios.

Yet a look at the relative exogenous fundamentals in Figure 4.6 shows a striking characteristic. The relative French/German capital/employment ratio, k, has tended to rise over the period, while the relative French/German social saving ratio, s, has fallen. The two variables are expected to have opposite long-run effects on the bilateral NATREX, R, a rise in k appreciating R and a fall in s depreciating R. We suggest that the comparative stationarity of the real exchange rate (R 3) in response to non-stationary fundamentals may result from these opposite movements, with one fundamental cancelling out the effects of the other.

6.2 Econometric Results

We now address ourselves to the question: what is the explanatory power of our model which claims that the real exchange rate converges to the NATREX which, in turn, is determined by the relative saving ratios s in France less that in Germany, and the relative productivity variable k measured as the capital intensity in

France/Germany. The model is dynamic, in the form of equation (4.8) for the real exchange rate R. The exogeneous variables are $Z = (s, k)$.

$$R(t) = a_1 R(t-1) + a_2 Z(t) + a_3 Z(t-1). \tag{4.8}$$

The steady-state value $R(Z(t))$, conditional upon the fundamentals $Z(t)$ is equation (4.9). We seek to estimate vector B, so that we have a long-run relation between $R(t)$ and $Z(t)$, which is the cointegrating equation.

$$R(Z(t)) = [(a_2 + a_3)/(1 - a_1)] Z(t) = BZ(t) \tag{4.9}$$

The basic equation used to estimate B is equation (4.10).

$$R(t) = BZ(t) + a_1[R(t-1) - B(Z(1-1))] - a_3[Z(t) - Z(t-1)] + e(t), \tag{4.10}$$

The Phillips–Loretan procedure estimates this through non-linear least squares, where B is constrained to be the same in the first and second terms. The Engle–Granger method used two steps. First, it estimates B by regressing $R(t)$ on $Z(t)$. Let the estimate of $B = B'$ in equation (4.11), where h is the residual.

$$R(t) = B' Z(t) + h(t) \tag{4.11}$$

The lagged residual $h(t-1) = R(t-1) - B'Z(t-1)$ is used as the second term in (4.10). This second term is the error correction, which we call the 'drawback'. Thus the Engle–Granger method yields, as a second step, equation (4.12).

$$R(t) = B' Z(t) + b\, h(t-1) + c\, DZ(t) + e(t). \tag{4.12}$$

It is essential for the cointegration technique that each variable $R(t)$, $Z(t)$ be integrated of order 1 and that the residuals from the cointegrating equation be integrated $I(0)$. The exogenous variables Z are $I(1)$ but the real exchange rate $R3$ may or may not be stationary. Hence, using $R3$ as the real exchange rate attenuates the significance of the cointegration analysis.

Tables 4.2 and 4.3 present the results. In Table 4.2, the saving ratio has not been corrected for the possible endogeneity, whereas it has been corrected in Table 4.3. There are no significant differences in the results. Column 1 reports the results from the first step of the Engle–Granger estimation, equation (4.11). The residual $h(t)$ is shown to be stationary, so we may have a cointegrating equation. Column 2 is an OLS estimate of equation (4.8). Column 4 is the estimate of equation (4.10), using the NLS estimation. Column 3 is the second step estimation of equation (4.12). For the innovation

TABLE 4.2 Results of the Engle–Granger cointegration equation and error-correction for the level of the Real Exchange Rate FF/DM; relative social saving: exogenous plus endogenous part; France–Germany (period 1971.1–1990.4) and (t- statistics in parentheses)

	I Cointegration Engle–Granger equation (11)	II Ordinary LS equation (8)	III Error correction Engle–Granger equation (12)	IV Non-linear LS Phillips–Loretan equation (10)
Intercept	−0.208(−1.90)	−0.123(−1.77)	−0.012(−0.25)	−0.065(−0.866)
Real Exchange Rate $(t-1)$		0.740(10.81)		
$R^*(X(t))$ NATREX from Equation [4.11] column I			1.032(6.92)	
Drawback (Force) Residual $(t-1)$ from Equation [4.11] column I			0.710(8.73)	
Long-Term Impact	0.478(3.83)	0.263(3.23)		1.026(3.48)
Relative Social Time Preference France minus Germany (lag = −1)				
Long-Term Impact	0.248(4.74)	0.097(2.71)		0.242(2.02)
Relative Productivity France/Germany (lag = −1)				
Short-Term Impact			0.00034(0.92)	0.00090(1.88)
World Real Interest Rate long-term (United States); One Quarter Ahead				

	Equation [4.11]	Equation [4.8]	Equation [4.12]	Equation [4.10]
Root Mean Squared Error Mean Absolute % Error for the Fit on the sample 1970.1–1993.4	0.0176 4.280	0.007 1.860	0.009 2.275	0.0075 1.925

Equation [4.11]:
Residuals
$ADF(C, 1) = -3.26$
$ADF\ 10\% = -3.53$
$ADF(C, 2) = -3.12$
$ADF\ 10\% = -3.53$
$ADF(C, 4) = -4.01$
$ADF\ 10\% = -3.53$

Equation [4.8]:
Adjusted R^2:0.696
DW Statistic: 1.853
$F_{(8,59)}$: 57.93
Probability: 0.00

Equation [4.12]:
Adjusted R^2: 0.649
DW Statistic: 1.8534
$F_{(8,59)}$: 46.88
Probability: 0.00

Equation [4.10]:
Adjusted R^2: 0.709
DW Statistic: 1.848
$F_{(8,59)}$: 45.78
Probability: 0.00

Sources: See Table 4.1.

Notes: Total effect means that the *Relative social saving* is in the equation, while exogeneous part means that the residual of the OLS of *Relative social saving on Relative productivity* is in the equation instead. The correlation between the *Relative productivity* and the total effect (endogenous plus exogenous part) is 0.74, while the correlation between the *Relative productivity* and exogenous part is 0.06, the correlation between the total effect (endogenous plus exogenous part) and the exogenous part is 0.67. This decomposition is taking care of an eventual multicollinearity problem, which however the results show is not binding.

TABLE 4.3 *Results of the cointegration equation and error correction for the level of the Real Exchange Rate FF/DM; relative social saving: exogenous part only; France–Germany (period 1971.1–1990.4) (t-statistics in parentheses)*

	I Cointegration Engle–Granger equation (11)	II Ordinary LS equation (8)	III Error correction Engle–Granger equation (12)	IV Non-linear LS Phillips–Loretan equation (10)
Intercept	0.094(1.27)	0.0433(0.912)	−0.007(−0.16)	0.145(−2.186)
Real Exchange Rate $(t-1)$		0.734(10.53)		
$R^*(X(t))$ *NATREX* from Equation [4.11] column I			1.018(6.91)	
Drawback Force Residual $(t-1)$ from Equation [4.11] column I			0.714 (8.30)	
Long-Term Impact Relative Social Time Preference France minus Germany (lag = −1)	0.496(3.99)	0.269(3.27)		1.024(3.69)
Long-Term Impact Relative Productivity France/Germany (lag = −1)	0.103(2.93)	0.019(0.78)		−0.069(−0.76)
Short-Term Impact World Real Interest Rate long-term (United States) One Quarter Ahead			0.00033(0.89)	0.00098(2.04)

Root Mean Squared Error Mean Absolute % Error for the Fit on the sample 1970.1–1993.4	0.0117 2.910	0.0074 1.869	0.0079 1.957	0.0072 1.762
	Equation [4.11]: Residuals $ADF(C, 1) = -3.06$ $ADF\ 10\% = -3.53$ $ADF(C, 2) = -3.11$ $ADF\ 10\% = -3.53$ $ADF(C, 4) = -4.02$ $ADF\ 10\% = -3.53$	**Equation [4.8]:** Adjusted R^2: 0.693 DW Statistic: 1.816 $F(8,59)$: 56.54 Probability: 0.00	**Equation [4.12]:** Adjusted R^2: 0.648 DW Statistic: 1.812 $F(8,59)$: 45.33 Probability: 0.00	**Equation [4.10]:** Adjusted R^2: 0.710 DW Statistic: 1.833 $F(8,59)$: 45.85 Probability: 0.00

Sources: See Table 4.1.

TABLE 4.4 *Results of the Johansen procedure maximum likelihood (no trend case) cointegration test of the stochastic matrix; 80 observations; maximum lag in VAR = 2; Real Exchange Rated FF/DM with fundamentals; France–Germany (Period 1971.1–1990.4)*

Variables included in the cointegrating vector	Real exchange rate	Relative productivity	Relative social saving: endogenous plus exogenous part	Intercept
Coefficient Estimate	– 1.0	0.192	0.375	– 0.092

Null versus alternative	Statistic	95% critical value	90% critical value
$r = 0$ versus $r >= 1$	27.84	22.00	19.76
$r <= 1$ versus $r = 2$	11.18	15.67	13.75
$r <= 2$ versus $r = 3$	0.96	9.24	7.53

List of Eigenvalues in descending order	.29394	.13044	.011874

Variables included in the cointegrating vector	Real exchange rate	Relative productivity	Relative social saving: exogenous part only	Intercept
Coefficient Estimate	−1.0	0.078	0.375	0.147

Null versus alternative	Statistic	95% critical value	90% critical value
$r = 0$ versus $r >= 1$	39.98	34.91	32.00
$r <= 1$ versus $r = 2$	12.14	19.96	17.85
$r <= 2$ versus $r = 3$	0.956	9.24	7.52

List of Eigenvalues in descending order	.29394	.13044	.011874

Sources: See Table 4.1

term $DZ(t)$ we used the world real rate of interest one quarter ahead.

Table 4.4, using the Johansen procedure, shows that we have one cointegrating vector between the real exchange rate, relative productivity k and relative thrift s. Tables 4.2 and 4.3, column 1 using the Engle–Granger equation (4.11), show that relative saving $s = s$ (France) $-s$ (Germany) appreciates the real value of the French franc relative to the DM, and relative capital intensities $k = k$ (French)/k (Germany) also appreciates the French franc.

Table 4.2, column 4, using the NLS estimates gives the same results as Engle–Granger. However, using the NLS estimates in Table 4.3 (where the saving ratios are truly exogenous), the relative productivity effect is not significant. The same results occur using OLS in column 2 in Table 4.3.

The world real rate of interest has an effect in the shorter period. It is positive because a rise in the US rate shifts portfolios from DM denominated assets into $US denominated assets. The DM declines relative to the dollar so that the French franc appreciates relative to the DM. Portfolio adjustments lead to a convergence of both French and German real long-term interest rates to the US rate, so that the interest-rate effect is not present in the cointegrating equation.

Figure 4.1 compares the real exchange rate $R(t)$ with the estimate from the cointegrating equation (4.11) $R(t) = B'Z(t)$ using Engle–Granger, denoted Natural Real Exchange Rate $R[X(t)]$ and the forecast in equation (4.12) also using the error correction, denoted Estimated Real Exchange Rate. The period after German unification is to be ignored for the reasons cited above concerning the data after 1990.

7. CONCLUSION

We have shown that the bilateral French/German real exchange rate does respond to the real fundamentals of relative thrift and productivity as predicted by the NATREX model. Increases in relative thrift, measured by relative social saving/national product, and increases in relative productivity, measured by the relative capital/employment ratios, both produce long-run real appreciation of the French franc relative to the Deutsch mark. The economic logic was explained above in the text in connection, with Figure 4.5. A *decrease* in thrift which *depreciates* the real exchange rate is the movement from $R(0)$ to $R^*(1)$. A *rise* in productivity which *appreciates* the real exchange rate is the movement from $R(0)$ to $R^*(2)$ in Figure 4.5.

The sample period, 1971–90, includes a variety of nominal exchange-rate policies. The responsiveness of the real exchange rate to the fundamentals supports the NATREX assumption that real exchange rates will adjust, regardless of the nominal exchange-rate regime. When nominal rates are fixed, the necessary changes in the real exchange rate must be accomplished through adjustments in relative prices of goods. If differing national monetary policies, either actual or expected, prevent the adjustment of relative goods prices, then the pressures to change nominal exchange rates become irresistible, as seen in the disruption of the EMS exchange rates in 1992. Moreover, even with similar monetary policies, wage and price rigidity may slow the adjustment of the actual real exchange rate to the NATREX, increasing the economic costs of a fixed nominal exchange rate.

The empirical support we find for the NATREX model does not say whether France and Germany are ready for a fixed nominal exchange rate. It does suggest (1) that the bilateral real exchange rate has responded to changes in the fundamentals, whether through price adjustments or changes in the nominal exchange rate, during a period when nominal exchange rates were in varying degrees fixed but adjustable; and (2) that the NATREX will continue to change, with disturbances in the real fundamentals requiring future changes in the real exchange rate, no matter how well integrated are the two economies. Evidence for the NATREX approach for France and Germany states that any observed stationarity of a real exchange rate is a serendipitous effect, since the fundamentals, productivity and thrift, are not stationary. It turned out that these variables moved in opposite directions. If the NATREX is moving in one direction, because a linear combination of the fundamentals is not stationary, then the real exchange rate must change, regardless of what monetary policies the central banks seek to follow. This is the lesson that the NATREX model has for Europe.

REFERENCES

Cohen, D. and Wyplosz, C. 1989. 'The European monetary union: an agnostic evaluation'. In Ralph Bryant *et al.*, eds., *Macroeconomic Politics in an Interdependent World*, Washington, DC, Brookings Institution.

Crouhy-Veyrac, Liliane and Michel Crouhy. 1978. 'National economic planning, environmental policy and stochastic capital productivity'. *Time Studies in the Management Sciences*, 9, 171–83.

——, —— Jacques Melitz. 1982. 'More on the law of one-price'. *European Economic Review*, July.

—— and Michèle Saint Marc. 1991. 'The natural and the nominal exchange rate: the case of French franc and the Deutsche mark'. CNRS–HEC–Bundesbank workshop, Oct.

——, ——1992. 'Le couple Franc-mark du SME à l'UEM'. In 'Du franc Poincaré à l'Ecu', Colloque de Bercy, Dec.

——, —— 1993. 'The natural rate of exchange between the French franc and the Deutsche mark: a Wicksellian approach'. American Economic Association Meeting, Anaheim, Calif., Jan.

Crouhy, Michel and Melitz, J. 1976. 'Faut-il rejeter les thèses traditionelles de l'inflation?' *Revue Economiques*, 27 (6).

Davanne, Olivier. 1990. 'La dynamique des taux de change'. *Economie et Statistique*, 236, Oct. 37–50.

Dean, Andrew, Martine, Durand, John Fallon, and Peter Hoeller. 1989. 'Saving trends and behaviour in OECD Countries': Working papers, OECD, no. 67, June.

Dickey, D. A. and W.A. Fuller. 1981. 'The likelihood ratio statistics for autoregressive time series with a unit root'. *Econometrica*, 49, 1057–72.

Eichengreen, Barry. 1988. 'Coûts et avantages de l'unification monétaire de l'Europe'. In 'Vers l'Union économique et monétaire', Colloque Bercy 1990, La Documentation Française, Paris.

Engle, R. and C. W. Granger. 1987. 'Cointegration and error-correction: representation, estimation and testing'. *Econometrica*, Mar., 251–76.

Frenkel, Jacob A. and Morris Goldstein 1991. 'Monetary policy in an emerging European economic and monetary union'. IMF Staff Papers, no. 38, no. 2, June.

Granger, C. W. J. 1986. 'Development in the study of cointegrated economic variables'. *Oxford Bulletin of Economics and Statistics*, 48, 3.

INSEE. 1991. 'France-Allemagne'. In *Economie et Statistique*, 246, 247. Paris.

—— 1993. 'L'Union Economique et Monétaire'. In *Economie et Statistique*, 262, 263, Paris.

Léon, Pierre. 1980. *Histoire économique et sociale du monde*. Paris, A. Colin.
OECD. 1975–1993. Economics studies, France, Germany.
Phillips, P. C. B. 1987. 'Time regression with unit root'. *Econometrica*, Mar., 277–301.
Phillips, P. C. B. and Mico Loretan. 1991. 'Estimating long run economic Equilibria'. *Review of Economic Studies*, 58, 407–36.
Pollin, J.-P. and Fitoussi, J.-P. 1977. 'Grandeur et misère de l'économetrie'. *Revue Economiques*, 29 (4).
Saint Marc, Michèle. 1983. *Histoire Monétaire de la France: 1800–1980*. Paris, Presses Universitaires de France.
—— 1989. 'Monetary history in the long run: how are monetarization and monetarism implicated in France, in the UK and in USA?'. *Journal of European Economic History*, 18, (3), 551–82.
—— 1990. 'En France, la construction monétaire européenne, un défi pour l'équilibre extérieur'. *Revue du Marché Commun*, Apr.
—— 1990. 'Europe monétaire: excès de rigueur en France?'. *Revue Banque*, Apr.
—— 1993. *L'économie Allemande face à la réunification*. Vuibert ed. Paris.
Villa, Pierre. 1990. 'Une analyse macroéconomique de l'économie française au vingtième siècle' INSEE, juin.
Weiller, Jean. 1949. 'Les préférences nationales de structure et la notion de déséquilibre structurel'. *Revue d'Economie Politique*, 414–34.
Wicksell, Knut. 1898. *Geldzins und Güterpreise*, Iena, tr. A. Kahn. *Interest and prices*. MacMillan 1925.

5

The Equilibrium Real Exchange Rate: Theory and Evidence for Latin America

MICHAEL CONNOLLY AND JOHN DEVEREUX

1. INTRODUCTION

The determinants of relative national price levels, usually called the real exchange rate, have interested economists from David Ricardo to the present. Since Balassa (1964) and Samuelson (1964), most have acknowledged that real exchange rates appreciate in the long run with development due to the higher prices of services. More recently, however, economists in developed economies have focused on short-run fluctuations in real exchange rates arising from monetary and fiscal policies, while neglecting long-run factors such as growth and investment. Dornbusch (1989) has identified four approaches in the literature: the monetary approach, the new classical approach, the equilibrium approach, and the macroeconomic approach. These models and their shortcomings are discussed in Chapters 1 to 4 and the Appendix of this volume. Development economists, by contrast, have tended to emphasize real factors such as the external terms of trade, commercial policy, and growth as determinants of the real exchange rate.

It is no exaggeration to say that the real exchange rate is at the centre of much of development economics. It plays, for example, an important role in theoretical and in empirical work on the current account, export supply, and import demand, as well as in many other areas. It is also a crucial indicator for international organizations such as the International Monetary Fund and the World Bank. Moreover, the real exchange rate is also important in policy debates and popular discussions in Latin economies. Indeed, casual observation suggests that it plays a greater role in public debate in Latin America generally than in the US or other OECD countries.

As noted in the Appendix at the end of this book, the constancy of the real exchange rate is an important element in many open-economy models. By contrast, there is a widespread acceptance among economists in developing economies that the equilibrium real exchange rate is not constant and, furthermore, that its equilibrium value is a function of real factors that are constantly changing. The work of Sebastian Edwards (see Edwards 1988a and 1989a), has done most to establish this. A further contrast with the literature for developed economies is that empirical work in developing economies tends to emphasize real factors (see Edwards 1988b for a careful study). In addition, this work often attempts to quantify deviations from the equilibrium real exchange rate (see Edwards 1989a; Cottani, Cavallo, and Khan 1990).

In this chapter we discuss the determinants of equilibrium real exchange rates for Latin America. We also touch on the role played by the real exchange rate in development economics generally, with particular emphasis on similarities with NATREX. This chapter is not, however, intended as a survey, since there are already a number in existence (see Edwards 1988a and 1989a). Moreover, our treatment is by its nature incomplete, thereby ignoring important areas of research.[1] Rather, our goal is to derive some principles which can be used to determine the real exchange-rate effects of commercial policy and changes in the external terms of trade, on the one hand, and, on the other, of technological change, capital accumulation, and increasing returns. In doing so, our aim is to synthesize and extend existing work. The theoretical construct that we employ, the equilibrium real exchange rate, focuses upon the real or fundamental determinants of the price of domestic goods in terms of foreign goods.

At the outset, it should be stated that while we start from the same premise, that real factors play a crucial role in real exchange-rate determination, there are important differences between our model and NATREX. First, our model is derived from the pure or barter theory of international trade, whereas NATREX has a growth-theoretic setting. Second, and unlike NATREX, we do not analyse the dynamics of real exchange-rate determination. Nor do

---

[1] In particular, we ignore the speculative attack literature which is crucial to understanding short-run movements in real exchange rates. For a recent survey see Agenor, Bhandari, and Flood 1992.

we provide a fully worked-out model of investment. Finally, our model abstracts from capital flows so that the current account, which is identical to the trade balance, is always zero. But our model is complementary to NATREX in that it extends the results of earlier chapters to a multi-good setting with particular emphasis on the role of the non-traded price level in real exchange-rate determination.

To conclude this chapter, we provide empirical evidence on the long-run factors which have shaped real exchange rates in Latin America over the 1960–85 period. The results are supportive of the NATREX approach, since they suggest that real exchange-rate movements for these economies are largely explained by real factors as income per capita, openness, government spending, and the external terms of trade.

This chapter is organized as follows: the real exchange rate is introduced in Section 2. In Section 3, we discuss real exchange movements in Latin America over the last decade of so. We develop, in Section 4, a benchmark model of real exchange-rate determination for an open developing economy based upon optimization by producers and consumers. The next section uses this model to analyse the effects of growth on the real exchange rate. We find that technological progress and increases in overall size produce real appreciations. On the other hand, the real exchange rate effects of capital accummulation and changes in factor endowments rate cannot be signed. Section 6 derives some general propositions regarding the real exchange effects of terms-of-trade changes and commercial policy. We show that import protection tends to appreciate the real exchange rate while a deterioration in the external terms of trade leads to a real depreciation. These results are extended to an intertemporal setting in Section 7, where we emphasize the implications of our analysis for empirical work. The concluding section provides evidence on the determinants of the real exchange rate for Latin American economies using pooled time-series data for the 1960–85 period.

2. DEFINING THE REAL EXCHANGE RATE

Our definition of the real exchange rate is given by (5.1), where R is the real exchange rate, N is the nominal exchange rate defined in units of local currency per US dollar and P and P^* are the domestic and foreign price levels respectively. A real exchange appreciation is defined as an increase in this index while a real depreciation corresponds to a reduction. Note also that (5.1) is the real exchange-rate definition used by the IMF. In sum it compares the domestic and external price levels and is often referred to as the purchasing-power parity real exchange rate.[2]

$$R = \frac{P}{NP^*} \ \textit{The real exchange rate} \tag{5.1}$$

In (5.2) and (5.3), we specify exponential price indices for external and internal price levels. The domestic price level is measured using the consumer price index while the foreign price level is given by the US wholesale price index. Finally, we assume that the US WPI consists of traded goods only.

$$P = \prod_{i=1}^{n} p_i^{\alpha_i} \ \textit{Domestic consumer price index} \tag{5.2}$$

$$P^* = \prod_{i=1}^{n} p_i^{*\,a_i^*} \ \textit{Foreign price index} \tag{5.3}$$

3. LATIN REAL EXCHANGE RATES 1980–1992

Table 5.1 presents data on multilateral real exchange rates for selected Latin economies from 1979 to the present, where our real exchange rate is taken from the International Monetary Fund tapes. A striking feature of this table is that despite the great differences in institutions and economic policies in these economies, real exchanges rates show similar patterns. To us, this suggests that common external shocks are important in explaining real exchange-rate movements.

Large real depreciations for all countries coincide with the onset of the debt crises in 1981. This period also saw significant declines in the external terms of trade. After 1984, real exchange rates appreciate. This was a period of growth lasting roughly to 1988. It

---

[2] In theoretical work the real exchange rate is often measured as the internal relative price of non-tradables in terms of tradables. The use of both definitions has led to confusion in the literature. For a discussion, see Connolly and Devereux (1992).

was also a time when many Latin economies tightened trade restrictions. The world recession of the 1980s hit Latin economies hard and real exchange rates again depreciate. But growth returned in 1991 for most countries. Perhaps even more importantly, capital flows to Latin America after averaging about $8 billion throughout most of the 1980s, surged to $24 billion in 1990 and $40 billion in 1991. Recent years have seen real appreciations for some countries. Real appreciations, moreover, that have given rise to fears of overvaluation (see Calvo, Leiderman, and Reinhart 1993). It should be noted, however, that for most economies real rates are nowhere near their peaks of the early 1980s.

The volatility of these real exchange rates is extraordinary. It is much greater, for example, than that for developed economies. Notice also that volatility differs greatly between economies. There is little doubt that monetary and exchange-rate policies have important roles in explaining these differences. In particular, the large real depreciations are associated with nominal devaluations. But exchange-rate and monetary policy are not the whole story.

TABLE 5.1 *Multilateral real exchange rates for selected Latin American economies 1979–1992*

Year	Bolivia	Chile	Costa Rica	Ecuador	Paraguay	Uruguay	Venezuela
1979	100	100	100	100	100	100	100
1980	111	117	110	102	115	128	109
1981	148	142	71	116	141	152	124
1982	161	129	81	114	124	160	134
1983	148	105	93	108	116	98	122
1984	192	103	92	89	109	94	104
1985	329	83	90	93	94	91	99
1986	97	70	81	75	95	89	83
1987	93	65	74	57	76	87	60
1988	89	61	67	43	79	82	66
1989	85	62	70	50	60	86	57
1990	72	61	69	46	58	78	51
1991	74	62	63	48	68	88	54
1992	72	66	64	48	67	95	57

Source: IFS Tapes

Observe that despite the large nominal devaluations from 1981 to the present, real exchange rates tend to return towards their old levels. Second, while monetary and exchange-rate policies have differed greatly across economies, there are large real exchange-rate co-movements. In the remainder of this paper, we shall examine real shocks which we believe can explain such co-movements. We focus on growth, commercial policy, changes in the external terms of trade, and fiscal policy, all of which have tended to be correlated across Latin economies.

4. THE EQUILIBRIUM REAL EXCHANGE RATE

In this section, we present a benchmark long-run model of real exchange-rate determination. Our economy is a price taker in world markets producing one non-traded good (services) and a large number of traded goods. In addition, markets are competitive. The model is a real barter model of international trade in the tradition of Neary (1988). Throughout, we focus on the underlying structural or real determinants of the real exchange rate, and short-run fluctuations due to monetary and exchange-rate policy are ignored.

The economy consists of a single representative household. The demand side is captured by the expenditure function $e(\cdot)$, of (5.4). The function shows the minimum expenditure necessary to achieve a given level of utility. In (5.4), p_s is the price of services, p is a vector of traded goods prices, x is a vector of traded goods consumed, x_s is the consumption of services and U is a scalar representing welfare. Without loss of generality, let us choose one of the traded goods as our numeraire. Note that the expenditure function is linear homogeneous and concave in prices. In addition, its first derivative with respect to the i'th price, denoted by e_i, provides the compensated demand function for the i'th good. We assume that all goods are normal.

$$e(p, p_s; U) \equiv \underset{X, X_s}{\text{Min}} \; px + p_s x_s \; \text{Subject to} \; \bar{U} = U(x, x_s) \qquad (5.4)$$

Production functions are assumed to display constant returns to scale and the number of factors is greater than the number of goods produced. Given these assumptions, national income may be represented by the well-behaved GNP function $g(\cdot)$ of (5.5).

$$g(p, p_s; v) \equiv \underset{X, X_s}{\text{Max}} \; pX + p_s X_s \; \text{Subject to} \; X = f(X_s, v) \qquad (5.5)$$

In (5.5), X is the vector of traded goods produced, X_s is the production of non-traded goods while $f(\cdot)$ is the production possibility set, and v is a vector of factor endowments. The GNP function is convex and linear homogeneous in prices. In addition, its first derivative with respect to the i'th price, denoted by g_i, provides the output supply function for this good.[3]

For equilibrium, income must equal expenditure and the non-traded market must clear. Equation (5.6) sets expenditure equal to national income plus tax tariff revenue and transfers from abroad (F).

$$e(p, p_s; U) \equiv g(p, p_s; U) + t(e_p - g_p) + F \tag{5.6}$$

In (5.6), t is a vector of trade taxes. We assume that tariff revenue is redistributed in lump-sum fashion. Total demand for tradables is given by $e_p(\cdot)$ which is a vector of derivatives of the expenditure function with respect to traded prices. Tradables production is $g_p(\cdot)$, a vector of derivatives of the GNP function with respect to traded prices.

The second condition for equilibrium, that the non-traded goods market clear, is given by (5.7) which equates the demand and supply of non-traded goods. Let $e_s(\cdot)$ and $g_s(\cdot)$ indicate the first derivatives of the expenditure and GNP functions with respect to the price of non-traded goods.

$$e_s(p, p_s; U) = g_s(p, p_s; v) \tag{5.7}$$

We assume that all goods are substitutes in compensated excess supply. Complementarities, of course, do occur in models based on maximizing behaviour. But from the properties of expenditure and GNP functions, it can be shown that substitutability holds on average. To conclude, note also that this model embodies a general specification of technology. In particular, no restrictions are placed on the number of goods and factors nor on the degree of vertical integration in production.

Totally differentiating (5.7) and solving for the services price level, (5.8) is obtained, where e_{ss} is the slope of compensated demand for services, e_{si} is the cross effect in demand for services, assumed positive, with regard to the price of the i'th traded good, g_{ss} is the slope of the supply function for services goods, g_{si} is the cross effect of supply, assumed negative, with respect to the price of

---

[3] For further details of the GNP and expenditure functions, see Woodland 1982.

the i'th good, g_{sv_j} is the Rybczynski (1955) term for the supply of services with respect the j'th factor, y is real income and e_{sy} is the marginal propensity to spend on services. Following the literature, we define changes in real income, dy, as $e_u dU$, where e_u is the inverse of the marginal utility of income. The marginal propensity to spend on services, e_{sy}, is equal to e_{su}/e_u.

$$dp_s = (\phi_i + \theta_i) dp_i + \pi_j dv_j + \gamma dy \qquad (5.8)$$

where $\phi_i = \dfrac{e_{si}}{g_{ss} - e_{ss}} > 0$, $\theta_i = \dfrac{-g_{si}}{g_{ss} - e_{ss}} > 0$, $\pi_i = -\dfrac{g_{sv_i}}{g_{ss} - e_{ss}} \gtreqless 0$ and

$$\gamma = \dfrac{e_{sy}}{g_{ss} - e_{ss}} > 0$$

This model can be used to study the effects of a wide variety of shocks. We focus in this chapter on commercial policy, changes in the external terms of trade, fiscal policy, and growth. But it can just as easily be used to study topics as diverse as the real exchange-rate effects of price controls or public sector prices.[4]

The first term on the right-hand side of (5.8) gives the impact on the non-traded goods price level of changes in the price of the i'th traded good. At a constant level of real income, this increases the non-traded price level. The second terms shows the relationship between the non-traded price level and the supply of the j'th factor. This term can be positive or negative depending on the general equilibrium structure of the economy. The final term, γ, is positive since an increase in real income raises the demand for services.

5. GROWTH AND THE REAL EXCHANGE RATE

The last few years have seen rapid growth in a number of Latin economies, such as Chile and Venezuela. This section examines the effects of growth on the real exchange rate. Of course, the modern literature on this subject dates from Balassa (1964) and Samuelson (1964).[5] But subsequent work in this area has developed largely in isolation from the macroeconomic literature on real exchange rates

---

[4] See Devereux and Connolly 1993a.
[5] It should be noted, however, that this work represents a re-discovery of the earlier work of Cairnes (1874), Ohlin (1933) and Harrod (1933).

surveyed in the Appendix. The NATREX approach is, however, in this earlier tradition as it emphasizes that investment and productivity change are crucial determinants of the real exchange rate. The NATREX approach proceeds from an aggregate macroeconomic perspective. In this section, we pursue a more disaggregated microeconomic approach, where we distinguish between the effects of growth due to capital accumulation, increases in market size, and technological progress. Previous research has found that the role of these factors differs greatly between developing and developed economies. Typically, studies found that capital accumulation accounts for around two-thirds of growth per capita in Latin America. The corresponding figures for developed economies are, of course, much lower.[6]

From the small-economy assumption, external prices are fixed. Thus, changes in the real exchange rate with growth are due to changes in the non-traded price level. More formally, differentiating (5.1) and (5.2) and transforming into proportional rates of change where a ' $\hat{\ }$ ' represents a proportional rate of change, we have (5.9). Finally, to avoid the various paradoxes connected with immiserizing growth (see Bhagwati 1958, and Neary and Ruane 1988), we set all distortions in this economy equal to zero.[7]

$$\hat{R} = \alpha_s \hat{p}_s \qquad (5.9)$$

5.1 Capital Accumulation

To begin, let us consider the impact of capital accumulation on the real exchange. Capital accumulation is treated here as exogenous in contrast to the endogeneity of capital in the NATREX model. Totally differentiating (5.5), we obtain (5.10) which gives the change in real income due to a change in the supply of capital (K).

$$dy = g_k \, dK \qquad (5.10)$$

From the properties of the GNP function, the g_k term is the marginal product of capital which, under competition and constant

---

[6] For a discussion of this issue see the 1991 World Development Report, the World Bank.

[7] This approach can be extended to incorporate unemployment, see Neary (1985b). Also Devereux and Connolly (1993b) show how informal markets affect real exchange-rate determination.

returns to scale, is equal its market return r. Using (5.8) and (5.10) and solving for the non-traded price level, we obtain (5.11).

$$dp_s = (\gamma r + \pi_k)\,dK \qquad (5.11)$$

An increase in the capital stock raises income, thereby increasing the demand for services. This effect is given by the first term in parenthesis in (5.11). By contrast, the impact of capital accumulation on the supply of services is ambiguous as π_k, the Rybczynski term for capital, can be positive, negative, or zero depending on general equilibrium structure of the economy. We conclude that the *relationship between capital accumulation and the real exchange rate is ambiguous*. This result can be generalized to other factors. One important implication of (5.11) is that, contrary to a widespread impression, there is no general presumption that increases in land or mineral resources specific to traded sectors increase the non-traded price level.

5.2 Technical Progress

There is an old doctrine which holds that technological progress occurs at a faster rate in the traded sectors of an economy. Balassa (1964), Samuelson (1964), and Bhagwati (1984) argue that higher rates of technological progress in the traded sectors relative to the non-traded sector raises the non-traded price level. We incorporate technological progress into the GNP function by introducing a shift parameter τ which changes the GNP function to $g(p, p_s; v, \tau)$. To proceed, we need to impose more structure on the model. Here, we shall assume that technological change is product augmenting or Hicks neutral. In this case the GNP function becomes, $g(\tau p, p_s; v)$ where τp is a vector with elements $\tau_i p_i$. Recall that product-augmenting technological progress has the same effect on revenue as an increase in the price of output. Therefore $g_\tau(\cdot) = g_p(\cdot)$. Using this result, totally differentiating (5.5) and solving for income, we obtain (5.12) where $d\tau_i$ is the change in technology in the i'th sector.

$$dy = g_i\,d\tau_i \qquad (5.12)$$

Technological progress raises the demand for non-traded goods by increasing income. On the supply side, it reduces the supply of non-traded goods. Intuitively, this occurs because an expansion in the i'th sector attracts resources from the rest of the economy. Therefore, as shown by (5.13), technological progress in the i'th traded sector increases the non-traded price level. By contrast, technological progress in the non-traded sector reduces the non-traded price level.[8]

$$dp_s = (\theta_i + \gamma g_i) d\tau_i \qquad (5.13)$$

5.3 Increasing Returns

Panagariya (1988) has suggested that with increasing returns to scale in traded sectors, absolute size plays a role in real exchange-rate determination. To analyse the effects of increasing returns we shall make use of an important correspondence. If increasing returns are external to firms but internal to the traded sector then the following result holds: *the impact on the non-traded price level of an increase in overall size is equivalent to an increase in size combined with product-augmenting technological progress in the traded sector with constant returns to scale.*[9]

We assume that increasing returns occur at the traded sector as a whole because if there were increasing returns at the industry level, a good would tend to be produced entirely in one country, violating the small-country assumption. Furthermore, this assumption is consistent with the empirical evidence of Cabellero and Lyons (1992).

Using this correspondence, the impact of an increase in overall size on real income with increasing returns to scale in the traded sector is given by (5.14). For convenience, initial factor supplies are normalized at unity. Note that the T subscript refers to the traded sector.

$$dy = y dv + g_T d\tau_T \qquad (5.14)$$

As shown by (5.15), a sufficient condition for the price of services to rise with overall size is that the elasticity of demand for services, denoted by η_s, is greater than or equal to unity. As this condition is likely to be satisfied, we conclude that an increase in size appreciates the real exchange rate. To derive this result, the initial supply of non-traded goods is normalized at unity.

---

[8] If technological progress is factor augmenting then the effects on the non-traded price level are uncertain.

[9] The exact conditions under which this relationship holds are given in Helpman (1984).

$$dp_s = \left(\frac{\eta_s - 1}{g_{ss} - e_{ss}}\right) dv + (\theta_T + \gamma g_T) d\tau_T > 0 \qquad (5.15)$$

Throughout, we assume that the economy is a price taker on world markets. While this assumption is a reasonable one for Latin America, it is important to note that our results are altered if growth affects the external terms of trade. Growth can improve or worsen the external terms of trade (see Johnson 1958). And, as is well known from Bhagwati (1958), real income can fall with induced changes in the external terms of trade.[10]

6. COMMERCIAL POLICY, CHANGES IN THE EXTERNAL TERMS OF TRADE, AND THE EQUILIBRIUM REAL EXCHANGE RATE

In this section, we analyse the real exchange-rate effects of commercial policy, changes in the external terms of trade, and fiscal policy. These subjects are important in policy debates in Latin America. First, virtually all Latin economies remain dependent on the export of primary commodities. As a result, their terms of trade are volatile. More volatile indeed than any developed economy with the exception of Australia and Japan. Furthermore, economies in the region have seen huge swings in commercial policy over the last decade and a half. In particular, there have been dramatic moves towards free trade by many of the larger economies over the last four years.[11]

6.1 Commercial Policy and the Real Exchange Rate

Towards the end of the 1970s a number of Latin economies, particularly in the Southern Cone, liberalized their economies. Most of these reforms were reversed after the debt crises of the early

---

[10] Stein (1991) is one of the few papers to consider the impact of growth on the real exchange rate when the external terms of trade are endogenous.

[11] Moreover, there is a huge theoretical literature on these topics. The 'Dutch Disease' literature analyses the effects of changes in the external terms of trade on the real exchange rate. See Neary (1985b) and Corden (1984) for surveys. The literature on real exchange effects of commercial policy is surveyed by Edwards (1989a) and (1989b). Neary (1988) integrates both approaches. A recent real business-cycle treatment of these issues is found in Mendoza (1992).

1980s. (For an account of this period see Edwards 1991). But in the last couple of years, Argentina, Brazil, Colombia, Peru, and Uruguay amongst others have again dramatically liberalized their trade regimes, producing large changes in relative prices. The effects of trade policy on the real exchange rate is therefore a question of great policy relevance.[12]

Using (5.2) and (5.3), we obtain (5.16) and (5.17), which summarize the effects of commercial policy on price of non-traded goods and the real exchange rate. Let us assume that initial protection is zero. We do this to ensure that there are no first-order income effects. We relax this assumption later.

$$dp_s = (\phi_i + \theta_i)\,dp_i + \gamma dy \qquad (5.16)$$

$$\hat{R} = (\alpha_i + \alpha_s \omega_i)\,t_i + \alpha_s \mu \hat{y} \qquad (5.17)$$

In (5.17), ω_i is the compensated elasticity of the non-traded price level with respect to the i'th price. This parameter is positive and less than unity. Since the second term on the right-hand side of (5.16) is zero by assumption, a tariff raises the non-traded price level while an export tax reduces it. From (5.17), observe that a tariff increases the domestic price level relative to the external price level, thereby appreciating the real exchange rate. Export taxes, on the other hand, lower domestic prices, causing a real depreciation. Note that (5.17) implies that import and export restrictions have opposite real exchange-rate effects. Of course, from Lerner Symmetry, we know that their real effects are identical. This is important as it is our first indication that there is not a one-to-one correspondence between resource allocation and the real exchange rate.

When we allow for income effects, the second term on the right-hand side of (5.16) is negative. It follows that the impact of of import restrictions on the non-traded price level is a priori uncertain, as income and substitution effects tend to work in opposite directions. The empirical evidence, however, suggests overwhelmingly that protection increases the non-traded price level.[13] We therefore assume that substitution effects dominate income effects. Finally, income and substitution effects tend to work in the same direction for export price changes, so that there is no ambiguity.

---

[12] Hallberg and Takacs (1992) provide some details. To take just one example, nominal protection in Peru fell from an average of 67% to 15% in 1990.

[13] See Devereux and Connolly (1993c).

6.2 External Prices and the Real Exchange Rate

Latin economies are dependent on the export of primary commodities. As a result, their terms of trade are volatile. More volatile indeed than those of developing economies with the exception of Australia and Japan. Although experience differs across economies, the 1980s were a decade of sustained declines in the external terms of trade for most economies. This was especially marked for the oil exporters, Ecuador, Mexico, and Venezuela.

The impact of an increase in the world price of the i'th good on the non-traded goods price level is given in (5.18). For convenience, we assume that protection is zero, although it can be shown that our results are unaffected by this assumption.

$$dp_S = [\phi_i + \theta_i + \gamma(g_i - e_i)] dp_i^* \tag{5.18}$$

If this good is exported, income and substitution effects associated with a world price increase work in the same direction and the non-traded price level increases. By contrast, the non-traded price level effects of an increase in import prices are uncertain because income and substitution effects oppose.

The relationship between the real exchange rate and the external terms of trade is given by (5.19) where μ is the elasticity of the non-traded price level with respect to changes in real income.

$$\hat{R} = [(\alpha_i - \alpha_i^*) + \alpha_s \omega_i] \hat{p}_i^* + \alpha_s \mu \hat{y} \tag{5.19}$$

With changes in the external terms of trade, external and internal prices will, in most cases, move in the same direction. Yet equation (5.19) can still be signed. To see why, let us assume that the i'th good is exported. In this case the domestic price level increases as does the external price level. Note that the second term in (5.19) is positive. Turning to the first term, recall that for a typical developing country, the share of its export good in the external price level is small, consequently $\alpha_i^* < \alpha_i$. This is sufficient to ensure that improvements in the external terms of trade appreciate the real exchange rate. Moreover, unlike the trade policy case, it can be shown that there is no difference between the real exchange-rate effects of import and export price shocks.[14]

---

[14] This, however, requires balanced trade. Notice also that we have assumed that our measure of the foreign price level, the US WPI, excludes non-traded goods. This assumption is adopted for convenience, as our results continue to hold in the more general case.

These results have important implications for empirical work. For example, an opinion widely shared by economists is that an appreciation of the real exchange rate increases imports while it reduces exports. Our results are inconsistent with this hypothesis. To see why, note that a tariff *appreciates* the real exchange rate but at the same time it *reduces* imports, which is the opposite of the postulated relationship. Similarly, a rise in the external terms of trade *appreciates* the real exchange rate, but it *increases* exports. In fact it is only when shocks are due to monetary and fiscal policy or capital inflows that the conventional wisdom holds. Since to the external terms of trade, commercial policy as well as growth are important in developing economies, this implies that econometric attempts to uncover stable relationships between exports or imports on the one hand and the real exchange rate will fail because such correlations are by their nature unstable.[15] By contrast, the model does imply that there is a stable long-run relationship between the real exchange rate and the external terms of trade. It should be noted that Lim and Stein, Chapter 3 above, have provided powerful evidence that such a relationship exists for Australia which shares many economic characteristics with developing economies.

6.3 Government Spending

We conclude by discussing the real exchange-rate effect of government purchases. With government spending, the non-traded goods-market clearing condition becomes (5.20) where x_g^s is government spending on non-traded goods. We assume that spending is not productive in the sense that government output is valued at zero by the private sector and that it is financed by lump-sum taxes. For models where this assumption is relaxed, see Baily 1971 and Barro 1981.

$$e_s(p, p_s; U) = g_s(p, p_s; v) - x_s{}^g \qquad (5.20)$$

As shown by (5.21), an increase in government spending on non-traded goods raises the non-traded price level, whereas an increase in government spending on traded goods, denoted by x_t^g, lowers it.

$$dp_s = \frac{(1 - e_{sy})}{(g_{ss} - e_{ss})} \, dx_s{}^g - \frac{e_{sy}}{(g_{ss} - e_{ss})} \, dx_t{}^g \qquad (5.21)$$

[15] Tanner (1992), using data from a large number of developing economies, has shown that the real exchange rate and export volumes are not cointegrated.

Consequently, the real exchange rate appreciates with government spending on non-traded goods, and depreciates with government spending on traded goods.

7. THE REAL EXCHANGE RATE IN AN INTERTEMPORAL MODEL

In this section, we sketch how our results in regard to commercial policy and changes in the external terms of trade generalize to intertemporal models A two-period model will suffice to illustrate this. We show that a temporary tariff temporarily appreciates the purchasing-power-parity real exchange rate while a temporary export tax temporarily depreciates it. Along the same lines, temporary improvements in the external terms of trade are associated with temporary real appreciations. Formal proofs of these statements are given in the appendix at the end of this chapter.

Intertemporal models, in addition, help us understand the relationship between the real exchange rate and the current account. It is taken for granted in the empirical literature for developing and developed economies that improvements in the current account are associated with real exchange-rate depreciations. Surprisingly, this is not generally true, as there is no stable relationship between the real exchange rate and the current account. For example, we show in the appendix that if shocks to the current account arise from commercial policy or changes in the external terms of trade, improvements in the current account are associated with temporary *appreciations* of the purchasing-power-parity real exchange rate, while deteriorations in the current account are associated with temporary real *depreciations*. This is the opposite of the conventional wisdom. More generally, it can be shown that the correlation between the current account and the real exchange rate depends on the nature of the underlying shocks to the economy and on the definition of the real exchange rate used.[16] Only if shocks to the

---

[16] Moreover, as Polly Allen has pointed out to us, there is unlikely to be a stable correlation between the real exchange rate and the current account even in traditional open-economy models. For example, take the traditional Keynesian model of an open economy. One can show that a depreciation due to an exogenous fall in foreign demand for exports will depreciate the real exchange rate and worsen the current account.

current account arise from fiscal and monetary shocks or from capital inflows does the conventional wisdom hold.[17]

To understand the intuition underlying these results, let us consider the current-account and real exchange-rate effects of a temporary tariff. We have already seen that a temporary tariff temporarily appreciates the real exchange rate. Furthermore, it is known since Razin and Svennson (1983) that, starting from free trade and assuming that substitutability holds in excess supply, a temporary tariff improves the current account. Combining these results, observe that a temporary *real appreciation* is associated with an *improvement* in the current account. Recall, that temporary tariff improves the current account through intertemporal substitution. This is so since the price level and hence the real exchange rate must fall in the second period relative to the first.

8. EMPIRICAL RESULTS

Empirical papers on growth and the real exchange rate include Kravis and Lipsey (1983 and 1988), Clague (1986 and 1989), and Officer (1989). By contrast to this well-developed literature, there is a dearth of evidence concerning the real exchange-rate effects of changes in the external terms of trade or commercial policy, size, or other variables discussed in this paper. Using the results of the previous sections and the existing literature as a guide, this section presents empirical evidence on the determinants of long-run real exchange rates for Latin American economies.

Our model suggests that the real exchange rate is positively related to economic size, technological progress, and the external terms of trade, while the real exchange-rate effects of government spending, the capital stock, and endowments of primary factors such as land and minerals are theoretically ambiguous.

Table 5.2 reports the regressions for the purchasing-power-parity real exchange rate for a cross-section of 17 Latin American economies for five-year periods from 1960 to 1985. We adopt five-year periods because data on many variables are available only at this interval. The countries in the sample are Costa Rica, El Salvador,

[17] Our hypothesis that there is no stable relationship between the real exchange rate and the current account has received confirmation from Rose (1991), who found no evidence of such a relationship for OECD countries.

TABLE 5.2 *Real exchange-rate regressions*

	(1)	(2)
INTERCEPT	39.41	39.653
	(3.38)	(4.03)
Y REL	0.646	0.605
	(3.03)	(2.17)
POP	0.00092	−0.00096
	(0.19)	(−0.15)
SEC ED	−0.208	−0.207
	(−1.51)	(−1.15)
ADJOPEN	0.946	
	(7.94)	
URB	0.096	0.113
	(0.73)	(0.66)
GOV	0.783	0.776
	(3.67)	(2.79)
TOT	−0.140	−0.140
	(−5.30)	(−4.04)
PRIM	0.179	0.177
	(0.88)	(0.67)
65D	1.520	1.442
	(0.47)	(0.327)
70D	0.330	0.003
	(0.04)	(0.05)
75D	−3.055	−3.130
	(−0.77)	(−0.61)
80D	6.462	6.292
	(1.52)	(1.13)
85D	−5.350	−5.71
	(−1.08)	(−0.88)
ARD	88.54	89.563
	(8.72)	(6.72)
R^2	0.728	0.530
SEE	9.49	12.42
N	102	102

Note: since a rise in the real exchange rate indicates a real appreciation, significant positive coefficients indicate factors inducing a real appreciation.

Guatemala, Honduras, Mexico, Nicaragua, Panama, Argentina, Bolivia, Brazil, Chile, Colombia, Ecuador, Paraguay, Peru, Uruguay, Venezuela. The data were obtained from the International Comparison Project (Summers and Heston 1991), supplemented by the World Bank *World Tables*.

The dependent variable in each regression is the bilateral real exchange rate relative to the US (REAL). The Summers and Heston (1991) bilateral real exchange rate is a true purchasing-power-parity real exchange-rate measure which compares absolute price levels in the US and other countries. By contrast, most real exchange-rate measures compare real exchange-rate changes relative to some base period. Unfortunately, data on the capital stock are not available. Following earlier studies, relative income per capita in terms of the US (Y REL), calculated using a purchasing-power-parity conversion factor, was used as proxy for endowments of capital and technology levels.

Secondary-school enrolments (SEC ED) was used to measure for human capital. Market size was proxied by population (POP). Data on the external terms of trade (TOT), and secondary-school enrolments were obtained from the World Bank *World Tables* various issues.

Comparable data on commercial policy are not available on an annual basis for any of the countries. It is true that the World Bank (see World Bank 1987) has constructed trade-policy measures for some economies. Unfortunately, these indices are subjective and are not directly comparable across countries. Following Leamer (1987) and other studies, we measure trade policy as the deviation of the ratio of trade to GNP from the average for Latin America. Trade policy is proxied by the residuals of a regression which relates the ratio of total trade to GNP (measured at world prices from the Summers and Heston data set). We regressed openness against a set of variables including population, income per capita, the terms of trade, the share of the primary sector in GNP. A negative residual suggests that a country has a relatively restrictive trade policy while a positive residual suggests a relatively outward-looking policy. The results of this procedure accord well with information from other sources. For example, Panama, a relatively open economy by Latin American standards, always had positive residuals. By contrast, the residuals for Uruguay, a protectionist economy,[18] were consistently negative.

---

[18] See Connolly and de Melo 1993 for a study of protectionism in Uruguay.

The share of agriculture and mining in GNP(PRIM) is used as a proxy for endowments of land and mineral deposits. Finally, a measure of urbanization (URB) was added to the list of variables. As is well known, price levels are systematically higher in urban as compared to rural areas. Therefore, an increase in urbanization at constant income levels would be expected to increase the measured price level. Urbanization was not used in previous studies, but has been suggested by Sachs (1985).

Intercept dummies were included for each period (65D, 70D, 75D, 80D, 85D). Given the number of observations, the use of individual country dummies was not practical. A preliminary graph of the data revealed that the real exchange rate for Argentina in 1980 was an outlier. It is argued in Connolly (1986), Calvo (1986), and Corbo and De Melo (1989), amongst others, that inconsistent monetary and exchange-rate policies led to a huge and unsustainable real appreciation in 1980. Accordingly, a dummy variable was used for this observation (ARD).

In Table 5.2, *t*-statistics are in parenthesis. As in previous studies, bilateral real exchange rates are positively associated with income per capita suggesting that an increase in the capital–labour ratio and improvements in technology raise the real exchange rate. But there is no evidence that the real exchange rate increases with absolute size, since population is insignificant with a negative coefficient. This suggests that increasing returns are equally likely to be present in the traded and non-traded sectors.

The relationship between enrolments in secondary education and the real exchange rate is negative but insignificant. Data on secondary-school enrolments, however, may be a poor proxy for human capital. First, it is the stock of human capital rather than the flow, as measured by enrolment, which is important for real exchange-rate determination. Second, enrolment measures take no account of quality differences in education across countries.

The urbanization and natural resources variables are positive but insignificant. This suggests that increases in urbanization or factors specific to the traded sectors such as land and mineral deposits do not appreciate the real exchange rate. By contrast, the external terms of trade and government share in GNP are strongly significant, although the external terms-of-trade variable does not have have the a priori expected sign.

A striking feature of Table 5.2 is the performance of the commercial-policy variable ADJOPEN, which is strongly significant with a positive coefficient. Recall, that a higher value for the adjusted openness variable signals lower levels of protection. Thus our findings suggest that an increase in protectionism *depreciates* the real exchange rate. This finding could be rationalized on the basis that income effects dominate substitution effects, thereby depreciating the real exchange rate. A more plausible explanation is that openness also signals other factors such as high levels of technology in the traded sector.

Fortunately, the results are not sensitive to the exclusion of the adjusted openness variable, as when it is excluded, as in regression (5.2), there is little change. The effects of openness on the real exchange rate thus remain a question for further study. Turning to the period dummies, none is consistently significant. To sum up, the model appears to explain a surprisingly large portion of observed changes in Latin American real exchange rates.[19]

9. SUMMARY

This chapter presents a model of the equilibrium real exchange rate. As with NATREX in other chapters, we abstract from short-run monetary and fiscal factors that cause temporary deviations in the short-run real exchange rate from its natural equilibrium level. Our empirical results suggest that movements in real exchange rates for Latin American economies over the 1960–85 period can be explained in terms of growth, openness, government spending, and the external terms of trade. In particular, technical advance and increases in the capital stock tend to appreciate the real exchange rate, as does trade liberalization (paradoxically) by increasing adjusted openness. Similarly, government expenditure also appears to appreciate the real exchange rate by falling primarily on non-traded goods.

---

[19] Clague (1988) appears to be the only other empirical study of real exchange rates in Latin American economies that adopted a long-run structural approach. He found that the real exchange rate was positively related to the share of mining in GNP, relative income and an unadjusted measure of openness.

REFERENCES

Agenor, Pierre-Richard, Jagdeep S. Bhandari, and Robert Flood. 1992. 'Speculative attacks and models of balance of payments crises'. International Monetary Fund Staff Papers, 2, 357–94.

Baily, Martin. 1971. *National Income and the Price Level.* New York, McGraw Hill.

Balassa, Bela. 1964. 'The purchasing power parity doctrine: a reappraisal'. *Journal of Political Economy*, 72, 584–96.

Barro, Robert 1981. 'Output effects of government purchases'. *Journal of Political Economy*, 89, 1106–21.

Bhagwati, Jagdish. 1958 'Immiserizing growth: a geometrical note'. *Review of Economics and Statistics*, 25, 201–5.

—— 1984. 'Why are services cheaper in the poor countries'. *Economic Journal*, 94, 279–86.

Caballero, Ricardo and Richard Lyons. 1992. 'External effects in US procyclical productivity'. *Journal of Monetary Economics*, 29, 209–25.

Cairnes, J. E. (1874). *Some Leading Principles of Political Economy Newly Expounded.* New York.

Calvo, Guillermo. 1986. 'Fractured liberalism: Argentina under Martinez de Hoz'. *Economic Development and Cultural Change*, 34, 511–33.

—— Leonardo Leiderman, and Carmen Reinhart. 1993 'Capital inflows and real exchange rate appreciation in Latin America'. *International Monetary Fund Staff Papers*, 40, 108–51.

Clague, Christopher. 1986. 'Determinants of the national price level: some empirical results'. *Review of Economics and Statistics*, 68, 320–3.

—— 1988. 'Purchasing power parities and real exchange rates in Latin America'. *Economic Development and Cultural Change*, 36, 529–41.

—— 1989. 'The national price level: theory and estimation: a comment'. *Journal of Macroeconomics*, 11, 375–81.

Connolly, Michael. 1986. 'The speculative attack on the peso and the real exchange rate: Argentina, 1979–81'. *Journal of International Money and Finance*, 5, 117–30.

—— and Jaime de Melo (eds.) 1993. *Essays on the Effects of Protectionism in a Small Country: The Case of Uruguay.* World Bank Publications, The World Bank, Washington, DC.

—— and John Devereux. 1992. 'Commercial policy, the terms of trade, and real exchange rates'. *Oxford Economic Papers*, 44, 507–12.

Corbo, V. and J. de Melo, 1989. 'External shocks and policy reforms in the southern cone: a re-assessment', in G. Calvo, R. Findlay, P. Kouri, and J. De Macedo (eds.), *Debt Stabilization and Development*, New York, Blackwell.

Corden, W. M. 1984. 'Booming sector and "Dutch disease" economics, survey and consolidation'. *Oxford Economic Papers*, 36, 359–80.

Cottani, Jaoquin, Domingo Cavallo, and Shahbaz Khan. 1990. 'Real exchange rate behavior and economic performance in LDC's'. *Economic Development and Cultural Change*, 40, 61–76.

Devereux, John and Michael Connolly. 1993a. 'Economic reform and the real exchange rate'. *Economica*, 60, 295–309.

——,—— 1993b. 'Economic reform, public sector pricing and the real exchange rate in Peru'. Forthcoming from the North–South Centre University of Miami.

——,—— 'Commercial policy, the external terms of trade and the real exchange rate revisited'. Unpublished, University of Miami.

Djajic, S. 1987. 'Temporary import quota and the current account'. *Journal of International Economics*, 22, 349–62.

Dornbusch, Rudiger. 1989. 'Real exchange rates and macroeconomics: a selective survey'. *Scandanavian Journal of Economics*, 91, 401–32.

Edwards, Sebastian. 1988a. *Exchange Rate Misalignment in Developing Countries*. Baltimore, Johns Hopkins.

—— 1988b. 'Real and monetary determinants of real exchange rate behavior'. *Journal of Development Economics*, 29, 311–41.

—— 1989a. *Real Exchange Rates, Devaluation, and Adjustment: Exchange Rate Policy in Developing Economies*. Cambridge, Mass., the MIT Press.

—— 1989b. 'Economic liberalization and the equilibrium real exchange rate in developing economies'. In G. Calvo *et al.*, *Debt Stabilization and Development*. Oxford, Basil Blackwell.

—— 1991. 'Structural adjustment reforms and the external debt crises in Latin America'. In Patricio Mellor (ed.), *The Latin America Development Debate*. Boulder, Colo., Westview Press.

Hallberg, Kristin and Wendy Takacs. 1992. 'Trade reform in Colombia 1990–1994'. In Alvin Cohen and Frank Gunther (eds.), *The Colombian Economy: Issues of Trade and Development*. Boulder, Colo., Westview Press.

Helpman, Elhanon. 1984. 'Increasing returns, imperfect markets, and trade theory'. In R. Jones and P. Kenen (eds.), *Handbook of International Economics*. Amsterdam, North Holland.

Harrod, Roy F. 1933. *International Economics*. Cambridge Economic Handbooks. London, Nisbet, and Cambridge, Cambridge University Press.

Johnson, Harry. 1958. *International Trade and Economic Growth*. London, Allen and Unwin.

Kravis, Irving and Robert Lipsey. 1983. 'Towards an explanation of national price levels'. Princeton Studies in International Finance, no. 52.

—— ,—— 1988. 'National price levels and the price of tradables and nontradables'. *American Economic Review*, 78, 474–8.

Leamer, Edward. 1987. 'Measures of openness'. Unpublished Working Paper, University of California Los Angeles.

Lim, G. C. and Jerome Stein. 1991. 'The real exchange rate and balance of trade in a small open economy: the case of Australia'. Working paper no. 91–12, Department of Economics, Brown University, Providence, Rhode Island, Mar.

Lopez, Ramon and Arvind Panagariya. 1990. 'Temporary trade taxes, welfare and the current account'. *Economics Letters*, 33, 347–51.

Mendoza, E. G. 1992. 'The terms of trade and economic fluctuations'. Unpublished Paper. International Monetary Fund. Washington, DC.

Neary, J. P. 1985a. 'International factor mobility, minimum wage rates and factor price equalization: a synthesis'. *Quarterly Journal of Economics*, 3, 551–70.

—— 1985b. 'Real and monetary aspects of the Dutch disease'. In D. Hague and K. Jungfeld (eds.), *Structural Adjustment in Open Developed Economies*. London, Macmillan.

—— 1988. 'Determinants of the equilibrium real exchange rate'. *American Economic Review*, 78, 210–15.

—— and Francis Ruane. 1988. 'International capital mobility, shadow prices and the cost of protection'. *International Economic Review*, 29, 571–85.

Officer, Lawrence, 1989. 'The nontraded price level: theory and estimation'. *Journal of Macroeconomics*, 11, 351–73.

Ohlin, Bertil. 1933.. *Interregional and International Trade*, Cambridge, Mass., Harvard University Press.

Ostry, Jonathon D. 1988. 'The balance of trade, terms of trade, and real exchange rate: an intertemporal optimizing framework'. *IMF Staff Papers*, 35, 541–73.

—— 1990. 'Tariffs and the current account; the role of initial distortions'. *Canadian Journal of Economics*, 26, 348–56.

Panagariya, Arvind. 1988. 'A theoretical explanation of some stylized facts of economic growth'. *Quarterly Journal of Economics*, 103, 509–26.

Razin, Asif and Lars Svensson. 1983. 'Trade taxes and the current account'. *Economic Letters*, 13, 55–7.

Rose, Andrew. 1991. 'The role of exchange rates in a popular model of international trade'. *Journal of International Economics*, 30, 301–16.

Rybczynski, Tibor. 1955. 'Factor endowment and relative commodity prices'. *Economica*, 22, 336–41.

Sachs, Jeffrey. 1985. 'External debt and macro-economic performance in Latin America and East Asia'. *Brookings Papers on Economic Activity*, 2, 523–64.

Samuelson, Paul. 1964. 'Theoretical notes on trade problems'. *The Review of Economics and Statistics*, 46, 145–54.

Stein, Jerome. 1991. 'Fundamental determinants of real exchange rates'. Paper presented at the CNRS/HEC-Bundesbank Conference on the Real Exchange Rate, Oct.

Summers, Robert and Alan Heston. 1991. 'The Penn World Tables (Mark 5); an extended set of international comparisons, 1950–1988'. *Quarterly Journal of Economics*, 111, 327–69.

Tanner, Evan. 1992. 'The permanent component of export volumes in highly indebted LDC's'. Unpublished, University of Miami.

Woodland, Allan. 1982. *International Trade and Resource Allocation*. Amsterdam, North Holland.

World Bank. 1983, 1990. *World Tables*. New York, Oxford University Press.

—— 1987, 1991. *World Development Report*. New York, Oxford University Press.

APPENDIX: The Real Exchange Rate and the Current Account

The simplest framework in which we can consider intertemporal issues is a two-period model. To begin, we introduce some new notation. For two periods, it is convenient to work in terms of the intertemporal trade expenditure function $E(.)$ which is given by (5.1a).[20] This function measures the excess of discounted revenue from production over discounted consumer spending. This is given by (5.1a) where $e(.)$ is the intertemporal expenditure function and $g(.)$ is the intertemporal revenue function.

Equilibrium requires that trade balance over both periods and that the non-traded goods market clears. The former condition is given by (5.2a) and the latter is given by (5.3a) and (5.4a) where $E_s(\cdot)$ and $E_s(\cdot)$ are the compensated excess-supply functions for non-traded goods given by the first derivatives of the trade expenditure function, p_s and P_s are non-traded goods price levels, p and P are vectors of traded prices, t and T are vectors of trade taxes in the first and second period. The discount factor δ is equal to $l/(l+r)$ where r is the world and domestic interest rate.

$$E(p, p_s, \delta P, \delta P_S; U) = g(p, p_s, \delta P, \delta P_S) - e(p, p_s, \delta P, \delta P_S; U) \quad (5.1a)$$

$$E(p, p_s, \delta P, \delta P_S; U) - t E_p - \delta T E_p = 0 \quad (5.2a)$$

$$E_s(p, p_s, \delta P, \delta P_S; U) = 0 \quad (5.3a)$$

$$E_S(p, p_s, \delta P, \delta P_S; U) = 0 \quad (5.4a)$$

Totally differentiating, (5.2a) to (5.4a) and solving for the non-traded goods price levels, (5.5a) and (5.6a) are obtained. The $\omega_j{}^i$ parameters measure the elasticity of the non-traded price level in the i'th period with regard to the j'th traded price. Assuming substitutability, these parameters are positive and less than unity. The γ_j coefficients give the elasticity of the non-traded price level with respect to an increase in real income.

$$\hat{p}_s = \omega_j{}^i \hat{p}_j + \gamma_1 \hat{y} \quad (5.5a)$$

$$\hat{p}_S = \omega_j{}^2 \hat{p}_j + \gamma_2 \hat{y} \quad (5.6a)$$

1.1 Commercial Policy, Changes in the External Terms of Trade and the Real Exchange Rate in a Two-Period Model

For convenience, we assume that trade policy is imposed from an initial position of free trade. From (5.5a) and (5.6a) note that a temporary tariff

---

[20] For similar models see Edwards 1989a and Ostry 1988.

raises non-traded prices in both periods while a temporary export tax reduces them. Equation (5.7a) compares the resulting changes in the real exchange rate across periods. Note that a temporary tariff temporarily appreciates the purchasing-power-parity real exchange rate under the weak assumption that a temporary tariff has the larger effect on the first period non-traded price level. In (5.7a), the real exchange rate in the j'th period is denoted R^j.

$$\hat{R}^2 - \hat{R}^1 = [\alpha_s^1 (\omega_i^2 - \omega_i^1) - \alpha_i^1] t_i < 0 \tag{5.7a}$$

The effects of temporary changes in the world prices of import goods on non-traded goods prices are uncertain. But a temporary increase in the world price of an export good increases the non-traded price level. In addition, it can be shown that a temporary export price increase leads to a temporary appreciation of the purchasing-power-parity real exchange rate while a temporary import price rise leads to a temporary real depreciation.

1.2 The Current Account and the Real Exchange Rate

The intertemporal budget constraint implies that trade measured at world prices balances over both periods, that is $B^1 + \delta B^2$ where B^i is the trade balance in the i'th period. It follows from this that the effects of temporary changes in commercial policy or the external terms of trade on the first-period current account can be obtained from the second-period trade balance.

Our goal is to show that if shocks to the current account arise from commercial policy or changes in the external terms of trade, then improvements in the current account are accompanied by real exchange-rate appreciations. To begin, note that by definition the trade balance in the second period is equal to the excess supply of second-period output multiplied by world prices. This is given in (5.8a). Since relative prices of tradables are constant in the second period, we aggregate traded goods into a composite commodity, tradables.

$$B^2 = P^* E_p \tag{5.8a}$$

To determine the relationship between the real exchange rate and commercial policy, let us consider the effects of a temporary tariff imposed from free trade. Solving (5.8a) for the impact of a temporary tariff, we obtain:

$$dB^2 = P^* [E_{Pi} dt_i + E_{Ps} dp_s + E_{PS} \delta dP_S] \tag{5.9a}$$

If substitutability holds in excess supply, all three terms in this expression are negative. Consequently, a temporary tariff worsens the trade balance in the second period and improves the current account in the first period, the Razin–Svennson (1983) result. Combining this with our previous results, we see that: *temporary real exchange rate appreciations in the purchasing-power-parity rate are accompanied by trade surpluses, while temporary real exchange-rate depreciations are accompanied by current account deficits.*[21] It is straightforward to show that this proposition also holds for changes in the external terms of trade.

---

[21] With negative income effects or complementarities, the effects of a temporary tariff on the current account are uncertain. See Djajic 1987, Edwards 1989a, Lopez and Panagariya 1990, and Ostry 1990.

6

The Equilibrium Real Exchange Rate of Germany

JEROME L. STEIN

For very open economies like the Federal Republic of Germany the real exchange rate is an economic variable of major importance. The effects of the exchange rate on an economy are positively related to the degree of openness of that economy, and Germany is an extremely open economy. In 1992 the ratio of exports plus imports to GDP was 46 per cent, compared to 16 per cent in Japan and 17 per cent in the USA.[1] Furthermore, Germany is deeply integrated into the international financial markets. There is complete freedom of capital movements, and, as a reserve currency, the Deutschmark (DM) is second in the world after the US dollar. The strong dependence of the German economy on the international markets for goods and financial assets has induced the economic policymakers in Germany to give a high priority to exchange rate issues.

There is general agreement that exchange rates should reflect economic fundamentals and that excess volatility is undesirable. The main question that we address in this chapter is what the fundamental determinants of the medium-to longer-run movements in the real exchange rate are. We are not concerned with the short-run exchange rate movements, since they are the result of the highly volatile anticipations of monetary policy, and average out to zero with no long-run effects.

This chapter draws upon Stein and Sauernheimer (1997). We relate our analysis to the issues posed by the Deutsche Bundesbank *Monatsbericht* (Deutsche Bundesbank 1993, 1994, 1995). I thank Dr Willy Friedmann, Leiter der Abteilung Aussenwirtschaft of the Deutsche Bundesbank, for his criticism of an earlier draft.

[1] International Monetary Fund, *International Financial Statistics*, March 1994. The country index is GR for Germany and the suffix is the row in the *International Financial Statistics*. Thus DM/$US is GRae.

The equilibrium real value of the German Mark is also important for the viability of the European Monetary System (EMS) with fixed exchange rates. From 1987 to the autumn of 1992, nominal exchange rates in the EMS remained unchanged despite divergent rates of inflation. There were currency crises in the autumn of 1992 and summer of 1993. The resulting capital flights forced the governments to realign their currencies. The new parities agreed upon in September 1992 proved not to be sustainable, and on 16 and 17 September 1992 the British pound and Italian lira left the exchange rate mechanism. On 2 August 1993, after further speculative attacks, especially against the French franc, the EC finance ministers and central bank governors decided to enlarge temporarily the bands for the bilateral exchange rates from ± 2.25 per cent to ± 15 per cent.

Recent developments in foreign exchange markets have drawn renewed attention to the issue of exchange rate misalignments and imbalances in the balance of payments. In Europe, the ERM crisis and subsequent depreciation of some EMS currencies have led to suspicions that some currencies are now misaligned. This has given rise to a number of questions that are important in the context of the EMU. First, how can one evaluate whether or not a currency is misaligned? Second, what are the causes of the misalignment? Third, if there is misalignment, what are the policy options to remedy the situation? Fourth, what difficulties are implied for a successful move to Stage Three of the EMU? The only way that these questions can be answered is to have an empirically implementable, consistent theory that explains what the equilibrium exchange rate is. The NATREX model, developed in the preceding chapters, is the appropriate framework for the analysis.

It is essential to understand what the fundamental determinants of the equilibrium value of the Deutschmark are if we are to understand the conditions whereby the fixed nominal bilateral exchange rates within Europe are viable. The DM is the key currency in Europe. If the real value of the DM appreciates, say relative to the US dollar, then the DM must appreciate relative to the other European currencies. This is the result of arbitrage. Agents would try to avoid the appreciation of the DM relative to the dollar by using dollars to buy European currencies, and then sell the latter for DM. In this way, the DM would appreciate relative to all other currencies, and the US dollar would depreciate relative to the other currencies.

The real appreciation of the DM relative to the other currencies can occur in three ways: (1) the nominal bilateral value of the DM appreciates; (2) German prices and wages rise; (3) European prices and wages decline. Insofar as there are fixed bilateral nominal exchange rates, option (1) is excluded. If the Bundesbank will not permit inflation in Germany (option 2), then the remaining option is for European prices and wages to fall. Insofar as there is wage–price inflexibility downwards, there will be unemployment problems in Europe. Therefore, the bilateral value of a European currency could be misaligned because the real equilibrium value of the DM has changed.

It is often thought that if each European country maintains the same rate of inflation, there will be no problems of misalignment. This view assumes that the equilibrium real bilateral exchange rate is stationary and that nominal exchange rates are misaligned if and only if relative prices diverge. This PPP approach is equation (6.1), where the real exchange rate, $R(t)$, is the nominal exchange rate, $N(t)$ = foreign/domestic currency, times the ratio of domestic to foreign prices, $p(t)/p'(t)$. A rise is an appreciation, or, solving for the domestic price of foreign currency $(1/N)$, it is (6.2).

$$R(t) = N(t)p(t)/p'(t) \qquad (6.1)$$

$$1/N(t) = [1/R(t)][p(t)/p'(t)] \qquad (6.2)$$

$$\text{DM/foreign currency} = [1/R(t)](\text{German/foreign}) \text{ price index} \quad (6.2a)$$

Graphically, equation (6.2) is linear in the nominal price of foreign exchange $(1/N)$ and relative prices. The PPP hypothesis is that the equilibrium real exchange rate is stationary. The points are assumed to converge to a given straight line, with a constant slope. If the monetary authorities succeed in keeping relative prices stationary, then the bilateral equilibrium nominal exchange rate should be stationary.

Figure 6.1 plots the nominal DM per US dollar (as $1/N$ = GRae) against the ratio of German to US CPI indexes, p/p' = GRUSCPI. These variables are not co-integrated, and there is a weak relation between them. There is much more going on concerning the determination of the equilibrium nominal exchange rate than relative prices. Trying to keep the ratio of relative prices constant will not necessarily succeed in maintaining a fixed nominal bilateral exchange rate. There have been considerable variations in the equilibrium real exchange rate of Germany during the period of floating.

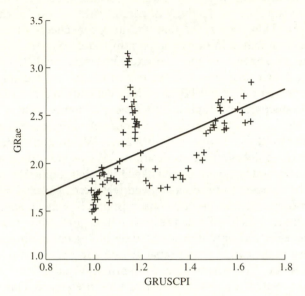

FIG. 6.1   *The DM per US dollar* (GRae) *plotted against the ratio of German to US CPI* (GRUSCPI) *during the floating-rate period*

The *basic questions* that we want to answer are: (1) What are the appropriate measures and determinants of the real exchange rate? (2) Which variables are exogenous to Germany and which are endogenous? (3) What are the longer-term and medium-term systematic determinants of the real exchange rate? (4) How can we sift out the effects of the longer-run fundamentals that affect fluctuations in the real exchange rate from the transitory ones?

We proceed as follows. First, we present the most important stylized facts relevant to our analysis and the issues of great concern to the Deutsche Bundesbank (DBB) as expressed in the *Monatsberichte*. We use these stylized facts in adapting the NATREX model to the German economy, which differs from the US economy. Second, we explain, within the context of our NATREX model, what the fundamental external and domestic determinants of the real exchange rate of Germany are. The fundamentals are time preference, measured as the ratio of social consumption to GDP, and the productivity of capital, theoretically reflected in the Keynes–Tobin *q*-ratio. The main determinants of the latter are the exogenous prices of imported materials, which affect the European terms of trade, the productivity of capital, and the rate of capacity utilization. Third, we show that the long-run effects of the fundamentals estimated in our co-integrating equations are consistent with the movements in the real exchange rate predicted by the model. Our conclusion is that the trends in the real exchange rate are determined by the NATREX, which depends in a dynamic way upon productivity of capital and time preference, which is the inverse of thrift, and the exogenous prices of imported materials.

Our approach is positive, not normative. We do not suggest that the derived equilibrium rate is desirable.[2] We do not advocate that the nominal rate should be managed or that domestic policies should be changed to produce a given real exchange rate. We take the sum of public plus private consumption/GDP as an exogenous fundamental, which we call the social time preference ratio. We show the effects of variation in the time preference ratio upon the trajectory of the equilibrium exchange rate and the evolution of the external debt. The sustainable equilibrium value of the debt is positively related to the social rate of time preference. Our equilibrium debt is sustainable, but unlike Williamson, who has a normative concept in mind, we do not discuss whether the social time preference ratio and resulting steady-state debt are desirable.

1. STYLIZED FACTS

Let us state some stylized facts that we use to adapt the NATREX model to the German economy. These facts show that several popular models are inappropriate for the analysis of the real exchange rate of Germany.

1.1 Measures of the Real Exchange Rate[3]

An important question is what the appropriate measure of the real exchange rate for modelling and policy analysis is. There are several

---

[2] The NATREX differs from the Fundamental Equilibrium Real Exchange Rate (FEER) of Williamson and the Desired Equilibrium Exchange Rate (DEER) of Bayoumi *et al.*, which are normative concepts. See Clark (1997) for an analysis of the relations among these three concepts.

[3] The basic data used here concerning $R(\text{CPI})$, $R(T)$, and $R(NT)$, which are defined below, come from the Deutsche Bundesbank and were used in the 1995 issue of the *Monatsbericht*. The data for $R(w) = \text{GRREU}$ come from the IMF *IFS*.

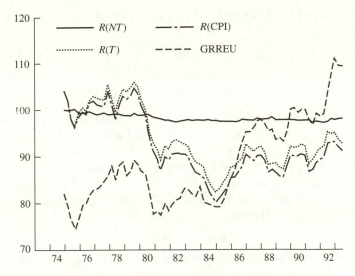

FIG. 6.2   *Alternative measures of the real exchange rate*

Notes: RCPI = the ratio of the German to foreign CPI, trade-weighted, adjusted for the nominal exchange rate; R(T) = the relative prices of traded goods at home and abroad, adjusted for the nominal exchange rate; R(NT) = the internal price ratio = the ratio of the German to foreign prices of non-traded/traded goods; GRREU = the real effective exchange rate = the ratio of German to foreign unit labour costs, trade-weighted and in a common currency.

concepts of the real exchange rate, with different implications for modelling. A broad measure is equation (6.3), the ratio of domestic to foreign CPI (p/p') in a common currency, denoted $R(p)$, where N is the index of the nominal exchange rate: a rise is an appreciation of the domestic currency. The foreign CPIs and the nominal exchange rates, N, are trade-weighted.

$$R(p) = Np/p' \qquad (6.3)$$

The CPI consists of traded goods with price index p_t and non-traded goods p_n for Germany, and p'_t, p'_n for the set of foreign countries. The CPIs are equations (6.3a) for Germany and (6.3b) for the set of foreign countries. When these are substituted into the real exchange rate equation (6.3), we obtain equation (6.4). The first term is the ratio of the prices of traded goods, call it $R(T)$, and the second term is the ratio of the prices of non-traded to traded goods in Germany relative to the same ratio in the set of foreign countries, denoted $R(NT)$. This term is referred to as the internal price ratio. We graph the relevant variables in Figure 6.2, based upon data provided by the Bundes-bank.[4]

$$p = p_t^{1-a} p_n^a \qquad (6.3a)$$

$$p' = p_t'^{1-b} p_n'^b \qquad (6.3b)$$

$$R(p) = (Np_t/p_t')[(p_n/p_t)a/(p_n'/p_t')b] = R(T)R(NT) \qquad (6.4)$$

Two sets of popular models claim that the relative price of traded goods, $R(T)$, is exogenous so that the mechanism of adjustment of the balance of payments is via the relative internal price ratio, $R(NT)$. The first term, $R(T)$, is viewed in different ways.

A 'law of one price' claims that the prices of traded goods are the same at home and abroad. The term $R(T)$ is unity or at least equal to a constant, C. The real exchange rate is:

$$R(p) = C \cdot R(NT). \qquad (6.5a)$$

An alternative view is that the term $R(T)$ represents the terms of trade, TOT, the ratio of German export prices to foreign prices, which are German import prices. This is:

$$R(p) = TOT \cdot R(NT). \qquad (6.5b)$$

The popular Balassa–Samuelson hypothesis claims that there is a faster rate of technical progress in traded goods than in non-traded goods. This is supposed to raise the internal price ratio, $R(NT)$, and appreciate the real exchange rate, $R(p)$. The appreciation will only occur if the internal price ratio rises faster at home than it does abroad.

This approach lacks explanatory power (see Figure 6.2). First, the relative price of traded goods, $R(T)$, is not stationary.[5] Second, the broad-based real exchange rate $R(p)$, denoted RCPI, is practically the same as the ratio of the relative prices of tradable goods, $R(T)$. The non-stationarity of $R(T)$, the relative price of tradable goods, indicates that the tradable goods are very heterogeneous. These facts make us reject equation (6.5a). Third, the internal price ratio, $R(NT)$, has hardly changed from 1975 to 1995. The reason is that, for virtually all industrial countries, the internal price ratio (the ratio of consumer prices of non-traded to traded goods, p_n/p_t) rose by similar proportions. It can be seen from Figure 6.2 that the same relative rate of technical progress occurred in Germany's trading partners and competitors. Hence the Balassa–Samuelson hypothesis

---

[4] See Deutsche Bundesbank (1995, p. 23).
[5] The ADF statistic for $R(T)$ using $(C,1) = -1.85$ is not stationary.

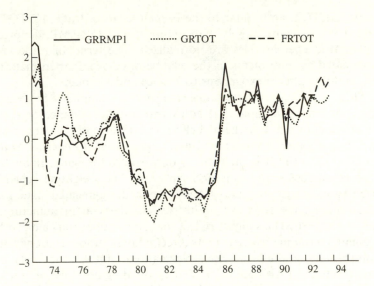

Fig. 6.3   *The German* (GRTOT) *and French* (FRTOT) *terms of trade move closely with the inverse of the relative price of imported materials to all imports* (GRRMP1)

cannot explain the movement in the real exchange rate, $R(p)$. Insofar as the relative internal price ratio, $R(NT)$, has hardly moved, it is not a likely candidate for being the variable that produces balance of payments equilibrium.

The terms of trade are very important. They are co-integrated with the broad-based real exchange rate, $R(p)$ = RCPI, but the correlation between them is very weak: $R^2 = -0.05$. The prices of German tradable goods are, to a large extent, externally determined. The major variations in the European terms of trade have been the result of the variations in the price of imported materials. In that case, we can view the ratio of the German import prices of raw materials to German prices of imports without materials (GRRMP) as the external fundamental.[6] Figure 6.3 shows that the German terms of

[6] In Stein and Sauernheimer (1997), the French terms of trade and the q-ratio were used as the external variable. Sauernheimer and Grassinger (1995), in their continuation of an earlier draft of the former, used GRRMP. Here we take the Sauernheimer and Grassinger measure of the external fundamental. The source for GRRMP = ratio of German imported prices of materials to German imported prices without raw materials is *Statistisches Bundesamt*, Fachserie 17, Reihe 8, taken from Sauernheimer and Grassinger (1995).

trade, GRTOT, are similar to the French terms of trade, FRTOT, and that both move closely with the inverse of GRRMP, denoted GRRMP1. The variables are normalized. The terms of trade are dominated by movements in the relative price of imported materials, and the latter is exogenous to France and Germany.

There is another real exchange rate that is a candidate for being the endogenous variable that adjusts to produce balance of payments equilibrium. It is the real effective exchange rate, as reported in the International Monetary Fund's *International Financial Statistics* (IMF *IFS*).[7] It is the ratio of domestic to foreign normalized unit labour costs in a common currency. The weighting scheme used to construct the rate is based upon disaggregated data for trade among the seventeen industrial countries in manufactured goods for 1980. The weights reflect the relative importance of both a country's trading partners in its direct bilateral trade relations and competition in third markets. Normalized unit labour costs in manufacturing (w, w') are calculated by dividing an index of actual hourly compensation per worker (W, W') by a five-year moving average index of output per manhour (A, A'). The real effective exchange rate, $R(w) = $ GRREU, is equation (6.6). Foreign variables are denoted with a prime. The nominal effective exchange rate is denoted by N, where a rise in N or REU signifies an appreciation.

$$R(w) = \text{GRREU} = N \cdot w/w' = (NW/A)/(W'/A') \qquad (6.6)$$

Figure 6.2 shows the dissimilar movements in the alternative concepts of the real exchange rate during the period from the third quarter of 1975 to the third quarter of 1993, denoted 1975(3)–1993(3). $R(p) = $ RCPI, $R(T)$, and $R(w) = $ GRREU are not stationary, but the internal price ratio, $R(NT)$, is stationary.

1.2 Interest-Rate Relationships

There is a convergence of the German real long-term interest rate, r, to the US real long-term rate, r', where the causality runs from the US to the German rate. We measure the *real* long-term rate of interest as the nominal yield on bonds less the rate of inflation of the CPI over the past four quarters. The *real long-term* rate of

---

[7] The data, which come from the IMF *IFS* March 1994, are denoted by a country prefix GR for Germany and a suffix which is the row in the *IFS*. Thus, the real effective exchange rate for Germany is GRREU, and the nominal effective exchange rate is GRNEU.

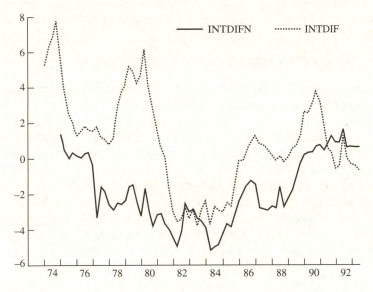

FIG. 6.4 *The real and nominal long-term interest-rate differentials (Germany less USA):* INTDIF *and* INTDIFN

interest differential, $(r - r')$ = INTDIF, plotted in Figure 6.4, is stationary at an expected value of zero[8] during the period. The German real long-term rate of interest has converged to the US real long-term rate of interest during 1974(3)–1993(3). The German real long-term rate of interest is Granger-caused by the US rate, and not the reverse.

The convergence does not occur for nominal long-term interest rates. The German (i) less US (i') nominal long-term bond yields, $(i - i')$ = INTDIFN = GR61 – US61, and the real differential, INTDIF, are plotted in Figure 6.4. The *nominal* interest-rate differential is not stationary over the entire period, though it has converged recently.

Finally, the theory of uncovered interest-rate parity with rational expectations claims that the rational expectation of the appreciation of the German Mark from one short period to the next is equal to the appropriate forward premium, which is equal to the appropriate foreign less German interest-rate differential, at the initial period.

---

[8] From 1974(3) to 1993(3), the INTDIF was stationary. ADF(N,1) = -2.6, which is highly significant (MacKinnon 5% = -1.9). No constant (N) was used because the constant was not significant.

This hypothesis is inconsistent with the evidence for Germany, as shown in Figure 2.2 in Chapter 2 for the one-month interest rate.

2.   THE NATREX MODEL APPLIED TO GERMANY

In this section, the NATREX model developed in Chapters 2 and 3 above is adjusted to make it applicable to Germany. Three major changes are made: (1) the appropriate real exchange rate is the real effective exchange rate; (2) little use is made of the dichotomy between traded and non-traded goods; and (3) the dynamic system is of the first order, rather than the second order, because the growth rate of Germany is stationary. With a first-order system, we are able to use a very simple diagram to show explicitly the difference between the medium-and long-run effects of changes in basic variables, such as time preference. This diagram highlights the difference between the NATREX and the conventional wisdom.

2.1   The Medium- and Longer-Run NATREX

The NATREX is the real exchange rate that is associated with both internal and external balance. The *medium-run* NATREX is the real exchange that satisfies the following four conditions. Internal balance means that: (1) the rate of capacity utilization is at its stationary mean; and (2) investment less saving plus the current account sum to zero, subject to condition (1) above. External balance differs according to the time-period considered. Conditions (3) and (4) refer to external balance: (3) changes in reserves and speculative capital flows are zero, so that the exchange rate is sustainable; and (4) there is portfolio balance, so that investors are willingly holding the stocks of net foreign assets. Thus the change in the stock of net foreign assets is willingly held in portfolios. We have seen that real long-term interest rates have converged. This means that there is no risk premium between German and US assets. Moreover, the asymptotically rational expected appreciation or depreciation of the real value of the DM is zero. The reason for this follows the logic developed in Chapter 2. Investors use all available information. The longer-run real exchange rate, $R^*(t)$, inherits its properties from the fundamentals: $R^*(t) = BZ(t)$. It follows that the rationally expected change in the real exchange rate, over the longer run, is based upon the expected change in the linear combination of the fundamentals. Agents know that the real effective exchange rate is of order $I(1)$, as are the fundamentals $Z(t)$ discussed below. Hence, the asymptotically rational expected change in the real exchange rate over the longer run is zero. Portfolio equilibrium leads to real interest-rate convergence. No widening of the real long-term interest-rate differential is required to absorb additions of net foreign assets.

The *longer-run* NATREX requires an additional condition: (5) the foreign debt intensity must stabilize. In a non-growing economy, the current account will be equal to zero. In a growing economy, current account/debt will converge to the long-run growth rate. Condition (5) is an intertemporal budget constraint. It means that the debt is sustainable insofar as the trade balance, B, is sufficient to pay the interest on the constant debt rF^*.

The determination of the exchange rate is described by equation (6.7). The real exchange rate, R, adjusts the current account to the *ex ante* difference between saving and investment, subject to conditions (1), (3), and (4) above.

$$S(k, F; Z) - I(q) = CA(R, F, k; Z) = B - rF \qquad (6.7)$$

We use the same saving and investment functions described in Chapter 3, with the difference that the German real long-term rate of interest converges to the exogenous US real long-term rate. The presentation here is simpler than the one in Chapter 3. Investment theoretically depends upon the q-ratio. Saving, $S(k,F;Z)$, depends positively upon wealth per unit of effective labour: the capital intensity, k, less foreign debt intensity, F, and exogenous factors, Z. The current account, $CA = CA(R,F,k;Z)$ is the trade balance, $B(R,F,k;Z)$, less net interest payments to foreigners, rF, and exogenous factors, Z. The appropriate real exchange rate in the current account is understood by considering the profit function discussed in the next section. The mechanism of adjustment, and the appropriate definition of the exchange rate, depend crucially upon the nature of the current account function, which we discuss in Section 2.3.

2.2 The Profit Function

We use the profit function[9] to obtain an equation for both the trade balance and the investment function. The profit function is the

---

[9] See Varian (1978), ch. 1 for a discussion of cost and profit functions.

maximum profit that a firm can earn given the price p of output and vector (w,v) of input prices, where w is the labour cost and v the price of materials. Consider the sectors producing tradable goods. The profit function is non-decreasing in output prices, non-increasing in input prices, homogeneous of degree one in (p,w,v), and convex in these prices. This is equation (6.8), where Π represents profits. Optimal output, y, is the partial derivative of profits with respect to output price, equation (6.8a); and optimal input is the negative of the partial derivative of the profit function with respect to the input price.

$$\Pi = \Pi(p,\ w,\ v) \qquad (6.8)$$
$$y = \delta\Pi/\delta p \qquad (6.8a)$$

Let us consider the tradable goods sector. Equations (6.8b) are based upon the law of one price for the same good that is traded internationally.[10] The output price is p, and the price of materials is v, which are equal to the respective world prices (equation 6.8b). The unit labour cost is w. The price of imported materials, v, is equal to the world price (equation 6.8b). The nominal effective exchange rate is N. The real effective exchange rate[11] is $R(w) = Nw/w'$, relative unit labour costs in a common currency. Define v^* as the ratio of the world price of materials to foreign unit labour costs (equation 6.8c). Let the ratio of foreign wages to price, w'/p', equal a, which is constant.

$$p' = Np;\ w' = ap';\ v' = Nv \qquad (6.8b)$$
$$v^* = Nv/w' = v'/w' \qquad (6.8c)$$

The homogeneity property of the profit function, and the equations above, imply equation (6.8d), where we use foreign labour costs as the scalar.[12]

$$\Pi(p,\ w,\ v) = (w'/N)\Pi(pN/w',\ Nw/w',\ Nv/w') = (ap)\Pi[1/a,\ R(w),\ v^*] \quad (6.8d)$$

Profits, Π, depend upon the endogenous real effective exchange rate in terms of unit labour cost, $R = R(w) = wN/w'$, the exogenous relative price of materials, v^*, and the domestic price.

---

[10] The ratio $R(T)$ in Section 1.1 above was an index, which we saw consists of heterogeneous goods.

[11] $R = Nw/w'$ is the IMF measure, which we denote as GRREU in the empirical work.

[12] This follows from $\Pi(p,w,v) = (w'/N)\Pi(pN/w',Nw/w',Nv/w') = (w'/N)\Pi(pN/w', R(w),v^*) = (ap'/N)\Pi(p'/w',R(w),v^*) = (ap)\Pi(p'/w',R(w),v^*).$

2.3   The Current Account Function

The trade balance is the net output of tradable goods. Output, y, is the partial derivative of the profit function with respect to the output price. Hence optimal output of tradables is:

$$y = a\Pi[1/a, R(w), v^*] \qquad (6.9)$$

The optimal output of tradable goods, y, depends upon the profit function (equation 6.8d). This approach takes explicit account of all of the input costs, including labour and materials.[13]

Therefore, write the trade balance, B, as equation (6.10), a function of the output of tradable goods, y, given by (6.9), and German demand factors, which determine consumption and investment. The latter are related to the German GNP = $Y(k;u) - rF$, where $Y(k;u)$ is GDP and rF is interest payments to foreigners if positive, and income received if negative.

$$B = B[R(w), v^*, Y(k; u) - rF; Z] \qquad \delta B/\delta R < 0, \ \delta B/\delta v^* < 0 \quad (6.10)$$

The current account, CA, is the trade balance, B, less net investment income earned by foreigners, rF. The current account function[14] is equation (6.11). The real effective exchange rate, $R(w)$, is not a sufficient statistic by which one can measure the competitiveness of the economy. It must be considered in conjunction with the other variables in the trade balance equation.[15]

$$CA = B - rF = CA(R, v^*, k, F; Z) \qquad (6.11)$$

The endogenous variable is the real effective exchange rate, $R = R(w)$; the exogenous variables, Z, are the external prices of imported materials, which strongly affect the exogenous terms of trade, and the US real long-term rate of interest.

---

[13] The Bundesbank *Monatsbericht* articles seek a real exchange rate that also takes into consideration the prices of imported materials and other non-labour costs. That is why they prefer broad-base indexes such as $R(p)$ to the real effective exchange rate, $R(w)$. The use of the profit function shows that we do take into account the imported price of material, which is contained in exogenous vector Z, but that the endogenous variable for balance of payments adjustment is $R(w)$.

[14] The average rate of return is profits, $\Pi(p,w,v)$, divided by the value of capital, p_k. In the long run, the average rate of return in the tradable goods sector should be equal to its cost of capital, say r. Therefore, define competitiveness as the difference between the average return and the cost of capital: $\Pi(p,w,v)/p_k - r$.

[15] This is my response to the Bundesbank articles on the appropriate measure of competitiveness.

2.4   The Investment Function

Investment is a function of the Keynes–Tobin q-ratio, as described in Chapter 3. The q-ratio is the expected present value of quasi-rents divided by the supply price of the investment good, denoted by p_k. The quasi-rents are the profits of the firm. Therefore, we may write the q-ratio as:

$$q(t) = \int_t^\infty (p/p_k)\Pi[R(w), v^*]\exp(-rs)\,ds = q(R, k; Z). \qquad (6.12)$$

The q-ratio is positively related to the output price relative to the supply price of the capital good, and negatively related to the real effective exchange rate and relative price of materials. The output price/price of the capital good is positively related to the terms of trade. Hence, we write the q-ratio as the last term in equation (6.12).

The rate of investment, $I = dk/dt$, is positively related to the q-ratio, as explained in Chapters 2 and 3. Therefore, we write the investment function as:

$$dk/dt = I(q) = J(R, k; Z) \qquad (6.13)$$

where the exogenous variables, Z, are the terms of trade or the relative price of materials, the US real long-term interest rate, and the level of technology.

2.5   The Exchange Rate Adjustment Mechanism

Until German reunification, the major disturbances were shifts in time preference owing to changes in government policy and variations in the exogenous relative price of imported materials. The dynamic system is similar to that used in Chapters 2 and 3. The exposition here will be simpler, insofar as we shall focus solely upon the endogenous real exchange rate and foreign debt and ignore the endogenous variation in the capital intensity. The reason is that the growth rate is stationary, and its variations are the result of variations in the rate of capacity utilization. Thus our dynamic system is only of the first order.

The medium-run NATREX equates the sum of planned investment less saving plus the current account to zero, conditional upon the factors mentioned in Section 2.1 above. This is equation (6.14). The change in the foreign debt, dF/dt, is investment less saving, equation (6.15). Vector Z of the fundamentals includes German time preference, the relative price of imported materials, the real long-term US interest rate, and the productivity of capital.

$$J(R, k; Z) - S(k, F; Z) + CA(R, k, F; Z) = 0 \qquad (6.14)$$

$$dF/dt = J(R, k; Z) - S(k, F; Z) = L(R, k, F; Z) \qquad (6.15)$$

Equations (6.14) and (6.15) are described in Figures 6.5 and 6.6. The vertical axis plots the real exchange rate, R. The horizontal axis plots saving less investment, $S - I$, and the current account, CA. Saving less investment is denoted by curve SI. An appreciation raises saving less investment. The SI curve shifts with changes in the debt, capital, and exogenous vector Z in the manner described below. The current account is negatively related to the real exchange rate via the profit function for tradables discussed above. An appreciation of the real exchange rate is an appreciation of the nominal exchange rate, N, or a rise in domestic/foreign unit labour costs, w/w'. Given the externally determined output price and relative price of imported materials, profits in the tradable sectors are reduced, which decreases the trade balance and current account.

The parameters of the current account function are endogenous debt, F, and capital, exogenous terms of trade or relative price of imported materials, and the world real long-term rate of interest. The disturbances to consumption, the current account, and the investment function will also affect the current account function.

The real exchange rate, the NATREX, adjusts the current account to *ex ante* saving less investment, where each decision is made independently by different agents. The equilibrium exchange rate, R, is where the curve SI intersects the negatively sloped current account curve CA. The NATREX is equation (6.16), derived from equation (6.14). Output is evaluated at capacity. When there is portfolio balance, the real long-term rate is equal to the world rate.

$$R = R(k, F; Z). \qquad (6.16)$$

The evolution of the foreign debt dF/dt is given by equation (6.15). The dynamic system converges to a steady state conditional upon the fundamentals. The system will be dynamically stable if a rise in the debt raises saving $S_F > 0$, and hence $L_F < 0$, in equation (6.15).

The longer-run solution[16] implies that the foreign debt must converge to a constant, so the current account—equal to saving less investment—must be zero in a non-growing economy.

---

[16] Table 3.2 in Ch. 3 describes the longer-run solution and comparative steady states in a small open economy. The analysis in this chapter is similar.

First, we examine the dynamics of the real exchange rate and foreign debt when there is a change in time preference (Figure 6.5). Second, we do the same for changes in the relative price of imported materials—the exogenous terms of trade (Figure 6.6). Time preference (MAGRQCON) and the relative price of imported materials (GRRMP), graphed in Figure 6.7, explain quite well the movement of the real exchange rate in the pre-unification period.

The graphs used in Figures 6.5 and 6.6 are simple and powerful ways of seeing how the dynamics of the real exchange rate produce different effects in the long run from those in the medium run, which is the contribution of the NATREX model.

2.6   Changes in Social Time Preference

In Figure 6.5, the saving less investment curve is initially $SI(0)$, and the current account curve is $CA(0)$. The initial equilibrium real exchange rate is $R(0)$. Let saving less investment decrease as a result of a rise in social time preference: the ratio of public plus private consumption to GDP rises. The SI curve shifts from $SI(0)$ to $SI(1)$. Fraction $0A''/0A'$ of the increase in social consumption is directed to foreign goods, and the CA function shifts from $CA(0)$ to $CA(1)$.

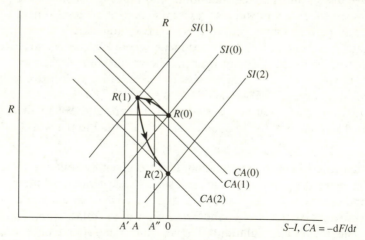

Fig. 6.5   *A rise in social time preference (social consumption/GDP) initially appreciates the real exchange rate from $R(0)$ to $R(1)$ and produces a current account deficit of $0A$. The long-run effect is a depreciation of the real exchange rate to $R(2)$*

At the initial real exchange rate $R(0)$, saving less investment, $0A'$, is less than the current account $0A''$. There is an excess demand for goods, or the *ex ante* capital outflow equal to $0A'$ is less than the current account $0A''$. Either the nominal exchange rate appreciates or domestic unit labour costs rise relative to foreign unit labour costs. Either way, the real effective exchange rate in terms of unit labour costs appreciates. The appreciation of the real effective exchange rate reduces profits and the optimal output in the tradables sector. The trade balance declines. The decline in the current account to $0A$ produced by the appreciation to $R(1)$ is the adjustment to the decline in saving less investment. This is the medium-run effect.

The current account deficits increase the foreign debt: dF/dt initially rises by $0A$. The rise in the foreign debt has two effects. First, it decreases the subsequent current account because of an increase in interest payments abroad. The CA curve shifts down towards $CA(2)$. Second, the rise in the debt lowers wealth, which raises social saving. Either households feel poorer and increase their saving or the government is troubled by the rise in the foreign debt and reduces its high-employment deficit. This stability condition shifts the SI curve to the right.

The decline in the current account to $CA(2)$ and rise in saving less investment to $SI(2)$ depreciate the real exchange rate to $R(2)$, below the initial rate $R(0)$. The NATREX model shows how the results of the 'conventional wisdom model', whereby a rise in social consumption produces an appreciation from $R(0)$ to $R(1)$, are reversed in the longer run. Graphically, the steady-state current account curve declines to $CA(2)$, below the initial level $CA(0)$, and saving less investment shifts to $SI(2)$. The trajectory of the real exchange rate is $R(0)$–$R(1)$–$R(2)$. Table 3.2 in Chapter 3 describes the longer-run effect. A decline in thrift—a rise in time preference—raises the debt and depreciates the real exchange rate.

2.7   The Exogenous Relative Price of Imported Materials

The external forces affecting the current account function are the exogenous prices for German imports and exports. The major variations in the European terms of trade have been the result of variations in the price of imported materials. Thus, we can view the ratio, v^*, of German import prices of raw materials to German prices of imports without materials, denoted GRRMP, as the

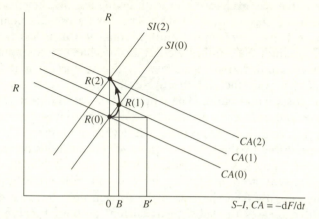

FIG. 6.6 *An improvement in the terms of trade initially shifts the current account curve from CA(0) to CA(1). The medium-run effect is an appreciation from R(0) to R(1) and a current account of 0B. In the longer run, the decline in the debt shifts the CA curve to CA(2) and the SI curve to SI(2). The long-run effect is an appreciation to* R(2)

external fundamental in the figures. Figure 6.3 shows that the German terms of trade, GRTOT, move closely with the inverse of GRRMP, denoted GRRMP1, when the variables are normalized.

Figure 6.6 describes the effects of a decline in the relative price of imported materials or a rise in the European terms of trade. Initially, let saving less investment be curve *SI*(0) and the current account curve be *CA*(0). The NATREX is *R*(0). Let there be an improvement in the external terms of trade, resulting for example from a decline in the price of imported materials. The current account, at exchange rate *R*(0), shifts to the right to *CA*(1) as the prices of imported materials decline.

Both saving and investment will be affected. Saving is GDP less transfer income to foreigners less consumption. Output, *y*, is negatively related to the price of imported materials, as shown in equation (6.9), derived from the profit function. A decline in the relative price of materials increases the quantity of materials used per unit of capital. Since the input of materials increases, output/ labour rises. Since GDP per worker rises, so does saving.

The decline in the relative price of imported materials will also increase the *q*-ratio. The rent per unit of capital rises because the quantity of materials/capital has increased. The rate of investment will rise for the reasons discussed in connection with equation (6.12). Assume that saving and investment rise by equal amounts so that the *SI* curve remains at *SI*(0).

The net effect of the improvement in the exogenous terms of trade is that, at the original exchange rate $R(0)$, the current account exceeds saving less investment by $0B'$. The real exchange rate appreciates to $R(1)$. At the appreciated exchange rate, there is an improvement in the current account—equal to saving less investment—to $0B$. This is the medium-run effect.[17]

The current account $0B$ means that the foreign debt is declining: $dF/dt = -CA = -0B$. The foreign debt declines, reduces the interest payments, and further increases the current account, thereby shifting the current account curve even more to the right towards $CA(2)$. Similarly, the decline in the foreign debt raises wealth and consumption and decreases saving. The *SI* curve therefore shifts to $SI(2)$. The net longer-run effect[18] is that the debt declines and the real exchange rate appreciates further to $R(2)$. The trajectory of the real exchange rate is $R(0)$–$R(1)$–$R(2)$.

3. DATA[19]

The econometric results are consistent with the theoretical model developed above. First, we discuss the data. We use quarterly data that correspond as closely as possible to the variables in the theoretical analysis. The source, measurement, and history of the evolution of the exogenous variables in vector Z is the subject of this section. All of the series we use are plotted in Figure 6.7, covering the sample period 1975(2)–1993(3). We use the same econometric methodology as we did in Chapters 2 and 3 above.

3.1 The Real Exchange Rate

The equilibrium real exchange rate in the model is the relative price that equates the current account to saving less investment generated

[17] Until unification, there were positive relations among the German terms of trade, current account/GNP, and the real effective exchange rate. This is consistent with the analysis in Figure 6.6.

[18] See Table 3.2 in Ch. 3.

[19] The basic data are graphed in Figure 6.7. Appendix Table 6A.1 describes the order of integration of basic variables.

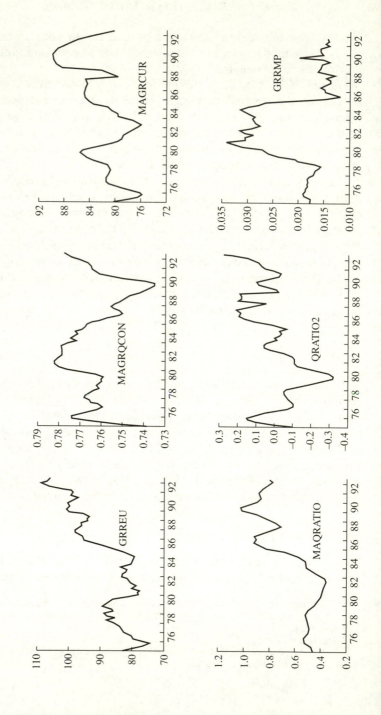

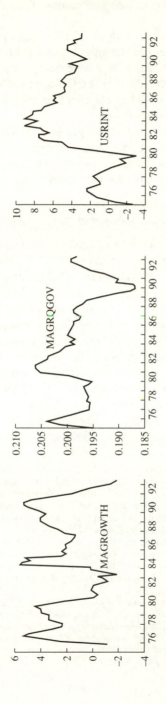

Fig. 6.7 Basic data

Notes: GRREU = real effective exchange rate in terms of unit labor cost; MAGRQCON = four-quarter moving average of social consumption/GNP for West Germany prior to, and all of Germany after, unification; MAGRQGOV = four-quarter moving average of government consumption/GNP for West Germany prior to, and all of Germany after, unification; MAQRATIO = four-quarter moving average of the q-ratio; QRATIO2 = cyclically adjusted q-ratio; GRRMP = ratio of German prices of imported materials to all import prices; MAGRCUR = four-quarter moving average of the rate of capacity utilization; MAGROWTH = four-quarter moving average of the growth rate of GDP by the fundamentals, when output is at capacity and there is portfolio balance. Since the terms of trade are exogenous to Germany, we use as the real effective exchange rate[20] the ratio of nominal unit labour costs adjusted for the nominal exchange rate, $R(w) = Nw/w' = $ GRREU. The real effective exchange rate is not stationary, the ADF equals -0.848.

The exogenous variables are time preference measured by the ratio of social consumption to GNP, the productivity of capital measured by the Keynes–Tobin q-ratio, and the exogenous relative price of imported materials or the European terms of trade.

3.2 The Measurement and Evolution of Time Preference

Time preference in the model is social time preference, which is public plus private consumption as a fraction of GNP. Social consumption/GNP and government consumption/GNP move together.

Our data refer to West Germany prior to unification and to all of Germany after unification.[21] Our measure of social time preference is a four-quarter moving average of social consumption/GNP for West Germany prior to unification and for all of Germany post unification. It is a moving average of the sum of *private plus government* consumption divided by GNP. The series, referred to as MAGRQCON, is stationary with an ADF of -2.99.

The history of the time preference variables reflects the German political situation. From 1969 to 1982 the Social Democratic party was in power, led from 1974 by Schmidt. After a period of

---

[20] Chapter 4 stressed the importance of both time preference and productivity in determining the franc/DM real exchange rate. That rate was based upon French and German GDP deflators, $R = R(p) = Np/p'$. Here we use the real effective exchange rate, $R = R(w) = Nw/w'$, based upon unit labour costs. Since unit labour costs are highly correlated with productivity, we cannot use productivity as an explanatory variable in our regressions. Instead, we have used the q-ratio. As a check, Appendix Table 6A.2 uses the real exchange rate based upon the CPI index, $R(p)$, as the dependent variable and as regressors the relative price of imported materials (GRRMP), social time preference (MAGRQCON), plus the rate of capacity utilzation (MAGRCUR) and a unification dummy. The results are qualitatively similar to those reported in the regressions above.

[21] The source of the underlying data is *Volkswirtschaftliche Gesamtrechnungen des Statistischen Bundesamtes*, Fachserie 18, Sonderdruck 8; Faschserie 18, Reihe 3, Ausgabe 1/87, 1/89, 1/91, 2/92; and *Vierteljahresergebnisse der Inlandsproduktberechnung* (March 1995). We thank Robert Grassinger for supplying us with these data. The national income accounts in the IMF *IFS* refer solely to West Germany. This measure is not stationary.

expansionary fiscal policies in the first half of the 1970s, during the period 1977–9 the Schmidt government tried to stabilize the share of government consumption/GDP. Define government time preference as the sum of West and East German *government* nominal consumption divided by the sum of West and East German nominal GNP. The derived series is called GRQGOV, where the Q refers to all of Germany post unification. The four-quarter moving average, to correct for seasonality, is MAGRQGOV. This is stationary with an ADF of – 3.12.

Government debt, which grew rapidly in the mid-1970s, could not be reduced by that strategy, but its growth could be slowed down. At the Bonn summit in mid-1978, however, Schmidt agreed that Germany should be a locomotive for growth. He put into force government expenditure programmes, and government consumption/GNP began to rise again in the period 1980–2. The time preference graphs of MAGRQGOV and MAGRQCON in Figure 6.7 show this clearly.

Social time preference, MAGRQCON, shows a rapid rise until 1982 for an additional reason. After Brandt's election, his government promised not to accept any unemployment. This promise made it impossible for trade union leaders to oppose wage demands from the rank and file. As a result, there were large wage increases in 1973–5, especially in the public sector,[22] which raised social time preference.

From 1982 to 1990 government time preference, MAGRQGOV, declined drastically. This decline coincided with the switch from a Social Democratic government to a Conservative government led by Kohl. It was part of Kohl's government programme to slow down public deficits.[23] This reduced government time preference, MAGRQGOV. In addition, wage pressures remained weak, possibly as a result of the severe 1981–2 depression and the substitution of Kohl for Schmidt. During the Kohl period prior to unification, 1982–90, we see a decline in both measures of time preference, government MAGRQGOV and social MAGRQCON.[24]

---

[22] In 1974, one year after the oil-price increase, wage increases of 12% were negotiated.

[23] This is consistent with the feedback control parameter $\delta S/\delta F > 0$ in our saving equation. See also Boltho (1994).

[24] We shall discuss the post-unification period later.

3.3   The Keynes–Tobin q-ratio

Theoretically, the driving force behind capital formation is the Keynes–Tobin q-ratio, equation (6.12). It is the capitalized value of the quasi-rents derived from an investment divided by the reproduction cost of the investment. The quasi-rents depend upon the value of the marginal product of capital, which has several components. It is negatively related to the ratio of capital to the complementary inputs, such as imported materials, labour, and infrastructure. It is positively related to the ratio of the price of output to the supply price of the investment good.

Empirically, it is the ratio of the capital value of an asset to its reproduction cost. We calculate it as the ratio of industrial share prices (GR62) to the prices of industrial products (GR63), using the IMF *IFS* data. This variable is seasonal so we use a four-quarter moving average, denoted MAQRATIO. This variable is not stationary: ADF = -1.14. The implication, supported by Table 6.1, is that the q-ratio is positively related to the rate of capacity utilization and negatively related to the price of imported materials. Alternatively, the q-ratio is positively related to the terms of trade and rate of capacity utilization.

3.4   External Forces

There are two main movements in the German terms of trade series (see Figure 6.3). The price of imported materials is the factor producing the large swings in the terms of trade. The German terms of trade index declined from 1978–80 as a result of the second oil shock. This conformed to the decline in GRRMP1, the inverse of the ratio of prices of imported materials to prices of other imports. The German terms of trade rose from 1984 to 1986 because GRRMP1 rose, the dollar prices of imported materials declined, and the value of the dollar also declined relative to the Mark.

3.5   Cross-Correlations

The cross-correlations among the variables are very important in our attempt to separate the exogenous from the endogenous variables and to have a better idea of what to include in our vector of exogenous variables, Z. These cross-correlations are described in Table 6.1. The suffixes of the mnemonics are in the first column.

TABLE 6.1   *Cross-correlations among exogenous variables*

	Social time preference	Govern-ment time preference	q-ratio	Capacity utilization	TOT trade	GRRMP
QCON	1	0.82	− 0.71	− 0.62	− 0.72	0.72
QGOV		1	− 0.68	− 0.73	− 0.58	0.64
QRAT			1	0.78	0.69	− 0.71
CUR				1	0.42	− 0.48
TOT					1	− 0.96
GRRMP						1

The moving average (MA) and German (GR) prefixes are implicit. There are several points that we must emphasize from these cross-correlations. First, there is no Ricardian equivalence insofar as government and social time preference are positively correlated ($r = 0.82$). Second, the German terms of trade are very strongly negatively correlated ($r = - 0.96$) with the relative price of imported materials. Third, the q-ratio is negatively correlated with the relative price of imported materials ($r = - 0.71$) and positively correlated with the rate of capacity utilization ($r = 0.78$). Fourth, German growth is stationary (shown in Table 6A.1 at the end of this chapter) and is not related to any of the other variables in Table 6.1. Fifth, the rate of social time preference and the relative price of imported materials are positively correlated ($r = 0.72$).

4. ECONOMETRIC METHODOLOGY AND RESULTS

4.1 Methodology[25]

The NATREX is the real exchange rate that equates *ex ante* saving less investment to the current account, subject to medium-run conditions (1)–(4) and longer-run conditions (1)–(5) in Section 2.1 above. The vector Z contains the exogenous variables that affect the saving, investment, and current account functions.

Econometric equation (6.17) corresponds to the dynamic system in equations (6.15) and (6.16), which was described by the analysis in Figures 6.5 and 6.6. Equation (6.17) can be written as (6.18).

---

[25] This is the same analysis used in Chs. 2–4 above.

$$R(t) = a_1 + a_2 R(t-1) + b_1 Z(t) + b_2 Z(t-1) + e'(t) \qquad (6.17)$$
$$R(t) = BZ(t) + b[R(t-1) - BZ(t-1)] + cZ'(t) + e(t) \qquad (6.18)$$

The longer-run effect is described by term $BZ(t)$. In the longer run, the foreign debt stabilizes at a constant level and the trade balance is sufficient to pay the interest on the debt. This is our intertemporal budget constraint. The medium-run adjustment adds the error-correction term $b[R(t-1) - BZ(t-1)]$ to the longer-run effect.

In terms of Figures 6.5 and 6.6, the medium-run effect of a change in the fundamentals $Z(t)$ implies that the real exchange rate moves from $R(0)$ to $R(1)$. At $R(1)$ conditions for internal and external balance (1)–(4) in Section 2.1 above are satisfied. The longer-run effect is the movement from $R(0)$ to $R(2)$. At $R(2)$ all of the conditions (1)–(5) for external–internal balance cited in Section 2.1 are satisfied. The dynamic adjustment is in the error-correction term.

The estimation of the longer-run effects is by non-linear least squares, so that vector B is constrained to be the same in the long-run and error-correction terms.[26] The analysis contains several steps. (1) Perform the NLS estimation of equation (6.18). (2) Examine the residual, error $e(t)$, to see whether it passes the usual diagnostics. Is it serially correlated? Is there heteroskedasticity? (3) Are the residuals normal? If the residuals pass the usual test, then we may have confidence in the t-statistics. (4) Then examine the errors $R(t) - B^*Z(t)$, where B^* represents the estimates from the NLS regression. Are these errors stationary? We report the results below.

The NATREX model claims that: (1) A rise in time preference (Figure 6.5) appreciates the medium-run NATREX from $R(0)$ to $R(1)$, as in the conventional wisdom, but depreciates the long-run value from $R(0)$ to $R(2)$; (2) a rise in the exogenous terms of trade, or a decline in the exogenous relative price of imported materials, (Figure 6.6) appreciates the medium-run NATREX from $R(0)$ to $R(1)$ and the longer-run NATREX to $R(2)$.

4.2　Results

The dependent variable is the real effective exchange rate, $R = R(w) = $ GRREU. (1) Exogenous time preference, a 'tastes'

[26] The Engle–Granger two-step method of first regressing R upon Z does not provide us with efficient estimates. As can be seen from equation (6.18), the residual of such a regression would contain the lagged adjustment term $[R(t-1) - BZ(t-1)]$. Hence the errors of a regression of R on Z would be serially correlated. See Lim (1997) for an excellent analysis of how to estimate dynamic economic models.

variable, is measured as either social consumption/GNP or government consumption/GNP. (2) The exogenous external variable, which affects the current account, is measured as either the relative price of imported materials (GRRMP) or the terms of trade (GRTOT). The external variable also affects the investment function through the q-ratio, measured as a four-quarter moving average (MAQRATIO). (3) Theoretically, the q-ratio is related to the marginal physical product of capital, the external terms of trade or relative price of imported materials, and the world real rate of interest. (4) We know from the cross-correlations in Table 6.1 that the q-ratio is positively related to the rate of capacity utilization (MAGRCUR) and the external terms of trade. In view of these interrelations, and the possible arbitrariness of the measurements, several regressions are presented below. (5) The pre-unification and post-unification periods are sometimes distinguished by a dummy variable (DUM), which is 0 for pre- and 1 for post-unification. The variables are graphed in Figure 6.7.

A summary of four regressions is presented in Table 6.2. The results are similar and consistent. Columns (2)–(4) are from both Stein and Sauernheimer (1997) and our unreported regressions. Table 6.3 is an explicit presentation of the regression that we shall be using.

TABLE 6.2   *Summary of effects of the fundamental determinants of the German real effective exchange rate*

Variable	Regression			
	(1)[a]	(2)	(3)	(4)
MAGRQCON	– **	– **	– **	
MAGRQGOV				– **
GRRMP		– **		
GRTOT			+ **	
MAQRATIO	+ **			+ **
Error correction	0.88	0.98	0.98	0.90
MAGRCUR	ns	ns	ns	ns
DUM	+ **			+ **
Adj. R-squared	0.97	0.96	0.96	0.96

[a] See Table 6.3
** = significant at 5% level
ns = not significant
Note: the error correction is coefficient b in equation (6.18).

(1) Both measures of time preference (MAGRQCON and MAGRQGOV) depreciate the real exchange rate in the longer run. This is precisely the situation described theoretically in Figure 6.5. (2) The q-ratio appreciates the real exchange rate in the longer run. (3) The relative price of imported materials depreciates, and the German terms of trade appreciate, the real exchange rate in the longer run. Point (3) is what was described theoretically in Figure 6.6. (4) The capacity utilization rate does not seem to be significant. This may simply be the result of the correlation with the q-ratio. (5) The unification dummy is significant. Moreover, in the regressions, there is indeed a significant structural break-point at the time of the German unification. (6) The conclusion is that the real exchange rate is not an arbitrary stochastic process but responds in a systematic way, as explained by the NATREX, to the explicit neo-classical fundamentals of time preference and externally determined variables.

The diagnostics are reported in Table 6.3. The error $e(t)$ from the entire equation (6.18) is not serially correlated, there is no

TABLE 6.3   *Non-linear least squares estimation of the real effective exchange rate, GRREU*[a]

	Coefficient	Std. error	t-statistic	Prob.
$C(1)$	352.8552	66.11372	5.337094	0.0000
$C(2)$	11.72452	6.251636	1.875432	0.0650
$C(3)$	− 334.3230	74.58878	− 4.482216	0.0000
$C(4)$	− 0.210713	0.192762	− 1.093124	0.2782
$C(5)$	0.888088	0.049096	18.08899	0.0000
$C(6)$	0.273025	0.939003	3.485638	0.0009

R-squared	0.967011	Mean dependent var	88.76473
Adjusted R-squared	0.964586	S.D. dependent var	9.150449
Std. error of regression	1.721997	Akaike info criterion	1.164574
Sum squared resid.	201.6385	Schwartz criterion	1.351390
Log likelihood	− 142.0907	F-statistic	398.6617
Durbin–Watson stat.	1.699704	Prob(F-statistic)	0.000000

[a] GRREU = $C(1) + C(2) \cdot$ MAQRATIO + $C(3) \cdot$ MAGRQCON + $C(4) \cdot$ MAGRCUR + $C(5) \cdot$ [GRREU(-1) − $C(1)$ − $C(2) \cdot$ MAQRATIO(-1) − $C(3) \cdot$ MAGRQCON(-1) − $C(4) \cdot$ MAGRCUR(-1)] + $C(6) \cdot$ DUM
Notes: Sample: 1975(2)–1993(3); *Included observations*: 74 after adjusting endpoints.

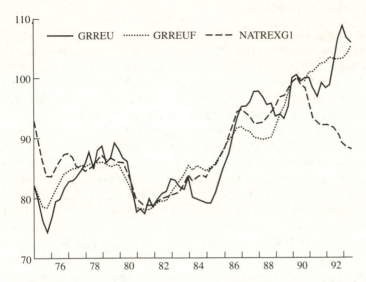

FIG. 6.8   *Actual real effective exchange rate* (GRREU), *estimate of medium-run NATREX from entire equation* (GRREUF), *and long-run* NATREX (NATREXG1)

heteroskedasticity, and it is normally distributed. The residual from the long run equation, $e^*(t) = R(t) - B^*Z(t)$, is stationary in the pre-unification period, but not over the entire period. Despite the attempt to filter out the effect of unification by a dummy variable, the post-unification period shows drastic changes.

The NLS estimate of the entire equation is labelled GRREUF in Figure 6.8. This is the medium-run NATREX. Define the long-run NATREX as $B^*Z(t)$, where B^* is the estimated value in Table 6.3. It is graphed as NATREXG1 in Figure 6.8. The actual real effective exchange rate, GRREU, converges to the medium-run NATREX. Until unification, the real effective exchange rate did converge to the long-run NATREX. Since unification (to be discussed below) the real exchange rate and medium-run NATREX have been higher than the long-run NATREX. The non-stationary error $e^*(t)$ since unification is seen by the difference between the curves GRREU and NATREXG1. It is not clear to what extent the real value of the DM is overvalued relative to its long-run value and to what extent the error is the result of the profound structural break.

4.3   German Unification

The treaty of economic and currency unification of 1 July 1990 integrated the two parts of Germany. It was expected that the German unification would present a laboratory situation to study the consequences of a rise in the productivity of capital and a rise in time preference. The econometric results above show that there was a structural break at the time of the unification.

Time preference rose for several reasons. The East Germans were endowed with German Marks from the currency conversion, and they had access to Western goods. The massive transfers from West to East, giving the East Germans access to Western goods, further increased the overall time preference measure. In East Germany after unification,[27] consumption plus investment exceeded GDP. East Germany's net imports were 92 per cent of its GDP in 1991, 82 per cent in 1992, and 66 per cent in 1993. A very large part of these imports was financed from West German transfer payments. These transfers consisted of payments from the federal government, the West German social security system, and a special 'German Unity' fund. In 1993, the fiscal transfers to East Germany amounted to 6 per cent of West German GNP. West German consumption did not decline to offset the higher East German consumption. The time preference for unified *West and East* Germany (MAGRQGOV and MAGRQCON) rose significantly[28] after unification.

The q-ratio depends upon the exogenous terms of trade, the marginal physical product of capital, and the rate of capacity utilization. Before unification, the main movements in the q-ratio were the result of movements in the terms of trade and rate of capacity utilization. After unification, the rate of capacity utilization declined, which led to a decline in the observed q-ratio, MAQRATIO. For this reason we also graph a cyclically adjusted q-ratio in Figure 6.7, denoted QRATIO2. Whereas the MAQRATIO declined, the cyclically adjusted ratio rose significantly[29] with

[27] We are drawing upon Clausen and Willms (1994), especially their tables 1 and 2, for the description of East Germany. See Sinn and Sinn (1992), Clausen and Willms (1994), and Friedmann and Herrmann (1994) for the effects of unification.

[28] The use of national income accounts, based upon West German data, does not reflect the significant rise in time preference in unified Germany.

[29] The non-cyclically adjusted MAQRATIO declined owing to the recession. Compare the MAQRATIO with QRATIO2 in Figure 6.7. The latter is the residual of a regression of the q-ratio on the rate of capacity utilization.

no significant rise in the terms of trade or decline in the relative price of imported materials (GRRMP).

There were three reasons for the rise in the cyclically adjusted q-ratio after unification. There was a rise in the marginal physical product of capital. Since the capital intensity in East Germany was very low compared with that in West Germany, German capital intensity in the unified Germany declined substantially after unification. There was a technology transfer from West to East, and the rebuilding of the East German infrastructure has raised the productivity of private capital. These factors should have raised the q-ratio significantly in the unified Germany.

There was a large increase in investment in East Germany. In 1993, per capita investment was the same in both parts of Germany. Government investment in East Germany is mainly in infrastructure, carried out by the German Federal Post Office and Railway Company. Private investment is almost exclusively in capital-intensive labour-saving activities. These private investments are subsidized by 20 to 30 per cent. The rise in domestic expenditure in East Germany has been a mixture of private and public increases in time preference. Part of the rise in investment has been engendered by a rise in the cyclically adjusted q-ratio and part of it has been a result of subsidies.

The medium-run effects of the rise in either time preference or the q-ratio increase investment less saving. In terms of Figures 6.5 and 6.6, the *SI* curve shifts to the left from $SI(0)$ to $SI(1)$ and appreciates the DM from $R(0)$ to $R(1)$. The appreciation of the Mark produces a current account deficit of $0A$ and the foreign debt rises. This is the medium-run effect. The longer-run effect of a rise in time preference is a depreciation of the real exchange rate to $R(2)$, as described in Figure 6.5.

The longer-run effect of a rise in the q-ratio owing to the rise in the productivity of capital is to increase the capital intensity monotonically. The debt first rises and then declines below its initial level. The trajectory of capital and debt, resulting from a rise in the productivity of capital, is $A-D-E$ in Figure 2.5 in Chapter 2.

The effect upon the long-run real exchange rate is ambiguous.[30] The rise in capital will lead to a rise in saving out of the higher GDP, and the *SI* curve in Figure 6.6 will shift to the right. The

---

[30] See the summary discussion in Table 2.1 of Ch. 2.

longer-run effect will depend upon what happens to the current account function, *CA*, evaluated at a given real exchange rate. Will it rise or decline?

There are counterbalancing effects. (1) The steady-state debt will decline, as shown in Table 2.3 and Figure 2.5, because the rise in capital will increase GDP and saving and lower investment. The lower debt, or greater income payments from abroad, will increase the current account and shift the *CA* curve to the right in Figure 6.6. This is a force for appreciation. (2) The rise in capital will increase GDP and imports and tend to reduce the current account. This shifts the *CA* curve to the left and down and leads to depreciation. (3) The German export sector is capital-intensive. In 1992, manufactured products accounted for almost 97 per cent of West German merchandise exports.[31] Insofar as the terms of trade are exogenous, the accumulation of capital will increase exports, which will tend to shift the current account upwards to the right. This will tend to appreciate the German Mark above its initial level. In view of these different effects, there is ambiguity about the long-run effect of German unification upon the real effective exchange rate.

On the basis of Figure 6.8, for the post-unification period the actual real value of the Mark is close to the medium-run NATREX (GRREUF). The model explains the medium-run movements quite well. However, for the long run, the time preference effect seems to be dominant. The longer-run real value of the NATREX (NATREXG1) is below the medium-run NATREX (GRREUF). There is considerable uncertainty concerning the longer-run NATREX in the post-unification period. The error $R(t) - BZ(t)$ between the actual real exchange rate GRREU and NATREXG1 is stationary until unification, but it is not stationary when the post-unification period is included.[32]

Grassinger and Fischer (1997) updated Stein and Sauernheimer with data covering the period up to 1996(4) and used the Johansen method of estimation to obtain an estimate of the long-run NATREX. They found that the real exchange rate converges to their estimate of the long-run NATREX, even during the post-unification period. Their results are more supportive of the NATREX than are the earlier results reported in this chapter.

---

[31] Deutsche Bundesbank (1994), p. 50.
[32] See Table 6.3 in the section on diagnostics.

5. NATREX AND PURCHASING POWER PARITY (PPP)

The Purchasing Power Parity (PPP) hypothesis was briefly discussed in connection with Figure 6.1 above. There are two components to PPP. The first is that the equilibrium real exchange rate is
stationary in the long run. This means that the real exchange rate
reverts to a constant mean. The reversion should occur in the
medium run, say within five years, if it is to have policy significance.
The second is that, in the longer run, relative prices are proportional[33] to the ratio of the domestic to the foreign ratio of money
to GDP. Both are long-, rather than shorter-run, relationships.[34] In
this section we explain why NATREX is a generalization of PPP.

The equilibrium nominal exchange rate $N(t)$ is equation (6.19),
the product of the equilibrium real exchange rate and the ratio of
foreign to domestic money/output, denoted $m'(t)/m(t)$. The NA-
TREX claims that the longer-run equilibrium real exchange rate is
not a constant, but $R^* = R[Z(t)]$, a function of the fundamentals
$Z(t)$ described above.

$$N(t) = R[Z(t)]m'(t)/m(t) \qquad (6.19)$$

Figure 6.9 plots the nominal exchange rate, $N(t)$—where a rise is an
appreciation—against the ratio of domestic to foreign money to
output, or relative prices. The level of the rectangular hyperbola is
the equilibrium real exchange rate, $R[Z(t)]$, the NATREX. The
longer-run real exchange rate, R^*, inherits its properties from the
fundamentals. Insofar as the fundamentals $Z(t)$ vary between $Z(1)$
and $Z(2)$, with a mean value of $Z(0)$, the NATREX varies between
rectangular hyperbolas $R[Z(1)]$ and $R[Z(2)]$, with a mean value
$R[Z(0)]$.

The PPP hypothesis is that the equilibrium real exchange rate is
stationary at $R[Z(0)]$. Variations in the nominal exchange rate from
$N(0)$ to $N(1)$ are the result of variations in relative money from $0b$

---

[33] Normalize the factor of proportionality at 1.

[34] The monetary theory of the balance of payments, which was popular in the
1970s, viewed these as short-run relations. This school of thought lost its influence
as a result of the emprical evidence concerning the floating-rate period. There are
hardly any exponents of this school left. The price level is proportional to
money/GDP in the longer run, but there is no direct shorter-run relation between
annual inflation and annual money growth. The longer-run relationship is $p = vm$,
where v is a constant. See Stein (1994) for an analysis of the relation of inflation to
money growth and the extent to which a central bank can control the rate of
inflation.

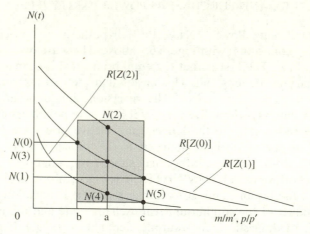

FIG. 6.9   *The nominal exchange rate is $N(t)$, the NATREX equilibrium real exchange rate is $R[Z(t)]$, relative prices are $p(t)/p'(t)$, relative money per unit of output is $m(t)/m'(t)$, and the real exogenous fundamentals are $Z(t)$. Each NATREX corresponds to a rectangular hyperbola*

to $0c$. The NATREX approach concerns the sources of variation in the equilibrium real exchange rate. Insofar as the fundamentals $Z(t)$ of time preference, the terms of trade, and the q-ratio vary between $Z(1)$ and $Z(2)$, when the relative money stocks are constant at $0a$ the equilibrium nominal exchange rate will vary between $N(4)$ and $N(2)$. Insofar as there are variations in both the fundamentals and relative money stocks the nominal exchange rate will lie in the shaded rectangle. Hence there will be no apparent relation between the nominal exchange rate and relative money stocks. This indeed is the case when the exchange rate of a currency is measured relative to the US dollar—a free rate.

There are two ways in which a researcher may find that the PPP hypothesis is consistent with the data. First, some researchers find support, in the very long run, for a stationary real exchange rate. The NATREX model can explain this result. Variations in social time preference, a component of $Z(t)$, produce variations in the steady-state foreign debt $F(t)$ and longer-run real exchange rate. The stabilizing feedback control on the social saving function concerns the effect of the foreign debt on the ratio of social consumption to GDP. This means that variations in $Z(t)$ must be bounded. For example, there may be a period when social consumption/GDP rises from $Z(2)$ to $Z(1)$ in Figure 6.9. The foreign debt will rise, and the real exchange rate will depreciate—from $R[Z(2)]$ to $R[Z(1)]$. Given relative money stocks at $0a$, the nominal exchange rate depreciates from $N(2)$ to $N(4)$. The rise in the foreign debt produces a feedback control that reduces the time preference. The lower time preference $Z(0)$ reduces the value of the foreign debt and appreciates the nominal exchange rate to $N(3)$. The very-long-run stationarity of the real exchange rate may arise because the very-long-run value of social time preference is stationary owing to the feedback control in the saving function.

Formally, the steady-state value of the foreign debt, F^*, and the real exchange rate, R^*, depend upon Z. Insofar as the feedback control only permits the foreign debt to vary between $F(1)$ and $F(2)$, this requires that social time preference, Z, be permitted to vary only between $Z(1)$ and $Z(2)$, with a mean value of $Z(0)$. Insofar as this occurs, the real exchange rate varies only between the two rectangular hyperbolas $R[Z(1)]$ and $R[Z(2)]$. The mean value $Z(0)$ means that the mean value of the real exchange rate is rectangular hyperbola $R[Z(0)]$, as drawn in Figure 6.9. Thereby, the mean very-long-run real exchange rate is stationary.

Second, the bilateral nominal exchange rates within Europe, say the French franc and the DM, are often close to their PPP values.[35] This may simply be a reflection of how the adjustable peg is determined and is unrelated to any equilibrium concept. Let the nominal exchange rate be $N(0)$ and relative price be $0b$. Then let the NATREX depreciate from $R[Z(0)]$ to $R[Z(1)]$ and relative prices rise from $0b$ to $0c$. The equilibrium nominal exchange rate declines from $N(0)$ to $N(5)$. There is an exchange crisis because nominal bilateral exchange rate $N(0)$ is overvalued. The political authorities do not know what the equilibrium real exchange rate is and assume that PPP is 'the only game in town'. So they realign the nominal exchange rate at $N(1)$ to conform to PPP. It looks as if one can explain bilateral European exchange rates by PPP. However, $N(1) > N(5)$ is an overvalued exchange rate. The observation that bilateral European nominal rates are close to PPP does not mean that they are equilibrium rates. It just means that the adjustable pegs are set at PPP and that there will be repeated exchange rate crises.

---

[35] See Ch. 4 above concerning the franc/DM. There, the real exchange rate is measured as $R(p) = Np/p'$.

6. THE TRADE BALANCE AND THE COMPETITIVENESS OF THE GERMAN ECONOMY

6.1   The Simultaneous Determination of the Real Exchange Rate and Trade Balance

German exports are primarily manufactured goods. Over the longer run, the ability to remain competitive in international markets is determined chiefly by the movement of relative cost, since there is a law of one price of internationally traded identical goods. In this section we ask what determines the trade balance or competitiveness of the German economy. Unit labour costs in manufacturing in Germany have been rising faster than those of its foreign trading partners; nevertheless, the German competitive position has been holding up well. The Bundesbank (1995; Friedmann and Clostermann 1997) was puzzled by this phenomenon and attempted to determine the appropriate statistic whereby one can measure the competitiveness of the German economy.

The NATREX model explained the simultaneous determination of the real exchange rate and current account in equations (6.14) and (6.15) and Figures 6.5 and 6.6. These show why there is no direct relation between these two *simultaneously determined—* endogenous—variables. In Figure 6.5, a rise in time preference appreciates the real exchange rate from $R(0)$ to $R(1)$ and reduces the current account from zero to $0A$, which is negative. In Figure 6.6, an improvement in the terms of trade, say a decline in the relative price of imported materials, appreciates the real exchange rate from $R(0)$ to $R(1)$ and increases the current account from zero to $0B > 0$. Similarly, a rise in the GDP of the G7 shifts the CA curve to the right and simultaneously appreciates the real exchange rate and increases the trade balance.

6.2   Estimation of the Trade Balance/GNP

Equation (6.10) states that the trade balance relative to German GNP, denoted GRTBGNP,[36] depends upon the real effective exchange rate, $R = $ GRREU, and external variables in vector Z.

---

[36]   GRTBGNP = 400 · (GR77acd · GRae)/GR99ac, using IFS data. The trade balance, GR77acd, is measured in US dollars and is quarterly, and GR99ac is measured in DM and at an annual rate. Hence the trade balance was converted into DM on an annual rate.

TABLE 6.4a   *Cointegration analysis: trade balance/GNP*
GRTBGNP, GRREU, GRRMP, *and* G7GDP

Eigenvalue	Likelihood ratio	5% critical value	1% critical value	Hypothesized no. of CEs
0.335045	53.08592	47.21	54.46	None*
0.194555	24.52337	29.68	35.65	At most 1
0.123918	9.378187	15.41	20.04	At most 2
0.001678	0.117536	3.76	6.65	At most 3

* rejection of the hypothesis at 5% significance level.
Notes: *Sample*: 1973(1)–1993(3); *Included observations*: 70; *Test assumption*: linear deterministic trend in the data; *Lags interval*: 1 to 1; L.R. test indicates 1 cointegrating equation(s) at 5% significance level.

TABLE 6.4b   *OLS regression of the trade balance/GNP*[a]

Variable	Coefficient	Std. error	*t*-statistic	Prob.
GRREU	− 0.104069	0.044376	− 2.345131	0.0220
GRRMP	− 162.1300	32.33166	− 5.014591	0.0000
G7GDP	0.000359	6.26E–05	5.729842	0.0000
DUM	− 5.134808	0.511477	− 10.03918	0.0000
C	13.76670	3.989495	3.450737	0.0010

R-squared	0.664255	Mean dependent var		3.832646
Adjusted R-squared	0.644211	S.D. dependent var		1.803030
Std. error of regression	1.075472	Akaike info criterion		0.212435
Sum squared resid.	77.49493	Schwartz criterion		0.370537
Log likelihood	− 104.8112	F-statistic		33.13912
Durbin-Watson stat.	1.149873	Prob(F-statistic)		0.000000

[a] Dependent Variable is GRTBGNP
Notes: *Sample*: 1975(1)–1992(4); *Included observations*: 72; *Excluded observations*: 0 after adjusting endpoints.

These external variables are the relative price of imported materials (v^* = GRRMP) and foreign demand, which we measure as the GDP of the G7: Z = (GRRMP, G7GDP). Table 6.4a shows that these four variables, each of which is $I(1)$, are cointegrated. Table 6.4b is an OLS regression of the trade balance/GNP upon: the relative price of imported materials, the GDP of the G7, and a dummy variable that is 0 prior to unification and 1 after unification.

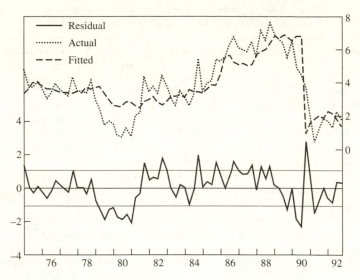

FIG. 6.10   *The trade balance/GNP: actual, fitted from Table 6.4b and residual*

It can be seen that the real effective exchange rate reduces the trade balance/GNP, the relative price of imported materials decreases the trade balance, and the GDP of the G7 increases the trade balance. The unification dummy shows how there was a structural shift in the trade balance. Figure 6.10 graphs the actual and forecast trade balance/GNP on the basis of Table 6.4b.

The conclusion is that the competitiveness of the German tradable sector, reflected in the trade balance/GNP, must be viewed in terms of both foreign demand and all input costs: the real effective exchange rate and the relative price of imported materials. The real effective exchange rate is an endogenous variable that equilibrates the trade balance to saving less investment. The fundamental determinants of the real exchange rate are time preference in Germany, as well as the external factors.

6.3   Conclusion

We may now answer the basic questions posed at the beginning of this chapter. First, the longer-term systematic determinants of the real effective exchange rate are both domestic and external. The main domestic determinants are time preference, the ratio of public plus private consumption to GNP, and the q-ratio. The main external determinants are the European terms of trade, whose variations are produced primarily by the relative price of imported materials, and the GDP in the G7. The equilibrium real effective exchange rate produced by these fundamentals in the medium to the longer run is referred to as the Natural Real Exchange Rate (NATREX). The NATREX model explains how these fundamental determinants determine the evolution of the equilibrium real effective exchange rate and the current account/GNP in the medium to longer run. The actual real exchange rate of the German Mark converged to both the medium-run and longer-run values of the NATREX. The medium-to longer-run real effective exchange rate does not follow a random walk but inherits its properties from the fundamentals. The PPP theory is a special case of the NATREX when a linear combination of the fundamentals is stationary.

The depreciation of the real value of the DM from 1979 to 1980, and its appreciation from 1985 to 1986, were primarily the result of the external factors: the decline in the terms of trade (rise in the relative price of imported materials) in the first period, and the rise in the terms of trade (decline in the relative price of imported materials) in the second period.

The differences in social policy under Schmidt and Kohl, and German reunification, produced changes in time preference. The rise in time preference under Schmidt from 1980 to 1982 produced shorter-run appreciation and longer-run depreciation. The decline in time preference under Kohl from 1982 to 1990 produced shorter-run depreciation and longer-run appreciation. The high and rising current account surpluses/GNP from 1981 to 1989 generated investment income that was an important factor in explaining the trend appreciation of the real effective exchange rate from 1985 to 1992.

In the post-unification period, the medium-run NATREX increased owing to the rise in time preference and the cyclically adjusted q-ratio, which reflects a rise in the productivity of capital. Time preference rose from the reunification in 1990 until 1994, and then declined in 1996 to the 1984 level. The actual real exchange rate appreciated as it converged to the medium-run NATREX.

The second question is what determines the ratio of the current account to GDP. The trade balance/GNP and real exchange rate are both endogenous variables, determined in the manner graphed in Figures 6.5 and 6.6. The current account function has as parameters the following external factors: the European terms of trade or relative price of imported materials, and the GDP of the G7. The saving-less-investment function has as parameters time preference and the q-ratio. A decline in the relative price of imported materials or a rise in G7GDP will appreciate the real exchange rate and increase the trade balance. A rise in time preference will decrease saving less investment, appreciate the currency in the medium run, diminish the trade balance and current account, and increases the foreign debt. In the longer run, the real exchange rate will depreciate to generate the trade balance sufficient to pay the higher interest on the foreign debt. Thus it is misleading to view the real effective exchange rate alone as a measure of competitiveness. It is when the real effective exchange rate appreciates without rises in G7GDP and declines in the relative price of imported materials that the economy is losing competitiveness.

The deviations of the actual real effective exchange rate from the medium-run NATREX are the result of cyclical factors, union pressures on unit labour costs, and speculative capital flows. The latter result from anticipations of policy changes in Germany and the G7. These short-run produce significant but temporary deviations from the NATREX. The real exchange rate converges to the time-varying NATREX.

TABLE 6A.1   *Order of integration of variables, 1975(4)–1993(3)*[a]

Variable	$I(1)$	$I(0)$
$R(w) = Nw/w' = $ GRREU	− 0.848	
$R(p) = Np/p' = $ RCPI	− 1.899	
$R = Np_t/p'_t = R(T)$	− 1.446	
MAGRGOV(W)	− 1.11	
MAGRQGOV(WE)		− 3.12*
MAGRQCON(WE)		− 2.99*
MAGRDIS(W)	− 1.55	
MAGRCUR		− 2.8*
GRRMP	− 1.93	
GRTOT	− 1.41	
MAQRATIO	− 1.147	
MAQRATIO1	− 1.149	
MAGROW		− 4.86*

[a] UROOT(C,2)

Notes: The variables were defined in the text above. The W and E symbols refer to West Germany (W), or East and West combined (WE). MAGRDIS(W) is the time preference of West Germany. MAGROW is a four-quarter moving average of the growth rate of GDP. The RCPI and RT exchange rates came from the Bundesbank.

TABLE 6A.2   *Non-linear least squares estimation of RCPI*[a]

	Coefficient	Std. error	t-Statistic	Prob.
$C(1)$	− 51.45645	563.4001	− 0.091332	0.9275
$C(2)$	− 218.2553	108.6966	− 2.007932	0.0487
$C(3)$	− 174.6481	57.02724	− 3.062539	0.0032
$C(4)$	0.978612	0.032696	29.93072	0.0000
$C(5)$	0.071748	0.056630	1.266951	0.2096

R-squared	0.943867	Mean dependent var	92.02254
Adjusted R-squared	0.940465	S.D. dependent var	6.625324
Std. error of regression	1.616563	Akaike info criterion	1.028424
Sum squared resid	172.4761	Schwartz criterion	1.187768
Log likelihood	− 132.2537	F-statistic	277.4457

[a] RCPI = the real exchange rate, $R = Np/p'$, in terms of the CPI deflators = $C(1) + C(2) \cdot$ GRRMP + $C(3) \cdot$ MAGRQCON + $C(4) \cdot$ [RCPI(− 1) − $C(1)$ − $C(2) \cdot$ GRRMP(− 1) − $C(3) \cdot$ MAGRQCON(− 1)] + $C(5) \cdot$ MAGRCUR
Notes: *Sample*: 1975(2)–1992(4); *Included observations*: 71 after adjusting endpoints; *Diagnostics*: (1) Breusch–Godfrey LM test for serial correlation, $pr = 0.11$; (2) ARCH test, $pr = 0.97$; (3) Jarque–Bera test for normality, $pr = 0.93$.

REFERENCES

Boltho, Andrea. 1994. 'Why do countries change their fiscal policies?' *Journal of International and Comparative Economics*, 3: 77–100.

Clark, Peter. 1997. 'Concepts of equilibrium exchange rates'. In *The Globalization of Markets*, ed. Jerome L. Stein, Heidelberg, Physica-Verlag.

Clausen, V. and Manfred Willms. 1994. 'Lessons from German monetary union for European monetary union'. *Journal of International and Comparative Economics*, 3: 195–228.

Deutsche Bundesbank. 1993. 'Trends and determining factors for the external value of the Deutsche Mark'. *Monatsbericht* (Nov.).

—— 1994. 'Real exchange rates as an indicator of international competitiveness'. *Monatsbericht* (May).

—— 1995. 'Overall determinants of the trends in the real external value of the Deutsche Mark'. *Monatsbericht* (Aug.).

Friedmann, W. and J. Clostermann. 1997. 'Determinants of the real D-Mark exchange rate', paper presented at a conference on Real Exchange Rates and European Monetary Union, Johannes-Gutenberg University, Mainz and the Deutsche Bundesbank, May 22–23.

—— and H. Herrmann. 1994. 'A review of Gerlinde and Hans- Werner Sinn: *Jumpstart*'. *Journal of International and Comparative Economics*, 3: 309–20.

Grassinger, R. and C. Fischer. 1997. 'The real DM exchange rate in the NATREX model', paper presented at a conference on Real Exchange Rates and European Monetary Union, Johannes-Gutenberg University, Mainz and the Deutsche Bundesbank, May 22–23.

Lim, G. C. 1997. 'A note on estimating dynamic models of the real exchange rate'. In *The Globalization of Markets*, ed. Jerome L. Stein, Heidelberg, Physica-Verlag.

Sauernheimer, K. and R. Grassinger. 1995. 'The long run determinants of the real exchange rate: the case of Germany'. Working paper, University of Munich.

Sinn, Gerlinde and Hans-Werner Sinn. 1992. *Jumpstart: The Economic Unification* of Germany. Cambridge, MA, MIT Press.

Stein, Jerome L. 1994. 'Can the central bank achieve price stability', Federal Reserve Bank of St Louis, *Review* 76, no. 2 (March/April): 175–204.

—— and Karlhans Sauernheimer. 1997. 'The real exchange rate of Germany'. In *The Globalization of Markets*, ed. Jerome L. Stein, Heidelberg, Physica-Verlag.

Varian, Hal. 1978. *Microeconomic Analysis*. New York, Norton.

APPENDIX: International Finance Theory and Empirical Reality

JEROME L. STEIN

1. QUESTIONS TO BE ANSWERED AND THE SUCCESSION OF THEORIES

We have developed the NATREX approach, with all of its diffi-culties and limitations, because of the serious problems with the contemporary models. An evaluation of these contemporary models provides the justification for taking a different approach. This appendix summarizes the underlying rationale of these models and shows why economists have been so disappointed in their ability to explain the determination of exchange rates and capital flows.

Good economic theory should explain with simplicity and clarity the complex world of experience. Its propositions should be logical and mutually consistent and should imply testable propositions that are consistent with empirical reality. Ultimately, the usefulness of any scientific theory depends on the quality of its answers to important empirical questions. In studying exchange-rate determi-nation, we would like a theory to answer questions Q1–Q5. *The answers one gets to these questions differ depending upon the theory (model) that is used.*

(Q1) Have exchange rates been as stable as the macroeconomic fundamentals? What are these fundamentals? If there has been 'excess volatility', what has produced it? (Q2) What determines the real exchange rate? (Q3) Has the purchasing-power-parity (PPP) theory been valid under floating rates? Do deviations from PPP indicate over-or under-valuation of a currency? (Q4) Are variations in real exchange rates caused by changes in the fundamentals or merely by noise? (Q5) Are variations in nominal exchange rates explained primarily by monetary factors that produce changes in relative nominal prices or also by real disturbances that change the equilibrium real exchange rate?

The failure of flexible exchange rates to perform as economists had expected raised a number of important questions about how exchange rates actually do behave in the real world, and about the validity of various models. The performance of these theories in explaining exchange rates has not been encouraging, particularly for the period of the 1980s. The failure of the models gave rise to a succession of new models of exchange rate determination. De Grauwe states, in his 1989 study summarizing the developments of exchange-rate theories and their application to empirical reality, that the current

models are unable to explain either the long swings in the exchange rate or the systematic bias in the forward rate as a predictor of the future. In the past we economists have tried to explain, and even predict, how particular disturbances in the 'fundamental' variables affect exchange rates. We should reduce our ambitions in this field. Movements of the real exchange rates are, within certain bounds, unexplainable. All we can hope to do is to analyse the nature of the variability, without necessarily being able to explain why a particular movement (for example the appreciation of the dollar from 1982 to 1985) occurred. (1989: 179)

Meese (1990) has concluded that 'economists do not yet understand the determinants of short-to medium-run movements in exchange rates'. It is our contention that the focus on the short-run of recent empirical studies of exchange rates is responsible for this state of affairs.

In the decade before the move to floating exchange rates in 1973, the Mundell–Fleming model was the standard view of balance-of-payments and exchange-rate determination. The Mundell–Fleming model was the open-economy version of the Hicks *IS–LM* model. Because prices were assumed to be fixed during the period of adjustment, changes in nominal and real exchange rates were identical. The Mundell–Fleming models emphasized the role of the goods market and the trade balance in determining the real exchange rate, and gave little attention to modelling the asset markets.

The move to floating exchange rates in the early 1970s and the ensuing growth of international financial markets pointed up the importance of asset markets in determining the nominal exchange rate. Subsequent theoretical developments shifted the emphasis away from the real exchange rate to the nominal exchange rate and to the roles of asset markets and money in its determination. A variety of monetary and asset-market models have been used in recent years to to try to explain the short-run determination of nominal exchange rates. The essential feature of all of the contemporary monetary models is that the nominal exchange rate depends only on relative prices in the two countries, which in turn depend on relative money stocks per unit of output.

Portfolio models, based on the theory of optimal portfolio selection of Markowitz and Tobin, emphasized the imperfect substitutability among assets, requiring the specification of markets for a number of financial assets, one of them being money. Given the difficulties of estimating a wide array of asset demands, empirical estimates of portfolio models have often been limited to looking for measures of a risk premium to explain deviations from open-interest rate parity. Whereas portfolio models depict demands for several assets, monetary models focus almost all attention on money. Assumptions of perfect capital mobility and perfect substitutability among assets permit summarizing the non-money assets with a simple open-interest-parity condition. Assumptions guaranteeing neutral money and ignoring real disturbances lead to the assertion of a constant real exchange rate, and that the nominal exchange rate depends upon relative money stocks per unit of output.

The simple monetary models were extended to include exchange-rate and monetary dynamics with rational expectations, beginning with Dornbusch's 1976 paper. In these models, prices are assumed to be sticky in the short run, so that an increase in the money supply initially depreciates both the nominal and real exchange rates. The real exchange rate is viewed as stationary, however, in the sense that it converges to a constant as prices gradually move to their equilibrium values. The long-run equilibrium is consistent with the monetary model, but the dynamics of these models offered a rationale for wide fluctuations in exchange rates in markets with rational participants. By 1988 these 'overshooting' models dominated explanations of nominal exchange-rate determination.

Several factors have led more recently to the popularity of intertemporal optimization models of exchange-rate determination. Among these factors have been the desire to support macroeconomic models with explicit microeconomic foundations based on optimizing behaviour, growing awareness of the importance of intertemporal budget constraints for behaviour over time, and a recognition of the need to include forward-looking behaviour more explicitly. The intertemporal optimization models (IOM) apply well-known theories and analytical techniques of intertemporal pricing of storable commodities to international finance. Yet, in spite of their dynamic optimizing properties, most intertemporal optimization models of exchange-rate determination are in many ways quite similar to the monetary models. They incorporate assumptions of a stationary real exchange rate and a simple demand for money. Not surprisingly, many also end up claiming that the nominal exchange rate is proportional to relative prices, which, in turn, are proportional to relative supplies of money per unit of output.

Each of these asset and monetary models is logical within its own set of assumptions and constraints and also captures some aspect of exchange-rate determination that appears to describe the real world. But empirical tests of these models as a means of explaining recent movements of nominal exchange rates have been notably unsuccessful. Neither their structural nor reduced form equations are consistent with the evidence, giving rise to the views expressed by Meese and De Grauwe, cited above. The paradox is that, although the empirical failure of these models and their structural equations is well known (Boughton 1988), they continue to be offered as the dominant explanation of nominal exchange determination. Although most scholars are aware of the deficiencies of these models, the profession continues to use them wholly or partly because they do not have a logically satisfactory substitute.

Given the continuing popularity of these contemporary models of exchange-rate determination, which are based on *monetary dynamics with rational expectations*, we summarize first their basic properties in Part 2 and then their failure empirically to explain the movements in nominal exchange rates in Part 3. Part 4 addresses the limitations of the intertemporal optimization models for empirical explanation of exchange rates.

2. THE LOGIC OF THE STATE OF THE ART THEORIES: THE CRUCIAL ROLE OF THE ASSET MARKETS, MONETARY DYNAMICS WITH RATIONAL EXPECTATIONS

The contemporary models we are evaluating focus on the short-run determinants of the nominal exchange rate in asset markets dominated by speculative capital flows. In today's international financial markets, with $1,000 billion traded every day in the world's foreign-exchange markets, expectations of future nominal exchange rates dominate the fundamental determinants of the real exchange rate in any short-run analysis. These expectations are standardly modelled as rational expectations, defined below. The logic of all of these models is that *the considerable variations in the nominal exchange rate can be explained by current and rationally expected monetary factors.* All of these models contain three crucial equilibrium relationships: (a) Fisher open interest-rate parity with rational expectations, (b) a stationary real exchange rate, and (c) dependence of relative inflation rates on relative rates of growth of money supplies. Each of these crucial assumptions will be evaluated in this appendix.

We first define the real and nominal exchange rates. The nominal exchange rate N is defined as the foreign-currency price of domestic currency, so that a rise in N is an appreciation. The real exchange rate R is the product of the nominal exchange rate N and relative prices (p/p'), where p is the domestic GDP deflator, and p' the foreign GDP deflator. The real exchange rate is simply the ratio of domestic to foreign prices, measured in a common currency, making it an inverse measure of competitiveness.

$$R = Np/p' \tag{A.1}$$

$$N = R/(p/p') \tag{A.2}$$

There are three crucial equations (A.3)–(A.5) underlying the contemporary models. Equation (A.3) is the Fisher Open Rational Expectations (FORE), or uncovered interest-rate parity–rational expectations equation.[1] Equation (A.4) is the stationarity of the real exchange rate. Equation (A.5) is the monetary explanation of relative prices.

Fisher open interest-rate parity states that the subjectively *expected* (by the market) percentage change in the nominal exchange rate will equal the difference between the foreign and domestic nominal interest rates, implying perfect capital mobility and perfect substitutability between comparable domestic and foreign assets. If, in addition, expectations are assumed to be rational in the sense of Muth (MRE = Muth Rational Expectations), then the difference between the subjectively expected change and the realized change is

---

[1] Below, we discuss the portfolio balance theories which imply that assets are not perfect substitutes.

random variable z' which is iid with a zero expectation. Fisher open interest parity with rational expectations (the FORE hypothesis) can then be expressed in terms of observed changes in the exchange rate, equation (A.3) or the regression equation (A.3a). They state that short-term capital flows occur to produce equality in the rationally expected rates of return on domestic and foreign assets. The nominal interest rate on the domestic asset is $i(t-1)$ and on the foreign asset of comparable risk it is $i'(t-1)$, at time $t-1$. The percentage appreciation of the domestic currency from $t-1$ to t is $\log N(t) - \log N(t-1)$, denoted Dlog N. Thus the rationally expected percentage change in the nominal value of the domestic currency is equal to the foreign less domestic nominal interest rates on comparable assets. In regression (A.3a) coefficient $\beta = 1$ and term z' is an iid term with a zero expectation. Refer to this as the FORE hypothesis.

$$\text{Dlog } N = \log N(t) - \log N(t-1) = [i'(t-1) - i(t-1)] + z' \qquad (A.3)$$

$$\text{Dlog } N = \log N(t) - \log N(t-1) = a + \beta[i'(t-1) - i(t-1)] + z'; \qquad (A.3a)$$

Equation (A.4) states the hypothesis that the real exchange rate is stationary at a *constant* value C. At any time, the real exchange rate may not equal the constant C, for example because prices are sticky in the short run, but it will converge to this value. Term z'' is an iid term with a zero expectation, coefficient b is a positive fraction significantly different from zero.

$$[R(t) - C] = b[R(t-1) - C] + z''. \quad 1 > b > 0 \qquad (A.4)$$

This is the Purchasing Power Parity (PPP), or 'law of one price', assumption with a lagged adjustment, due possibly to sticky prices, in the shorter run. The smaller is the value of $1 > b > 0$, the faster is the convergence[2] to PPP.

The third assumption is that relative prices are *ultimately determined* by ratios of money per unit of output m (home country) and m' (foreign country), equation (A.5), where the P's are functions, which need not be the same in both countries. If the relative money supplies stabilize at m, m' then relative prices will converge to $(P(m)/P(m'))(T)$ at more distant date T. This terminal date is a transversality condition.

---

[2] The solution of (A.4) is that the expected value of the deviation $[R(t) - C] = [R(0) - C](b)^t$. It half of the deviation has been reduced at time T, then time $T = \log 0.5/\log b$. If $b = 1$, equation (A.4) has a unit root, the denominator is zero, and convergence never occurs.

$$\log(p(T)/p'(T)) = \log(P(m(T)/P(m'(T)))$$ (A.5)

The models containing these assumptions continue to be used to 'explain' why exchange rates are volatile. The volatility of the current nominal exchange rate $N(t)$ will be produced by *rationally expected temporary and permanent changes* in relative money supplies during the interval from the present (time t) to the more distant date T. To understand this we must invoke forward-looking rational expectations over a sufficiently long interval of time from the present time t to the longer-run equilibrium at time T. This is done as follows.

Sum the rationally expected percentage changes in the real exchange rate in equation (A.3) from time t to later date T, and derive (A.6), which states that the average percentage change in the nominal exchange rate per unit of time from t to T is equal to the average nominal interest rate differential $(i' - i)$ during that interval.[3] (The index s goes from $t-1$ to $T-1$).

$$[\log N(T) - \log N(t)]/(T-t) = \Sigma[i'(s) - i(s)]/(T-t) = i' - i.$$ (A.6)

The transversality condition is that the nominal exchange rate is close to its equilibrium at time T. The expected real exchange rate will be stationary at C, given in (A.4). This means that the nominal exchange rate at time T is (A.7). This is our fixed (equilibrium) point. The time $h = T - t$ that it takes to reach the equilibrium, where the real exchange rate is at its stationary value, depends upon the degree of price flexibility in the economy. When prices are extremely flexible (as in the models of the monetary approach to the balance of payments) h is small, and when prices are very sticky (as in Dornbusch's 1976 model), h is large.

$$\log N(T) = \log C + \log P(m'(T)) - \log P(m(T))$$ (A.7)

Substitute (A.7) into (A.6) and derive the essence of the contemporary models, equation (A.8). This equation is drawn in Figure A1, where $\log N(t)$ is plotted as a function of time between t and T. The fixed point, or transversality condition, $\log N(T) = \{\log C + \log P(m'(T))/P(m(T))\}$ is where the economy is heading rationally, and it precludes 'bubbles'.

$$\begin{aligned}\log N(t) &= \log N(T) - (T-t)(i' - i)\\ &= \{\log C + \log(P(m'(T))/P(m(T)))\} - (T-t)(i' - i)\end{aligned}$$ (A.8)

[3] Since we are summing the rationally expected percentage changes, the error terms z' are zero.

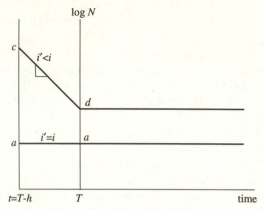

FIG. A.1 $\log N(T) = \log N(t) + (T-t)(i'-i)$

The economic content of (A.6) or (A.8) can be expressed in several ways. (a) The percentage difference between the current and equilibrium nominal value of the currency $\log N(T) - \log N(t)$ is the product of the average nominal interest differential $(i' - i)$ between these two dates, and the time $h = T - t$ that it takes for the nominal exchange rate to converge to its equilibrium value. (b) The average rate of appreciation, measured as a per cent per annum, $[\log N(T) - \log N(t)]/(T-t)$ is equal to the average interest-rate differential $(i' - i)$ between these two dates, which is the slope of the curve in Figure A1.

The 'beauty' of the FORE/PPP model is that it has an explanation of exchange-rate volatility, which may be independent of anything that is observed at the present. The *rational expectations assumption* is that at time $t < T$ people know the expectation of $\log N(T)$, based upon their knowledge of (a) the stationary real exchange rate C, (b) the rationally expected relative price levels, $p'(T)/p(T)$, (c) how long it will take for $N(t)$ to attain its equilibrium value $N(T)$, and (d) the average nominal interest-rate differential $(i' - i)$ during the interval from t to T. The trajectory is from $\log N(t)$ to $\log N(T)$. The current nominal exchange rate $N(t)$ is obtained by moving backwards from the fixed point $N(T)$. The exchange rate appreciates at rate $(i' - i)$ to $\log N(T)$. Since the exchange rate remains steady at the equilibrium $\log N(T)$, then nominal interest rates must be equal from T on.

The causes of variations in the nominal exchange rate are easily 'explained' in this model. The current exchange rate varies because either the rationally expected fixed point $\log N(T) = C + \log P'(T)/P(T) = C + P(m'(T))/P(m(T))$ varies, or because the rationally expected slope, average interest rate differential $(i' - i)$, varies. A *temporary* monetary change just changes the slope; and a *permanent* change in monetary policy changes both the fixed point and the slope. There can be considerable variations in nominal exchange rates even though current policies have not changed, as long as they are rationally expected to change.[4]

An example of this forward-looking rational expectations process will prepare the way for an evaluation of empirical testing. Suppose that initially the exchange rate $N(t)$ is equal to its equilibrium value $N(T) = a$, which requires that the interest-rate differential equal zero. This is curve *aa*. Let there be a rationally expected permanent rise in the relative foreign to domestic money supplies, which *will occur some time in the future*. Consider both the fixed point at time T and the slope, representing the average rationally expected interest-rate differential during the interval (t, T). The rationally expected change in money stocks is rationally expected to change the relative price levels. Since the real exchange rate is assumed to be stationary, the rationally expected fixed-point changes from $\log N(T) = a$ to $\log N(T) = d$. The rationally expected steady-state value of the currency will appreciate by *ad* per cent. This is the intercept effect.

Moreover, the effect of the rationally expected rise in foreign money per unit of output relative to the domestic money is to lower the foreign less domestic interest rate during the period when prices are sticky. Therefore, the rationally expected average foreign less domestic interest rate differential, the average slope, is now negative. Since the rationally expected average domestic interest rate exceeds the foreign rate, there is a capital inflow and the domestic currency immediately appreciates above its steady-state value. The net effect is to move the trajectory from *aa* to *cd*. Both the slope and intercept are changed. This has several important implications.

(1) The nominal exchange rate will appreciate immediately as a result of rationally anticipated changes in relative money stocks

---

[4] This is the so-called peso problem: the market is reacting rationally to an expected policy change.

which will occur *sometime in the future*. (2) The initial appreciation *ac* exceeds the steady-state appreciation *ad*, because of the temporary decline in the foreign less domestic interest rate (decline in slope) during the period of price stickiness. The inequality *ac > ad* is called 'overshooting'. (3) The expected change in relative price levels is produced by rationally expected permanent changes in money per unit of output. Thus nominal exchange-rate volatility is explained by rationally anticipated monetary policies *either now or sometime in the future*. (4) A rationally expected *temporary* change in relative money supplies will not change the steady-state value $N(T)$ but will change the average interest rates during the interval. This changes the slope of the trajectory. Hence the current value of the nominal exchange rate $N(t)$ will change because there is a rationally expected temporary change in interest rates sometime in the future. That is, the exchange market reacts at present to anticipated changes in monetary policy. (5) The moral of the story, according to the proponents of this theory, is that there can be considerable exchange-rate volatility even though there are very few current changes in monetary magnitudes, if future policies are rationally expected to be volatile. Therefore, credible stable money-supply policies in the future will lead to stable nominal exchange rates[5] in the present. Volatility in nominal exchange rates is attributed to volatility in rationally expected money-supply policies in the future. Unless this hypothesis is quantified, it can easily become a tautology. The major issue is whether this forward-looking rational-expectations monetary view is consistent with the evidence. Does it have any explanatory power?

3. THE FORE/PPP MODELS ARE NOT CONSISTENT WITH THE EVIDENCE

Economists have been disappointed to find that the models based upon equations (A.3)–(A.5) lack explanatory power. Empirical studies have shown that both the structural and reduced-form equations are inconsistent with the evidence. Section 3.1 shows why we reject the (Purchasing Power Parity) hypothesis that the real

---

[5] A large literature concerning what are credible policies has developed from this approach.

exchange rate has been stationary during the period 1975.1–1992.2. Section 3.2 explains why the FORE hypothesis (uncovered interest-rate parity with Rational Expectations) is rejected. Moreover, we show in Section 3.3 the basis for rejecting the portfolio models, which contain an endogenous risk premium based upon relative asset supplies, adjoined to the Rational Expectations hypothesis. That is, one cannot explain the failure of the FORE hypothesis by invoking a risk premium which is a function of the ratio of domestic to foreign assets. The Sections 3.1, 3.2, and 3.3 concern the structural equations. Section 3.4 presents evidence why the reduced-form equations, relating monetary variables to the nominal exchange rate, lack explanatory power. This corpus of evidence explains the disillusionment of economists with the state of the art theories. Our presentation is consistent with published results, so we may be terse and intuitive.

3.1 The Stationarity of the Real Exchange Rate is Rejected

In this section we show that one may reject the hypothesis that there has been a fixed steady-state real exchange rate C to which the actual real exchange rate gravitates as price flexibility increases (equation A.4), during the period 1975.1–1992.2. In so far as $R(t)$ converges on average to the constant C, variations in the equilibrium nominal exchange rate (fixed point in Figure A1) are closely tied to variations in relative prices. The real exchange rate will be stationary if b in equation A.4 is significantly different from unity. If b is not significantly different from unity, then the real exchange rate has a unit root, is integrated of order one I(1), and is not stationary. The non-stationarity of the real exchange rate rejects the Purchasing Power Parity Hypothesis.

Table A1 presents the adjusted Dickey–Fuller (ADF) statistics for the real effective (trade-weighted) exchange rate for seven currencies, based upon quarterly data 1975.1–1992.2. The ADF is the t-statistic for $1-b$. For the seven currencies, $1-b$ is not significantly different from zero. Hence b is not significantly different from unity. The real effective exchange rate has a unit root, and we reject the hypothesis that the real exchange rate is stationary. This rejects the PPP hypothesis during the period considered. Although the levels R are not stationary, the first differences (Dlog R) are stationary.

TABLE A1 *Adjusted Dickey–Fuller statistics: unit root tests for the stationarity of the real effective exchange rate UROOT (C,1), quarterly 1975.2–1992.2*

Country	ADF(C,1)
United States	− 1.219
United Kingdom	− 1.6745
Canada	− 1.6638
Germany	− 0.7072
France	− 2.2817
Japan	− 1.7796
Italy	− 2.5035

Data: from data bank of Federal Reserve Bank of St Louis. Significance levels denoted by asterisk (MacKinnon values, 5% = − 2.9; 10% = − 2.58). ADF (constant, lag)

In the earlier chapters we explained what are the fundamental determinants (vector Z) of the steady-state real exchange rate, denoted by $R(Z)$. Vector Z consists of the exogenous disturbances: social thrift, the productivity of capital, the terms of trade, and the world real rate of interest, depending upon the size of the economy. The real exchange rate is not stationary because variables in Z are not stationary. We explained the historical evolution of the real exchange rate in terms of the observed values of Z. However, *it is impossible to predict the long-run evolution of* Z, *which has a unit root*, because the variance increases with the length of the forecasting horizon.

3.2 *The Fisher Open/Rational-Expectations Hypothesis*

Equation (A.3) the uncovered interest-rate parity with rational expectations (Fisher Open Rational Expectations, FORE) is rejected for every major pair of currencies. The percentage change in the nominal exchange rate from $t-1$ to t, $\mathrm{Dlog}\,N = \log N(t) - \log N(t-1)$, is unrelated to the nominal interest-rate differential $i'(t-1) - i(t-1)$ at initial time t-1. The interest-rate differential is

equal to the forward premium on the domestic currency[6] at time
$t-1$. Table A2 presents estimates of β, and the 95 per cent
confidence limits for coefficient b, in equation (A.3a) above. This is
based upon daily observations at non-overlapping monthly intervals, during the period 1981.05–1989.09. Figures 2.1 and 2.2 in
Chapter 2 plot the actual rate of appreciation of the currency
DlogN on the vertical axis against the forward premium
$i'(t-1)-i(t-1)$ on the horizontal axis for the the $US–$Canadian
and for $US–DM. A regression line is drawn for the reader's
convenience. The FORE hypothesis is that the observations lie
along a 45-degree line ($\beta = 1$) plus an iid term with a zero expectation. We observe that there is no relation between the two variables.
The OLS estimate of β is b in the first column, and the 95 per cent
confidence limits in the second column. Table A2 shows that for the
major currencies we may reject the FORE hypothesis that the slope
is unity and not zero (see column 2). The nominal value of the
exchange rate does not appreciate at a rate equal to the foreign less
domestic interest rate at time $t-1$. The FORE hypothesis is also
rejected for the major currencies at horizons of 1, 3, 6, and 12
months (Longworth, Boothe, and Clinton).

3.3 Portfolio Models with Endogenous Risk Premium

Equation A.3 presupposes that there is perfect capital mobility and
perfect asset substitutability; hence there is no risk premium. The
portfolio-balance models argue that there is an endogenous risk
premium which depends upon the ratio of foreign to domestic
assets. In the typical investor's portfolio the greater the fraction of
foreign-currency denominated assets relative to assets denominated
in the domestic currency, the greater must be the expected return
on foreign relative to domestic assets. Since we are drawing upon a
Bank of Canada study, let the two countries be Canada and the US
(world). In the FORE context, let B represent Canadian currency
outside assets, B' represents outside assets in US currency, and

[6] The covered interest-rate parity always holds for the major currencies. The
forward premium on the domestic currency is always equal to the foreign less
domestic interest rate in the Euro market. We measure the interest rate differential
$i'(t-1)-i(t-1)$ as the forward premium on the domestic currency, on a contract at
time $t-1$ maturing at time t. The model, however, in equation (A.3) concerns the
uncovered interest-rate parity/rational expectations.

TABLE A2 *Test of hypothesis concerning one-month nominal exchange-rate changes and initial one-month nominal interest-rate differentials 1981.05–1989.08*

	b(*s*)	$b \pm t(.05)s$	adj. R-square
Britain	– 5.43	[– 2.5, – 8.36]	0.11
	(1.478)		
Canada	– .2947	[.96, – 1.54]	– 0.008
	(.63)		
France	.826	[1.98,– .32]	0.01
	(.58)		
Japan	– 2.685	[– .82, – 4.55]	0.068
	(.938)		
Switz.	– .678	[2.24, – 3.59]	– 0.008
	(1.469)		
W. Germany	– 2.97	[1.85, – 7.79]	0.005
	(2.43)		

Notes: Column 1 is the estimate *b* and in parentheses, its standard error. Column 2 is the 95 per cent confidence interval for β. Column 3 shows that the current interest-rate differential (forward premium or discount) has no informational value concerning the subsequent evolution of the exchange rate

$N = \$US/\$CAN$, where a rise in N is an appreciation of the Canadian currency, i is the Canadian and i' is the US nominal interest rate. Then the FORE hypothesis, in the context of the portfolio-balance models, is (A.9) or (A.9a). The expected return on the Canadian dollar denominated assets $i(t)$ plus the appreciation of the Canadian dollar log $N(t+1)/N(t)$ must exceed the return on US dollar denominated assets $i'(t)$ by a risk premium which is a function of NB/B' the ratio of Canadian-dollar denominated outside assets to US-dollar denominated outside assets. This hypothesis has been examined, using several different measures of B and B', by the Bank of Canada (Boothe, Clinton, Côté, and Longworth, 1985).

$$i(t) + [\log N(t+1) - \log N(t)] = i'(t) + b(NB/B') + z'; \, b > 0 \quad (A.9)$$

$$\log N(t+1) - \log N(t) = [i'(t) - i(t)] + b[N(t)B(t)/B'(t)] + z' \quad (A.9a)$$

The Canadian–US interest rate $(i - i')$ differential is measured by the forward premium on the \$US. Three measures of the endogenous risk premium are used, based upon the portfolio theory. Regression equation (A.9c) is obtained.[7] B = Canadian federal debt; W = world wealth, in Canadian dollars; Wc = Canadian wealth. The period is 1971.01–1982.11.

The portfolio/MRE hypothesis is that in equation (A.9b) the coefficient of the Canadian–US interest rate differential is unity, and the coefficient of the ratio of Canadian to US denominated assets is positive.[8]

$$\log N(t+1) - \log N(t) = a[i'(t) - i(t)] + b(NB/B') + z'$$

$$\text{Ho: } a = 1, \, b > 0 \quad \text{(A.9b)}$$

$$\log N(t+1) - \log N(t) = +.011 + .51[i(t) - i'(t)] - .18(B/W) + .05(Wc/W)$$

| (t-stat) | (.74) | (.75) | (.88) | (.50) |

$$\text{(A.9c)}$$

The results reject the portfolio version of the FORE hypothesis. (i) We may reject the hypothesis that the coefficient of the interest-rate differential is unity, the foundation of the FORE hypothesis. (ii) We may reject the hypothesis that the ratios of outside assets are significantly positive.

The conclusions are cogently stated by the authors of the Bank of Canada study:

Rational expectations models generally do not provide statistically significant evidence that differences in expected rates of return on Canadian and US dollar short-term instruments are dependent on stocks of Canadian and US government bonds, as they would if such assets were imperfect substitutes. This implies that there is no evidence of a variable risk premium depending on asset stocks. Since recent empirical work has strongly rejected the joint hypothesis of rational expectations and a constant risk premium, our interpretation of the evidence is that there is likely a failure of the rational expectations hypothesis; indeed, it seems that expectations can often be of an adaptive or extrapolative nature. Longworth *et al.*, 1983: 4–5).

The MRE hypothesis *arbitrarily assumes* that the market always knows the objective expectation of a distribution, but it contains no theory to explain the speed of convergence. As we have shown, the

---

[7] Bank of Canada, table A3.
[8] The Bank of Canada study used as the exchange rate, the price of foreign exchange $S(t) = \$C/\$US$ and $s = \log S$. A rise in S is a depreciation of the $C. Their $s = \log S = -\log N$ in our notation. Hence, we reverse the signs in their regressions.

Muth rational expectations hypothesis (MRE), that people know the objective distributions of the stochastic variables, is rejected in markets for foreign-exchange and financial instruments. This implies that short-term capital flows are not reflections of rational expectations, but are noise. Figures 2.1 and 2.2 in Chapter 2 show that the difference in interest rates is small, but there are large variations in the exchange rate which are unrelated to the short-term interest-rate differentials. In the chapters above, we used the Asymptotically Rational Expectations hypothesis[9] (ARE), whereby the market uses all available information efficiently, and the speed of convergence to MRE depends upon the nature of the exogenous disturbances. When the latter are not stationary (i.e., have unit roots, see Table A1), the speed of convergence to MRE is slow. If the disturbances are stationary, the limit point of ARE is MRE.

The results of this section can be summarized with a quotation from the study by the Reserve Bank of Australia (Blundell-Wignall *et al.*) cited in Chapter 3 above.

No economic hypothesis has been rejected more decisively, over more time periods, and for more countries than UIP [uncovered interest-rate parity with rational expectations] . . . Many researchers interpret rejection of UIP as evidence of a time varying risk premium, while still maintaining the assumption of rational expectations. However, as the risk premium is then typically defined to be the deviation from UIP, this interpretation is merely a tautology.

3.4 Reduced-Form Equations: Effects of Monetary Policies

We have explained why the structural equations of the class of models discussed in Part 2 are inconsistent with the evidence. We now explain why the implied reduced form of the structural equations is also inconsistent with the evidence.

The crucial variable in explaining the variation in nominal exchange rates is the rationally expected inflation differential. The value of the expected inflation differential is then associated with expected differentials in the growth of money per unit of output: the expected growth of money per unit of output abroad EDlog

---

[9] See Chow 1989 for empirical tests which reject the MRE. See Stein 1992 and *Econ. Record* 1992 for the development of the ARE, and Harrison 1992 for tests of this hypothesis.

(M'/y'), which determines the foreign rate of inflation, less the expected growth of money per unit of output at home EDlog(M/y), which determines the domestic rate of inflation. The rationally expected inflation differential is equal to E[Dlog(M'/y') − Dlog (M/y)]. Reduced-form equation (A.10) is implied by[10] the structural equations in Part 2.

$$D(\log N) = -\,E[\text{Dlog } M/M'] + E[\text{Dlog } y/y'] \qquad (A.10)$$

Variations in the current nominal exchange rate are linked to rationally expected differentials in money growth per unit of output in the future. If these forward-looking rational expectations hypotheses are to have scientific content (be meaningful propositions), one must give empirical, non-tautological content to what is meant by rationally expected differentials in money growth per unit of output in the future. Some authors arbitrarily assume that money growth is a martingale such that $E(\text{Dlog } M(t)) = \text{Dlog } M(t-1)$. Others assume that expected money growth is a weighted average of past rates of growth $\sum_{0}^{h} a(t-i)\,D(\log M(t-i))$, which contains the martingale as a special case. In Table A.3 below, we consider a general version of equation (A.10), where the regressors are current and lagged values of the growth rate of money at home less that abroad $x(t-i)$, and the growth of real income at home less that abroad $w(t)$. The rationally expected rates of money growth

$$E(\text{Dlog } M/M') = \sum_{0}^{h} a(t-i)\,x(t-i).$$

This is statistical equation (A.11), which is the implication of theoretical equation (A.10)

$$D(\log N(t)) = \sum_{0}^{h} a(t-i)\,x(t-i)) + b\,w(t); \text{ where} \qquad (A.11)$$

$$x(t-i)) = D(\log M(t-i)/M'(t-i)); \; w(t) = D(\log y(t)/y'(t))$$

[10] The derivation of (A.10) is obtained in several ways. First: if the real exchange rate is stationary, equation (A.2) states that the nominal exchange rate will move with relative prices. Equation (A.5) states that relative prices depend upon money per unit of output. Second: from (A.6) the average proportionate rate of change of the exchange rate is equal to the average expected nominal interest-rate differential. The nominal interest rate is equal to a relatively constant real interest rate plus the rationally anticipated rate of inflation. Hence the average proportionate rate of change of the exchange rate is tied to the rationally expected differential in rates of money growth per unit of output.

The statistical hypotheses implied by this set of models are as follows. (1) Coefficients a sum to minus unity. Exchange-rate depreciation is produced by differential money growth. (2) Coefficient b is positive. Differential real growth appreciates the currency. (3) The 'overshooting' hypothesis, discussed in Part 2, is that negative coefficient $a(t)$ is greater than minus one in absolute value, since prices are assumed to be sticky in the short run.

Table A.3, based upon quarterly data, considers several exchange rates. The value of: the Canadian dollar, the DM, the French franc, the pound sterling, the Italian lira, and the Japanese yen, relative to the $US during the period 1973.2–1989.1. Thus the dependent variable is the percentage change in the nominal value of these six currencies relative to the $US. In each cell is the value of the regression coefficient $a(t-i)$ or b, and in parentheses the t-value. For each country, two regressions were performed. In the first case, just the current rate of relative money growth $x(t)$ was used: the martingale hypothesis. In the second case, current and lagged values of $x(t-i)$ were used. Table A.3 presents estimates[11] of the coefficients in equation (A.11).

The conclusions drawn from Table A.3 are as follows. (a) The evidence for five out of the six exchange rates (the Canadian dollar, the DM, the French franc, the pound sterling, and the Japanese yen) rejects the monetary hypotheses completely. (1) There is no explanatory power to the monetary models that imply equation (A.11). The adjusted R-squares are negligible, ranging from 0.000 to 0.24. (2.1) In the martingale case, where the contemporaneous relative money growth is used, there is not only no evidence of overshooting but the relative monetary variable $x(0)$ is not significantly different from zero. (2.2) Where current and lagged relative rates of monetary growth are regressors, one can reject the hypothesis that the sum of the coefficients $a(t-i)$ is minus one (using an F-test). Moreover, this sum is not significantly different from zero. (2.3) The coefficient for relative real income growth $b(t)$ is not positive, as hypothesized. (b) The evidence for the Italian lira is (1) consistent with the monetary aspect of the hypothesis. Relative money growth depreciates the lira. (2) The relative growth of real income is not a significant variable. (3) The adjusted R-square is only 0.22.

---

[11] The data source is the OECD and the table was prepared by Chi-Young Song.

TABLE A3 *Estimates of the relation between the percentage appreciation of the currency and relative rates of money growth* x, *and relative rate of real income growth* w, *sample period is 1973.2–1989.1. The* t-*statistic is in parentheses*

	$x(0)$	$x(1)$	$x(2)$	$x(3)$	$x(4)$	$w(0)$	adj-R^2
Canada	− .068					.322	.16
	(− .71)					(.18)	
	− .154	− .178	.224	.211	.172	− .14	.24
	(− 1.5)	(− 1.6)	(2.1)	(1.9)	(1.6)	(− .8)	
DM	− .325					− .227	.05
	(− .77)					(− .46)	
	− .37	− .19	.13	.16	.067	− .25	.00
	(− .83)	(− .42)	(.29)	(.35)	(.15)	(− .49)	
France	− .24					− .15	.18
	(− .9)					(− .25)	
	− .28	− .04	− .05	.069	− .036	.187	.00
	(− .92)	(− .13)	(− .17)	(.22)	(.12)	(.66)	
UK	.256					− .117	.008
	(.71)					(− .32)	
	.297	− .62	− .037	.156	.05	− .067	.00
	(.78)	(− 1.7)	(− .1)	(.42)	(.14)	(− .18)	
Italy	− .76					.42	.22
	(− 2.6)					(.88)	
	− .79	− .16	− .05	.2	.22	.39	.17
	(− 2.5)	(.53)	(− .17)	(.66)	(.7)	(.78)	
Japan	− .16					− .55	.09
	(− .49)					(.94)	
	− .19	− .47	− .45	.18	− .2	− .16	.098
	(− .57)	(− 1.4)	(− 1.3)	(.56)	(− .65)	(.27)	

The rejection of both the structural equations (stationarity of the real exchange rate, uncovered interest-rate parity/Muth Rational Expectations, with or without an endogenous risk premium) and the reduced-form equation are the reasons why economists who have examined the evidence are disillusioned with the state of the art theories. More complex models which continue to be based upon these structural equations are unlikely to succeed in explaining the empirical phenomena.

244   *Appendix: Finance Theory and Empirical Reality*

4. INTERTEMPORAL OPTIMIZATION MODELS

The authors of the Representative Agent Intertemporal Optimization Model (RAIOM)[12] argue that this model, which now dominates the theoretical literature, should supplant the MDF model as
the dominant paradigm in international finance to be used by
central banks, finance ministries, and international economic agen-
cies. We first present the basic logic of this model as an explanation
of the current account and real exchange rate. Second, we show
how the RAIOM responds to the questions in Section 1 above.
Then we show that this model lacks explanatory power and is not
consistent with the evidence. We share the views of Dornbusch and
Frankel and Krugman that the RAIOM is not a promising line of
approach.

4.1   The Logic of the Model

We present the basic model without the unnecessary complexities
so that its strengths and weaknesses are apparent. In the MDF
models, the real exchange rate adjusts the current account to
independent saving-less-investment decisions made by households,
government, and firms. The RAIOM rejects this approach. Instead,
the RAIOM assumes that there is a representative agent who
simultaneously makes the saving–investment decision without a
market mechanism to reconcile the different decisions of savers and
investors. The agent selects the profile of consumption over time,
$c(t)$, to maximize a time-separable utility function $u(c)$ over an
infinite horizon. The discount rate is δ. This is equation (A.12). In
the single-good model, there is an intertemporal budget constraint
(IBC) that the present value of the terminal debt be zero. There is
no loss of generality if we consider a two-period model,[13] the
present time t and the future time $t + 1$. Production or GDP is y,
the interest rate is r, and initial net foreign assets is $A(t)$. Insofar as
there are no terminal assets or debt, the IBC is equation (A.13).

$$\max U = u[c(t)] + u[c(t + 1)]/(1 + \delta) \tag{A.12}$$

---

[12] The basic references are Obstfeld and Rogoff (1995) and Rogoff (1992). I follow
these two papers for the exposition of the model and empirical results. My
interpretation of their contribution differs from theirs.
[13] A dynamic programming approach has this logic. The use of many periods is
an unnecessary complexity.

$$c(t + 1) = y(t + 1) + (1 + r)[y(t) + A/t - c(t)] \quad \text{(A.13)}$$

There is no theoretical reason to select one utility function rather than another. The authors arbitrarily select an isoelastic time-separable utility function. The authors cannot justify selecting either that function or the degree of relative risk aversion (elasticity of intertemporal substitution).[14] The logic of the model is clear if we select a logarithmic function $u[c(t)] = \log c(t)$.

The implied optimal consumption, $c(t)$, is given by equation (A.14). The present value of life-time GDP is $Y^*(t)$ in equation (A.14a), and one can call $\beta[Y^*(t) + A(t)]$ in equation (A.14b) permanent income, $Y_p(t)$. Parameter β (defined in equation A.14c) is positively related to the discount rate.

$$c(t) = \beta[Y^*(t) + A(t)] \quad \text{(A.14)}$$
$$Y^*(t) = y(t) + y(t + 1)/(1 + r) \quad \text{(A.14a)}$$
$$Y_p(t) = \beta[Y^*(t) + A(t)] \quad \text{(A.14b)}$$
$$\beta = 1/\{1 + [1/(1 + \delta)]\} \quad \text{(A.14c)}$$

The current account, $CA(t)$, is GDP less consumption, $y(t) - c(t)$. Using the equation for optimal consumption, that it is equal to permanent income in equation (A.14b), the current account is:

$$CA(t) = y(t) - c(t) = y(t) - Y_p(t) \quad \text{(A.15)}$$

There will be current account surpluses (deficits) when current GDP exceeds (is less than) permanent income, $Y_p(t)$. Over the complete horizon, the IBC equation (A.13) ensures that the sum of the present values of the current account plus the initial value of net foreign assets will be zero.

In the analysis above, consumption, $c(t)$, is social consumption: government consumption, $g(t)$, plus private consumption, $c'(t)$. No distinction is made between the public and private sectors. Often a dichotomy is made between private and public consumption. In that case, the current account equation (A.15) can be written as equation (A.15a).[15] From the optimization, private consumption,

---

[14] The degree of relative risk aversion determines whether a rise in the expected return on capital raises or lowers saving (see Merton 1990: 115–16). Hence, the arbitrary choice of the degree of relative risk aversion introduces another arbitrary assumption into their model.

[15] In the budget constraint equation (A.13), social consumption c is private plus government consumption. Hence, private consumption is $c - g$, and the resources available to the consumer are $y - g$. Then equation (A.15a) follows from the optimization.

$c'(t)$, is equal to permanent income less permanent government consumption, $Y_p(t) - G_p(t)$.

$$CA(t) = y(t) - c'(t) - g(t) = y(t) - [Y_p(t) - G_p(t)] - g(t)$$
$$= [y(t) - Y_p(t)] - [g(t) - G_p(t)] \qquad \text{(A.15a)}$$

Equation (A.15a) is the foundation of the equations used in the empirical studies. It states that the current account just depends upon the deviation of GDP from its permanent level $[y(t) - Y_p(t)]$ less the deviation of government consumption from its permanent level $[g(t) - G_p(t)]$. This is the 'forward-looking' contribution of the RAIOM models. Equation (A.15) or (A.15a) completely describes the logic of the RAIOM and its explanation of the current account. It is fundamentally different from the 'conventional wisdom'.

Unlike the MFD models, there is no real exchange rate in the current account equation. There is no such a thing as a current account deficit owing to an overvalued exchange rate. The reason for this 'anti-conventional wisdom' is that there are no independent saving and investment equations. The nation is just a representative consumer who can borrow and lend at a given world interest rate.

In order to include an exchange rate, it is necessary to introduce two sectors: a tradable and a non-tradable goods sector. Then, the real exchange rate is positively related to the ratio $p(t)$ of the price of non-tradable goods, $p_n(t)$, to the price of tradable goods, $p_T(t)$—equation (A.16). In this type of model, one can refer to the relative price of non-tradables as the real exchange rate.[16]

$$p(t) = p_n(t)/p_T(t) \qquad \text{(A.16)}$$

The representative agent is assumed to have a Cobb–Douglas utility function, so that the optimal pattern of consumption is such that the ratio of expenditures on consumption of tradables, $p_T(t)c_T(t)$, to non-tradables, $p_n(t)c_n(t)$, is constant $1/\alpha$ based on the utility function. This implies:

---

[16] The real exchange rate (a rise is an appreciation) is $R = Np/p'$, where nominal exchange rate N is foreign currency/domestic currency (a rise is an appreciation), p is the domestic GDP deflator, and p' is the foreign GDP deflator. Let the deflators be geometric averages of the prices of traded goods (subscript T) and non-traded goods (subscript n). Then $R = N[(p_T)^{1-a}(p_n)^a]/[(p'_T)^{1-a'}(p'_n)^{a'}]$. The weights are a at home and a' abroad. Let the ratio of the prices of non-traded to traded goods be p at home and p' abroad. Then $R = (Np_T/p'_T)p^a/p'^{a'}$. Using the law of one price for traded goods, the first term is unity and $R = p^a/p'^{a'}$. This is why the real exchange rate is positively related to the relative price of non-tradables.

$$p(t) = p_n(t)/p_T(t) = \alpha c_T(t)/c_n(t). \tag{A.17}$$

The consumption of tradables can be smoothed intertemporally by borrowing and lending via current account deficits and surpluses. Since the consumption of tradables must satisfy an intertemporal budget constraint involving tradable goods only,[17] it is equal to permanent income involving tradables. Continue to call it $Y_p(t)$. The consumption of non-tradables is equal to their production, $Q_n(t)$, less the government consumption, $g(t)$, which consists of non-tradables. Therefore, the real exchange rate, $p(t)$, is given by equation (A.18). This is the basic exchange rate equation of the model.

$$p(t) = \alpha Y_p(t)/[Q_n(t) - g(t)] \tag{A.18}$$

Only unanticipated shocks to permanent income of traded goods change the consumption of traded goods. If the shocks are transitory or anticipated, they have no effect upon permanent income. The consumption pattern is smoothed via international capital flows: current account deficits or surpluses. This leads to the smoothing of the price of traded goods. If the shocks to traded goods income are permanent, agents will use the capital markets to change the consumption of traded goods by more than the change in current income. In this case, consumption smoothing amplifies the volatility of the relative prices of non-traded goods. There is no way to smooth the consumption of non-traded goods in this model. Government purchases are assumed to be in non-traded goods, and hence appreciate the real exchange rate.

4.2 The Empirical Measures and Tests of the Predictions of the RAIOM

The RAIOM asserts that agents make their current decisions by looking forward to future developments and have rational expectations. The rational expectations hypothesis is that agents agree what is the correct model[18] and know the distribution functions of the exogenous variables. This is contrasted invidiously with the

---

[17] The constraint looks just like equation (A.13) except that it only involves traded goods. Hence, the optimal consumption of traded goods follows the same logic as before.

[18] If the rational expectations hypothesis was correct, why is there such a disagreement concerning the correct model in international finance?

conventional wisdom, which generally[19] emphasizes current variables. Hence, the concepts of 'permanent income', 'permanent government spending', and 'anticipated productivity growth' in the tradable sector are the essence of the RAIOM. To avoid tautological statements concerning why the current account changes from surplus to deficit, or why the real value of the currency rises and falls, there must be objective measures of what is 'permanent' or 'anticipated'. We first show how the authors of the RAIOM measure these crucial variables. It will be clear that there is nothing forward-looking about these measures, and that they are arbitrary methods of extrapolation similar to adaptive expectations. Thus, the empirical implementation of the RAIOM is subjective, and is no more forward-looking than adaptive expectations.

Obstfeld and Rogoff (1995)[20] measure permanent income as equation (A.19), which is proportional to the expected present value of the future income stream, where index i goes from the present time, t, to infinity. The expectation of future income is given by equation (A.20), which implies equation (A.20a). The expected growth rate of real income is ($\rho - 1$). Substitute (A.20a) into (A.19) and derive equation (A.21) as 'permanent income', where the interest rate must exceed the growth rate.

$$Y_p(t) = [r/(1 + r)][y(t) + \Sigma Ey(t + i)/(1 + r)^i] \qquad \text{(A.19)}$$

$$Ey(t) = \rho y(t - 1). \qquad \text{(A.20)}$$

$$Ey(t + h;t) = \rho^h y(t) \qquad \text{(A.20a)}$$

$$Y_p(t) = [r/(1 + r - \rho)]y(t) = my(t); \ m = r/[r - (\rho - 1)] \qquad \text{(A.21)}$$

The authors note that the measure of permanent income is extremely sensitive to what are assumed to be the values of the expected growth rate and the appropriate real rate of interest. They state that, in practice, estimates of ρ are close to unity. In that case, $m = 1$ and permanent income is equal to current income. Even if m is not unity, equation (A.21) states that permanent income is proportional to current income. This means that *nothing has been gained over the conventional wisdom, which just looks at current income.*

---

[19] The Dornbusch, but not Mundell/Fleming, model does contain the uncovered interest rate parity/rational expectations equation. Hence it does have anticipations of future monetary policy as a crucial variable. We know that the hypothesis of uncovered interest rate parity/rational expectations is inconsistent with the evidence.

[20] Equations (A.19), (A.20), and (A.21) in the text correspond to Obstfeld and Rogoff (1995) equations (48), (47), and (49), respectively.

The current account equation (A.15a), using equation (A.21), becomes:

$$CA(t) = [y(t) - my(t)] - [g(t) - G_p(t)] = (1 - m)y(t) - [g(t) - G_p(t)]. \quad (A.22)$$

The GDP component, $y(t) - Y_p(t) = (1 - m)y(t)$, should not be able to explain anything about the trend movement of the current account from surplus to deficit or vice versa. If $m = 1$ then this term is zero. If m is not unity, then there is no reason why component $y(t) - Y_p(t) = (1 - m)y(t)$ should change sign or produce trends in the current account.

Therefore, all of the explanation must be in the second term, the difference between government expenditure and its permanent level, $g(t) - G_p(t)$. To form an estimate of permanent government spending, Obstfeld and Rogoff use 'an autoregressive forecasting model of detrended government spending' (1995: fn. 57 in sect. 4.2.2).

The study by Ahmed (1986)[21] regressed the trade balance, $B(t)$, on the level of 'permanent government spending', $G_p(t)$, and the difference between the actual and permanent levels $[g(t) - G_p(t)]$—equation (A.23). The hypothesis is that coefficient a of 'temporary deviations of government spending' is negative and coefficient b of permanent government expenditures is zero. This conforms to equation (A.15a).

$$B(t) = a[g(t) - G_p(t)] + bG_p(t); \qquad \text{H}_0 = [a < 0; b = 0] \qquad (A.23)$$

Even before looking at Ahmed's results, we can see that this test is inappropriate. Suppose that permanent government expenditures are either irrelevant or incorrectly measured but the conventional wisdom is correct that current government expenditures reduce the trade balance. Then coefficient a would be negative and b would be zero. That is, if the RAIOM hypothesis were incorrect and the conventional wisdom were correct, then we would not be able to reject the null hypothesis that $a < 0$ and $b = 0$.

Ahmed found that he could not reject the null hypothesis. Obstfeld and Rogoff recognize that Ahmed's tests were incorrect and unable to differentiate between the RAIOM and the conventional wisdom. They run the regression of the current account on the deviation $[g(t) - G_p(t)]$ and the actual level of government spending, $g(t)$:

---

[21] I am following the exposition in Obstfeld and Rogoff (1995: sect. 4.2.2). I always follow their exposition faithfully but use a different notation.

$$CA(t) = a[g(t) - G_p(t)] + cg(t); \qquad H_0 = [a < 0, \ c = 0] \qquad (A.24)$$

The null hypothesis is, as before, that only the deviation of government spending from its permanent level is significant and negative; and the level per se is not significant. The empirical results are that neither coefficient is significant. The authors conclude that 'it is unclear whether the intertemporal approach is simply false, or whether the many extraneous simplifications and maintained hypotheses imposed by the econometricians are to blame'.[22]

In his attempt to see if the RAIOM can explain the Japanese real exchange rate, Rogoff[23] tests the following proposition: 'whereas perfectly anticipated shocks do not lead to changes in the real exchange rate, unanticipated shocks do.' This is based upon equations (A.17) and (A.18) above, in the following way. From (A.17) derive (A.25). The consumption of tradables is based upon permanent income in tradables. Its change results from unanticipated changes in the productivity of producing traded goods. The unanticipated component is random. Therefore the first term [log $c_T(t)$ − log $c_T(t - 1)$] in equation (A.25) is random.

$$\log p(t) - \log p(t - 1) = [\log c_T(t) - \log c_T(t - 1)] - [\log c_n(t) - \log c_n(t - 1)]$$
$$(A.25)$$

These equations imply that 'barring shocks to the supply of nontraded goods available for private consumption, the log of the real exchange rate would follow a random walk, *regardless of the serial correlation properties of the shocks to traded goods productivity.* By the same logic, even if there is trend productivity growth in the traded goods sector, there will not necessarily be any trend in the real exchange rate' (Rogoff 1992: p. 8; his italics).

To separate the unanticipated component from the anticipated component of productivity shocks, he uses a Box–Jenkins analysis. He states that for 'both oil and manufacturing productivity, a simple (1,1,0) process fits the data fairly well. The residuals from the regression were used to proxy for unanticipated changes in lifetime traded goods income' (pp. 24–5).

---

[22] Obstfeld and Rogoff (1995: last para. in sect. 4.2.2). In section 4.2.3 they discuss other statistical manipulations and indicate that they end up regressing the current account on its lagged values. To find that the current account is related to its lagged values cannot be construed as evidence in favour of the anti-conventional wisdom, the RAIOM.

[23] The following quotes and discussion are based upon Rogoff (1992: 24–5).

How forward-looking is this procedure such that it is rational rather than adaptive expectations? What is its theoretical justification? Peter Kennedy (1985: p. 205) describes the Box–Jenkins procedure as follows: 'The main competitor to econometric models for forecasting purposes is time-series analysis, also known as Box–Jenkins analysis. Rather than making use of explanatory variables to produce forecasts, the key to forecasting with econometric models, time-series models rely only on the past behaviour of the variable predicted. Thus it is in essence no more than a sophisticated method of extrapolation.'

Given that the measures of anticipation are just extrapolations without theory, what are Rogoff's results? He regresses the change in the real exchange rate on his measures of unanticipated changes in productivity and the price of oil, which should appreciate the currency, and government expenditures, which decrease the consumption of non-traded goods and should also appreciate the currency. The results (Rogoff 1992: p. 25) are most disappointing. First, Rogoff (1992: fig. 2) finds that a rise in the ratio of Japanese government consumption to GNP does not appreciate the real value of the yen. It seems to depreciate it, contrary to the RAIOM. Second, for the full sample period, 'The coefficient on the innovation to the world real price of oil is of the correct sign and is highly significant . . . However, neither the productivity differential innovation or government consumption differential . . . appear important.' For the latter half of the sample period, 1981(1)–1990(3), 'Despite the apparent high correlation between oil and the real exchange rate . . . the coefficient of the oil shock loses its statistical significance'.

The conclusions so far are the following. First, the measures of anticipated or permanent variables are based upon arbitrary assumptions and are just sophisticated methods of extrapolation from past values of these same variables. Despite the use of the term 'rational expectations', no economic theory is used in their construction. They are no different from adaptive expectations. Second, since these measures are arbitrary, it is difficult for independent researchers to apply the RAIOM to the analysis of other bilateral exchange rates, because they are unable to state that the measures used will be the same as those used by the advocates of the RAIOM. Third, even using their own measures of unanticipated variables, the econometric tests reject their hypotheses.

4.3 An Evaluation of the Answers the RAIOM Gives to the Questions

Initially we posed the questions to be answered by a scientific theory. Let us evaluate how the RAIOM answers these questions in a way different from the 'conventional wisdom' and the validity of those answers.

The RAIOM cannot explain the trends in either the current account or the real exchange rate, because it claims that both are random walks. The expected change in *permanent* income is zero, hence the expected change in the real exchange rate is zero.

Suppose that we are given the expected productivity of capital and government expenditures, either at the beginning of the Reagan period for the USA or, in the case of Germany, as the result of unification. What does the RAIOM predict compared with the Mundell–Fleming–Dornbusch (MFD) model?

The MFD model claims that there will be current account deficits and an appreciation of the real exchange rate owing in large measure to government budget deficits. These deficits are not sustainable, and the real exchange rate is overvalued. There is misalignment. The RAIOM denies this and claims that current account deficits are the result of deviations of the current level of government spending from its permanent level. There may have been an unanticipated rise in government expenditures at the beginning of the Reagan period, producing a current account deficit. But since this deviation is noise with a zero expectation, why should it persist? A similar argument applies to the current account resulting from German unification.

According to the RAIOM any fiscal policy is sustainable. It will affect only permanent government expenditures and hence not the current account. There is no such thing as an overvalued real exchange rate that produces an unsustainable current account and growth of the foreign debt. The foreign debt is not a problem, because it is the result of an intertemporal optimization with an intertemporal budget constraint.

The RAIOM cannot answer the questions posed at the beginning of this appendix. It is difficult to give this model empirical content since its key variables are not objectively measurable. When the authors attempt to test the model, it is rejected. The failure of the model stems from its basic theoretical structure. Obstfeld and

Rogoff derive an equation for the steady-state debt as a fraction of GDP. Using 'reasonable' estimates for the key parameters they conclude (1995: end of sect. 3.1.1) that the steady-state foreign debt will be 2,000 per cent of GDP and the economy's trade balance will be 80 per cent of GDP. They are aware of the fact that these implications of the model are incredible. This is a devastating result.

The main 'positive' contribution of the RAIOM is that they claim that the log of the real exchange rate should follow a random walk. We share the reaction of Dornbusch and Frankel (1988: 162–3): 'The ultimate extrapolation of the argument occurs when the modern macroeconomist derives pride from his failure to explain any movement . . . in . . . the real exchange rate . . . He then goes on to "test" his theory "empirically" by seeing whether he can statistically reject the hypothesis that the real exchange rate follows a random walk. Rather than being humbled or embarrassed about his statistical failure to explain any movement in the macroeconomic variable that he has been investigating, he proudly proclaims it as confirming his theory on the grounds that the theory did not explain any movement in the variable.'

We have explained why the RAIOM is not a satisfactory approach and cannot be recommended as a substitute for the 'conventional wisdom'. An alternative approach is called for.

5. CONCLUSIONS

First: we posed some of the most important questions that a theory should answer. Second: we examined the logical structure of the contemporary models of international finance. It is well known among the empirical researchers that these models are inconsistent with the evidence. The deficiencies of these models are not easily rectifiable. For example, Meese and Rose (1989) concluded their study as follows:

We have applied a battery of parametric and non-parametric techniques to five structural exchange rate models in an attempt to account for potentially important sources of non-linearities in exchange rate models. However, our results are quite negative. There is no evidence that time deformation is responsible for significant non-linearities in exchange rate models. There is also little evidence that inappropriate transformations of fundamentals are responsible for the poor performance of the models considered. We conclude that accounting for non- linearities in exchange rate models does not appear to be a promising way to improve our ability to explain currency movements between major OECD countries. (1989: 36)

That is why economists who have examined the evidence, such as De Grauwe (quoted at the beginning of the chapter) are unable to accept the state of the art models as scientific explanations. The rejection stems from the facts that: (1) The real exchange rate is not stationary; (2) the monetary explanations of nominal exchange-rate variation have no explanatory power; (3) the currently popular RAIOM with MRE have yet to demonstrate their improvements over their predecessors as positive economics, i.e., as offering explanations of evidence. The NATREX models continue where De Grauwe stopped and attempt to provide an explanation of the fundamental determinants of real exchange rates.

REFERENCES

Ahmed, Shagil. 1986. 'Temporary and permanent government spending in an open economy'. *Journal of Monetary Economics*, 17.

Andersen, P.S. 1990. 'Developments in external and internal balances: a selective and eclectic review'. Bank for International Settlements, Basle.

Boothe, Paul, K. Clinton, Agathe Côté, and David Longworth. 1985. 'International asset substitutability'. Bank of Canada, Ottawa.

Boughton, J. 1988. 'The monetary approach to exchange rates: what now remains?' *Essays in International Finance*, 171 (Oct.).

Chow, Gregory. 1989. 'Rational versus adaptive expectations in present value models'. *Review of Economics and Statistics*, 71.

De Grauwe, Paul. 1989. *International Money: Postwar Trends and Theories*. Oxford: Oxford University Press.

Dornbusch, Rudiger. 1976. 'Expectations and exchange rate dynamics'. *Journal of Political Economy*, 84 (Dec.), 1161–76.

—— and Jeffrey Frankel. 1987. 'The flexible exchange rate system: experience and alternatives', NBER Working paper no. 2464. Reprinted in *International Finance and Trade in a Polycentric World*, ed. Silvio Borner, London, Macmillan, 1988.

Friedman, Milton. 1953. *The Case for Flexible Exchange Rates: Essays in Positive Economics*. Chicago, University of Chicago Press.

Genberg, H. and A. Swoboda. 1992. 'Saving investment and the current account'. *Scandinavian Journal of Economics*, 94(2).

Harrison, G. W. 1992. 'Market dynamics, programmed traders and futures markets'. *Economic Record*, Special Issue on Futures Markets, J. L. Stein and B. A. Goss, eds., Price Discovery and Price Determination.

Kennedy, Peter A. 1985. *Guide to Econometrics.* Cambridge, MA, MIT Press.

Longworth, D., Boothe, P., and Clinton, K. 1983. 'A study of the efficiency of foreign exchange markets'. Bank of Canada, Ottawa, Canada.

Meese, R. 1990. 'Currency fluctuations in the post Bretton Woods era'. *Journal of Economic Perspectives*, 4(1), 117–34.

Meese, Richard A. and Andrew Rose. 1989. 'An empirical assessment of non-linearities in models of exchange rate determination'. International Finance Discussion Papers, Board of Governors of the Federal Reserve System, no. 367.

Merton, Robert J. 1990. *Continuous Time Finance.* Oxford, Blackwell.

Obstfeld, Maurice and Kenneth Rogoff. 1995. 'The intertemporal approach to the current account'. In *Handbook of International Economics*, eds. Gene M. Grossman and Kenneth Rogoff, vol. 3, Amsterdam, North-Holland.

—— and Alan C. Stockman. 1985. 'Exchange rate dynamics'. In *Handbook of International Economics*, eds. R. W. Jones and P. B. Kenen, Amsterdam, Elsevier.

Rogoff, K. 1992. 'Traded goods, consumption smoothing and the random walk behavior of the real exchange rate'. Bank of Japan, *Monetary and Economic Studies*, 10(2), Nov. 1992, 1–30.

Roubini, N. 1988. 'Current account and budget deficits in an intertemporal model of consumption and taxation smoothing'. NBER Working paper, no. 2773.

Stein, Jerome L. 1971. *Money and Capacity Growth.* New York, Columbia University Press.

—— 1992. 'Cobwebs, rational expectations and futures markets'. *Review of Economics and Statistics*, 74(1), 127–34.

—— 1992. 'Price discovery processes'. *Economic Record*, Special Issue on Futures Markets, J. L. Stein and B. A. Goss, eds., Price Discovery and Price Determination.

INDEX